**Contemporary
Scientific Psychology**

CONTRIBUTORS

Leonard Berkowitz

Albert R. Gilgen

Lewis P. Lipsitt

Melvin H. Marx

Karl H. Pribram

Stanley C. Ratner

Irvin Rock

Arthur W. Staats

D. D. Thiessen

Contemporary Scientific Psychology

Edited by ALBERT R. GILGEN

DEPARTMENT OF PSYCHOLOGY
BELOIT COLLEGE
BELOIT, WISCONSIN

ACADEMIC PRESS   New York and London   1970

ACADEMIC PRESS, INC.
111 Fifth Avenue, New York, New York 10003

United Kingdom Edition published by
ACADEMIC PRESS, INC. (LONDON) LTD.
Berkeley Square House, London W1X 6BA

LIBRARY OF CONGRESS CATALOG CARD NUMBER: 71-127683

PRINTED IN THE UNITED STATES OF AMERICA

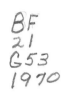
Contents

Part I.   SCIENTIFIC PSYCHOLOGY

Introduction: Progress, a Paradigm, and Problems in Scientific Psychology

ALBERT R. GILGEN

Observation, Discovery, Confirmation, and Theory Building

MELVIN H. MARX

Part II. THE RESEARCH AREAS

The Biology of Mind: Neurobehavioral Foundations

KARL H. PRIBRAM

Philosophy and Methods in Behavior Genetics: Its Relation to Biology

D. D. THIESSEN

Comparative Psychology

STANLEY C. RATNER

Developmental Psychology

LEWIS P. LIPSITT

CONTENTS

List of Contributors

Numbers in parentheses indicate the pages on which the authors' contributions begin.

LEONARD BERKOWITZ (283), Department of Psychology, University of Wisconsin, Madison, Wisconsin

ALBERT R. GILGEN (3), Department of Psychology, Beloit College, Beloit, Wisconsin

LEWIS P. LIPSITT (147), Department of Psychology, Brown University, Providence, Rhode Island

MELVIN H. MARX (13), Department of Psychology, University of Missouri, Columbia, Missouri

KARL H. PRIBRAM (45), Departments of Psychiatry and Psychology, Stanford University, Stanford, California

STANLEY C. RATNER (115), Department of Psychology, Michigan State University, East Lansing, Michigan

IRVIN ROCK (241), Institute for Cognitive Studies, Rutgers University, Newark, New Jersey

ARTHUR W. STAATS (183), Department of Psychology, University of Hawaii, Honolulu, Hawaii

D. D. THIESSEN (71), Department of Psychology, University of Texas, Austin, Texas

Preface

The integrating theme of this book is *the scientific method in action* in psychology. Each of the contributors, with the exception of Melvin Marx, was asked to write about his own interests, work, and background in such a way as to illustrate the process of psychological inquiry and at the same time provide the reader with an overview of his research area. Marx was asked to discuss the scientific method in a more general way. It was hoped that these papers would highlight the formal aspects of data gathering and theorizing as well as demonstrate the importance of other factors which determine the day-to-day activities of scientific psychologists—for example, the particular graduate training of an investigator, chance opportunities, the stage of development of an area of research, the vulnerability of a subfield to social pressures (the Zeitgeist), and the lure of fancy hardware and reliable but narrowly focused techniques.

The essays which resulted surpassed our expectancies. Taken together, they provide the desired overview of scientific psychology and the inquiry process; individually, each paper offers interesting and thought-provoking insights into the work and viewpoints of an accomplished research psychologist. The chapters by Pribram (Physiological Psychology), Staats (Learning), and Rock (Perception) include systematic statements, in considerable detail, of each man's theoretical position, while at the same time touching upon some of the problems characteristic of their respective areas of study. Ratner, on the other hand, selects as his emphasis the need in Comparative Psychology for a more well-defined research schema and a useful cross-species taxonomy of behaviors; what he has to say is of relevance to all psychologists engaged in investigatory activities. Thiessen's long essay presents an intriguing view of the important but until recently rather deemphasized field of Behavior Genetics, and in the process illustrates (as does Pribram's paper) the need for more interdisciplinary training and research. Lipsitt brings us up to date with regard to the exciting and significant work being done to determine the sensory and behavioral capacities of neonates and young infants. His chapter exemplifies dramatically how progress in one research area (in this case Learning) can open up new vistas in another (Developmental Psychology). Finally, Berkowitz, using some of his own studies to demonstrate his orientation, presents a short history of Social Psychology with particular concern for the roles played by problem-oriented and theory-generated investigations. The papers follow no rigid format. The variety of styles and emphases, in fact, convey a more accurate and interestingly presented picture of the professional activities of research psychologists and the types of problems with which they are confronted than would be possible in a treatise dealing with scientific psychology in a more abstract way.

In the first chapter, I summarize the characteristics and pitfalls of research dealt with in the seven chapters concerned with specific subfields of the discipline. I also found it appropriate to include a brief discussion of the question: Does the impressive work on the learning processes constitute a paradigm (as defined by Thomas Kuhn) for all of scientific psychology? This introductory paper, in conjunction with the chapter by Marx, comprises a sort of general frame of reference for reading subsequent chapters.

The book as a whole, or parts of it, can be used in teaching a variety of courses. It is most appropriate for courses in Experimental Psychology, History and Systems, Psychological Theories, the Philosophy of Science, honors sections in General Psychology, and seminars at both the undergraduate and graduate levels. Several of the chapters (Staats, Lipsitt, Pribram, Ratner, Berkowitz) might also be integrated into courses in Learning because they deal, in part, with the significant contributions made to psychology by investigators of the learning processes.

A. R. G.

Acknowledgments

I wish to thank the men who made this book possible for both their enthusiastic support and their cooperation in writing their chapters. I am grateful also for the financial support given by the National Science Foundation for the Summer Institute in Contemporary Psychology for College Teachers held at Beloit College in 1968 which I directed and at which the contributors served as instructors. The book was inspired by the success of that program. My wife, Carol, I thank for planning and serving as hostess at the Institute parties which facilitated the face-to-face interaction among instructors and participants, and for her patience, as I struggled, with her help, to complete this most rewarding project.

**Contemporary
Scientific Psychology**

Part I

SCIENTIFIC PSYCHOLOGY

Introduction: Progress, a Paradigm, and Problems in Scientific Psychology

ALBERT R. GILGEN

DEPARTMENT OF PSYCHOLOGY
BELOIT COLLEGE
BELOIT, WISCONSIN

In spite of the continuing controversy concerning the use and misuse of the scientific method in the social-behavioral sciences (Bugental, 1967; Kagan, 1967; Kessel, 1969; Merleau-Ponty, 1962; Polanyi, 1968; Severin, 1965), there can be little doubt that scientific psychology has evolved into an important and productive discipline. Particularly impressive (and this is reaffirmed by the papers which follow) has been the research on the learning processes as inferred from the observation of behavior change under laboratory conditions. Not only have the findings of investigators in this area found application in such diverse fields as clinical and physiological psychology, but techniques developed in conjunction with this work have opened up new research possibilities in almost all areas.

There have been, and of course still are, significant problems, and so far nothing has come along to unite the entire discipline around a common set of methodologies and principles. As many of the contributors to this volume indicate, psychologists (and probably all scientists) easily get into

3

ruts; for that reason there is a continual need for frequent reevaluations of the aims and procedural schemes of each area of study.

My purpose in this chapter is twofold: first, to argue that the research on the learning processes, important as it is, does not constitute a model or paradigm for all of scientific psychology; and second, to discuss some of the characteristics and needs of the research areas dealt with in the papers which comprise Part II of this book, and in the process to highlight factors which play a role in psychological inquiry. A list of topics for further study is presented at the end of this chapter.

I. Does Conditioning Research Constitute a Paradigm for Psychology?

Kuhn (1962) in his highly acclaimed book contends that the history of all mature sciences includes a pre-paradigmatic period, a paradigmatic period, and a succession of revolutions which occur when new paradigms replace old. According to Kuhn, the pre-paradigmatic period is characterized by rival schools, little agreement with regard to fundamentals or methodologies, and investigators busy studying casual, easily observed phenomena. Research generally is rather random. A science becomes paradigmatic when an achievement of such importance occurs that practitioners from the various schools accept it both as an integrative scheme and as a guide for future research. Kuhn cites Newton's work on optics and Franklin's theory of electricity as paradigms which appeared in the natural sciences. When a true paradigm emerges, the various schools either fade away or become isolated, and the members of the scientific community concern themselves with investigations suggested by the paradigm. As this "mop-up" work takes place, sophisticated hardware is developed, more precise hypotheses and observations become possible, and there is little squabbling over fundamentals or what constitutes the proper concern of the discipline. A paradigm is embraced until significant discrepancies between expectancies and observations appear; a revolution or radical reorientation, however, does not take place until another achievement provides a new focus for the science.

Keeping Kuhn's analytical scheme in mind, does the systematic study of behavior change, particularly the research on conditioning, constitute a true paradigm for all scientific psychology? Many contemporary psychologists evidently think so because psychology is today frequently defined as *the* scientific study of behavior. I believe, however, that psychology is still in the pre-paradigmatic stage, not only because the observation of behavior change is, in my opinion, a data source and not an end in itself (see also the chapters by Pribram and Rock), but also because psychologists still spend considerable time arguing over such fundamental questions as: What is psychology? What problems can psychologists legitimately investigate? What constitutes significant research?

A truly paradigmatic psychology, it seems to me, will be based on more than the study of behavior; many of the most important processes involved in organism–environment interactions (perceiving, thinking, emoting, feeling, sensing, etc.) are not highly correlated with gross behavioral changes and therefore require other data sources (biochemical, physiological, intro-spective) for their investigation. In a sense, physiological psychology has always represented the kind of multilevel approach which, in my view, is necessary for a paradigmatic psychology. Unfortunately, until rather recently, not enough was known about the functional organization of the nervous system to enable us to identify the mechanisms (biochemical and physiological correlates) underlying experiential states and transformation.

During the last fifteen years or so, however, physiological psychologists, neurophysiologists, and biochemists, equipped with new hardware and research techniques, have begun to unravel the mysteries of nervous system functioning, and although the work is far from completed, it is these develop-ments in conjunction with the methods and findings provided by behavioral psychology which may provide psychology with its first real paradigm. Psychology, after passing through a period of premature mentalism (1860–1915), and a period of fruitful, but limited, behaviorism (1915–1970) is, if my analysis is correct, entering a period of mature mentalism characterized by reliable procedures for studying the total functioning (behavioral as well as mentalistic) of the organism. Pribram's research and thinking (Chapter 3), which can be described as a physio-behavioral cognitive psychology, is a good example of this development.

I do not wish to leave the impression that future progress in psychology depends only on the discoveries of biochemists and neurophysiologists, and that we will all have to become physiological psychologists. Far from it, for if psychologists are to identify the physiological correlates of experience, there is much research yet to be done at the purely psychological level of analysis (see Rock, Chapter 8). It may be necessary, in fact, if we are to successfully match experiential events with bodily processes, for us to devise new taxonomies of awareness events; current categories such as feeling, perception, and cognition may not suffice. In this vein, I recently proposed a classification system of awareness events (Gilgen, 1969) consisting of two main categories: "diffuse" and "structured." It is my contention that diffuse changes in awareness are correlates of the neurophysiological activity of systems sensitive only to changes (flow, composition, concentration) in liquids (blood, cochlear fluid, hormones, mucus, etc.); therefore, sounds, tastes, feelings of hot and cold, and the common affects are all classified as diffuse. Structured events or changes, on the other hand, are considered experiential correlates of the activity of biological systems capable of extracting information about the shape and location of solids (including the bones of the body); these include the visual system, the limb-location detection system, the haptic system generally, the haptic and bone-location systems associated with the hands and mouth, the vestibular mechanism, the system controlling efferent activity, and the memory system. The primary virtue of reexaminations of systems of classification is probably that such inquiries may suggest new ways of organizing observations and data at other levels of analysis. New ways of categorizing our experiences, for example, may lead to new ways in classifying and organizing neurophysiological systems.

In summary, the paradigmatic discipline which I envision will be a truly cognitive psychology (it may even require that we again do some serious introspecting), but it will be a cognitive psychology based on reliable, multilevel data-gathering techniques. Other paradigms will, I am sure, also emerge; and if we expand our scope to the social-behavioral sciences as a whole, I should not be at all surprised if significant reorganizations of the disciplines as now constituted occur before the end of the century. In any event, the future of scientific psychology looks promising—that is, if we put what we learn to good use (see also Murphy, 1969).

II. CHARACTERISTICS AND NEEDS OF THE RESEARCH AREAS

My purpose in briefly summarizing certain aspects of the perspectives presented by the other contributors is to highlight some of the variables operative in scientific psychological inquiry. This is not an exhaustive analysis or a complete summary; it is, as I stated previously, meant primarily for the reader interested in the interaction between the scientific method and the concerns and needs of the various research areas.

Both psychology and neurophysiology, according to Pribram (Chapter 3 on *physiological psychology*), tend to be technique- rather than problem-oriented. This deficiency, he feels, would be remedied if the investigators in each discipline knew more about each others' work. Researchers become so enamored of their own conceptual frameworks and hardware, that they often fail to see the relevance of their work for problems which are the concern of more than one discipline. Interdisciplinary graduate and post-graduate training, as well as a willingness on the part of more seasoned investigators to read outside of their own areas, is necessary to avoid this type of problem. In short, a narrow perspective, though sometimes required, may stand in the way of discovery (see also Marx, Chapter 2). Pribram's own research, which involves methods and concepts from psychology, neurophysiology, biochemistry, physics, linguistics, the computer sciences, and mathematics, enabled him to derive a model of brain functioning, which not only has considerable power, but which would never have been forthcoming had he concerned himself only with physiological psychology as narrowly defined.

Thiessen (Chapter 4) calls for a new focus for *behavior genetics*—one which gets away from demonstrating the now well-verified fact that genetic factors and behavior are related, to a concern with the mechanisms developed by organisms as they evolved to cope with the important demands of their environments. Thiessen, in a sense, is suggesting to behavior geneticists (and I am sure that many of his colleagues agree) that they get out of a rut and concern themselves with a new unit of analysis, that unit being the organism (including its physiological mechanisms) and the environment within which it evolved. Such an emphasis requires more collaborative efforts among psychologists, geneticists, ethologists, neurophysiologists, and biochemists, and again reflects the apparent need for interdisciplinary training and research discussed previously with regard to Pribram's paper. Developments in this area, particularly at the biochemical and physiological levels, also illustrate another important characteristic of scientific inquiry, namely that systems of classification, no matter how universally accepted, eventually require modification. It is becoming increasingly clear that the line between purely genetic and strictly environmental factors is getting rather fuzzy. Conceptualizations are emerging which will, I am certain, have important implications for the recently revived nature–nurture controversy (Albee, *et al.*, 1969; Jensen, 1969a; 1969b).

Ratner (Chapter 5) contends that *comparative psychology* has been slow to develop for two reasons: first, because psychologists have not fully understood the relevance of evolutionary theory insofar as the comparative study of behavior is concerned, and second, because no effective general taxonomy of behaviors has been developed. Psychologists, according to Ratner, frequently do animal studies not knowing if the species they select is most appropriate (the best preparation) for the processes they want to investigate, and having very little knowledge of the behavioral capacities of either the animals studied or those animals to which they are interested in generalizing their findings. Such investigations are understandably of little value as comparative research. Furthermore, even when good comparative studies are attempted, researchers are hampered by the lack of a system of classifying behaviors which is applicable across all species. Ratner outlines a "stages" approach to research activity and presents a three-category taxonomy of behaviors which he hopes will help comparative psychologists overcome these difficulties. What he says, however, should be of interest to all scientific psychologists.

As was mentioned previously, the findings, concepts, and methodologies derived from, or involved in, conditioning studies have both created new research areas and revitalized others. Nowhere, with the possible exception of clinical and/or educational psychology, has the impact of this work been greater than in child psychology. In a sense, the field of experimental child psychology (or maybe more appropriately, experimental infant psychology) developed into a full-fledged area of study when conditioning methodologies made it possible, for the first time, to get some reliable information about the perceptual and behavioral abilities of preverbal infants.

Like Thiessen, Lipsitt (Chapter 6) feels that research in his area must take a new direction. In his opinion, enough time has been spent inventorying infant and child behavior; what is needed now are well-controlled laboratory investigations of the sensory, perceptual, and behavioral capabilities of neonates and infants. He suggests that individual differences in the condition-ability of very young infants may be useful in predicting differences in adult abilities. This is a particularly exciting possibility since investigators have until now failed to identify dimensions of infant behavior which correlate highly with variations in adult performance.

Lipsitt's paper illustrates the general point that the interests and activities of scientists are to some degree determined by the stage of development of their research area. Experimental child psychology, being a young enterprise, is, not surprisingly, primarily concerned with procedural matters and the acquisition of base-line data. There is little demand yet for high-level theorizing.

In contrast with experimental child psychology, the field of *learning* (characterized by sophisticated and reliable laboratory techniques, well-defined concepts, and a rather solid data base) is, in Staats' opinion (Chapter 7), ready for theoretical integration. He feels particularly strongly about the need for a symbol system which will tie together the concepts and principles of classical and operant conditioning, and thus provide a more effective framework for the investigation and explanation of complex processes such as language development. This call for theory building is interesting because, until recently, most psychologists working in this area (particularly operant conditioners) have taken the position that there is still much data to be gathered before useful multilevel theories of learning can be constructed. It may be that so much data has been collected that even hard-nose anti-theorists will agree with Staats that a little theorizing is now legitimate. On the other hand, it may be that recent challenges to conditioning explanations of language acquisition (Chomsky, 1965) and perceptual development (Bower, 1966; Rock, Ch. 8) require a reexamination of conditioning principles and their application. In any case it is refreshing to hear a respected experimentalist not only proclaim that there is a need for conceptual integration, but in fact, proceed to take a significant step in that direction. Staats' discussion of his "integrated learning theory" again demonstrates the important roles that taxonomies or classificatory schemes play in scientific work (see Ratner and Thiessen); it is also clear from reading his paper that the scientific method involves more than experimentation and data collection (see Marx, Chapter 2). This may sound like a truism, but with the great emphasis which has been placed on these aspects of scientific inquiry, particularly by operant conditioners, it may be well to state this point explicitly.

Shifting our attention to *perception*, one of the main points made by Rock in his chapter entitled "Toward a Cognitive Theory of Perceptual Constancy" is that he, as a perceptualist, sees behavior not as an end in itself, but as a data source from which inferences can be made about perceptual and cognitive processes. He also places considerable importance on his own subjective experiences and indicates that he generally refrains from making inferences about the experiences of others which are too discrepant with his own experiences in the same situation. I have already discussed this issue previously and, therefore, will say no more about it here. Rock, after presenting an interesting discussion concerning the nature of perceptual research, then demonstrates that investigations of complex perceptual phenomena (which are in themselves not observable) can be as scientific (objective, precise, reliable, communicable) as studies concerning the relationships between gross behavior and environmental change (both directly observable). He also makes the point (which I briefly referred to) that there is still much need for research at the purely psychological level, and that recent and continuing findings concerning brain functioning should not lure us all into becoming physiological psychologists. Although I consider the emerging multilevel psychology based on physio-behavioral methodologies so imporant as to comprise a paradigm for scientific psychology, I think that there is some danger that fad-prone American psychologists (see Marx, Chapter 2) will, as they did when they embraced behaviorism, go off the deep end and focus only on the one or two levels of analysis most characterized by fancy hardware. I certainly hope not.

One of the areas of psychological inquiry least vulnerable to the lure of microelectrodes, shiny stereotaxic gadgetry, and pulsating oscilloscopes is *social psychology*, at least that branch of the discipline (the mainstream) which is concerned with human, rather than animal, behavior. This, of course, is due to the fact that the level and units of analysis of social psychologists seldom extend to include biochemical and physiological observations. Other pitfalls, however, await the social psychologist (as well as sociologists, anthropologists, political scientists, etc.): Berkowitz (Chapter 9) contends that many social psychologists jump from one research interest to another, their latest concern being determined by either a promising new theory or a social issue which has become popularized. There are too few, he feels, who thoroughly investigate a problem or who stick around long enough to test the limits of a theoretical proposition. Furthermore, when evidence is reported that is discrepant with outcomes predicted by a theory, proponents of the theory frequently claim that the findings are a product of inappropriate or poorly conducted research, while skeptics are ready to abandon the theory completely. Social psychologists, of course, do not have a monopoly in so far as these problems are concerned; they are just less isolated from some of the pressures of the Zeitgeist which to some degree affect the work of all scientists. Berkowitz believes that there is need both for theory and a concern with social issues, but that those engaged in social psychological research should resist the temptation of the latest fad (see also Marx, Chapter 2) and get closure on projects already underway.

To summarize, the scientific method provides a set of formal guidelines for psychological research, but the interests and day-to-day activities of investigators are to a large degree a function of variables not explicitly dealt with in most treatises on the scientific method. These variables or factors include: (a) professional training and chance opportunities (see particularly the chapters by Lipsitt and Staats); (b) current taxonomies, theories, levels and units of analysis, and methodologies (Pribram, Thiessen, Ratner, Staats, Rock); (c) the tendency of investigators to become enamored of their conceptualizations, and/or research techniques (Pribram, Thiessen, Staats); (d) the stage of development of an area of investigation (Lipsitt, Staats); and (e) the vulnerability of research areas to outside pressures or lures (Berkowitz). These factors are in themselves neither good nor bad; they are intrinsic aspects of the scientific method in action, and as such are involved in both progress and stagnation. Only frequent reexaminations of the type conducted by the contributors to this volume will reduce the likelihood of the latter occurring. The demand for such reexaminations should be one of the formal rules of science.

III. GUIDELINE TOPICS

The topics listed below (some of which I have discussed in this chapter, but which can be researched in greater depth), concern issues and developments either directly dealt with in, or suggested by, the chapters which follow. They are intended to serve as focal points for discussion or further study.

1. The study of behavior: its role in psychology.
2. Is psychology a paradigmatic science?
3. The use and misuse of the scientific method in psychological inquiry.
4. Factors contributing to the narrowing of perspectives in scientific research and thinking.

5. The determinants of scientific activities (formal and informal).

6. Data-gathering and theory-building in the light of the stage of development of a research area (see particularly the chapters by Lipsitt and Staats).

7. The most important recent developments in scientific psychology.

8. Models: their roles in contemporary psychology (see particularly the chapters by Marx and Pribram).

9. The virtues and limitations of systems of classification (see particularly the chapters by Ratner, Thiessen, and Staats).

10. Multilevel research and the legitimation of mentalistic concepts (see chapters by Pribram and Rock).

11. Technique-, problem-, and phenomenon-oriented research (see chapters by Marx, Pribram, Thiessen, and Berkowitz).

12. American graduate training and creativeness in American psychologists. Is the European system better? [see Marx; let me also recommend Ben-David's short book (1968)].

13. The importance of evolutionary theory in contemporary psychology (Thiessen, Ratner, Lipsitt).

14. Is the field of learning ready for more theoretical integration? (Staats).

15. Hull's impact on psychology (see particularly chapters by Marx, Lipsitt, and Staats).

16. Research in perception is difficult because one must learn to think at several conceptual and observational levels (Rock; Pribram's chapter is also relevant).

17. The vulnerability of research to outside pressures (Berkowitz).

18. Expecting too much of theories (Berkowitz).

19. The recent revival of the nature–nurture controversy (Thiessen, and to some degree Lipsitt and Rock).

20. The need for the continual reexamination of the aims and methodologies of a research area.

REFERENCES

Albee, G. W., Back, K. W., Carter, L. F., Chin, R., Clark, K. B., Deutsch, M., Gamson, W. A., Gerard, H. B., Hammond, K. R., Hefner, R., Hollander, E. P., Kahn, R. L., Maccoby, N., Pettigrew, T. F., Proshansky, H. L., Smith, M. B., White, R. K., Zimbardo, P. G. Statement by SPSSI on current IQ controversy: Heredity versus environment. *American Psychologist*, 1969, **24** (11), 1039–1040.

Ben-David, J. *Fundamental research and the universities*. Paris: Organization for Economic Cooperation and Development, 1968.

Bower, T. G. R. The visual world of infants. *Scientific American*, 1966, **215**, 80–92.

Bugental, J. F. T. (Ed.) *Challenges of humanistic psychology*. New York: McGraw-Hill, 1967.

Chomsky, N. *Aspects of the theory of syntax*. Cambridge: M.I.T. Press, 1965.

Gilgen, A. R. Diffuse and structured awareness events. Paper presented at the meeting of the American Psychological Association, Washington D. C., 1969.

Jensen, A. R. How much can we boost IQ and scholastic achievement? *Harvard Educational Review*, 1969, **39**, 1–123. (a)

Jensen, A. R. Criticism or propaganda? *American Psychologist*, 1969, **24** (11), 1040–1041. (b)

Kagan, J. On the need for relativism. *American Psychologist*, 1967, **22** (2), 131–142.

Kessel, F. S. The philosophy of science as proclaimed and science as practiced: "Identity" or "dualism"? *American Psychologist*, 1969, **24** (11), 999–1005.

Kuhn, T. S. *The structure of scientific revolutions*. Chicago: University of Chicago Press, 1962.

Merleau-Ponty, M. *Phenomenology of perception*. London: Routledge, 1962.

Murphy, G. Psychology in the year 2000. *American Psychologist*, 1969, **24** (5), 523–530.

Polanyi, M. Logic and psychology. *American Psychologist*, 1968, **23** (1), 27–43.

Severin, F. T. (Ed.) *Humanistic viewpoints in psychology*. New York: McGraw-Hill, 1965.

Observation, Discovery, Confirmation, and Theory Building

MELVIN H. MARX

DEPARTMENT OF PSYCHOLOGY
UNIVERSITY OF MISSOURI
COLUMBIA, MISSOURI

The enterprise of science involves observation, discovery, confirmation, and interpretation or theory building. All of these activities are essential. Without observation and discovery, there can be nothing to confirm and nothing upon which to construct theories. Without confirmation, on the other hand, no systematic body of knowledge can be formed; and without theories, observations, no matter how well confirmed, remain disconnected and powerless to guide the course of future research and thinking.

13

It is my purpose in this chapter to discuss some of the guidelines, characteristics, and problems associated with these activities. In doing so I shall deal with the following issues: (*a*) the nature of "fact," (*b*) the virtues and limitations of individual-subject and group research, (*c*) some characteristics of data gathering which create difficulties for the researcher, (*d*) the "knowledge explosion," (*e*) training students to be creative, (*f*) the functions of theories, (*g*) the primary modes of theory construction, (*h*) the "bandwagon effect" (fads), (*i*) common fallacies concerning science, and finally (*j*) the current status of theory in psychology.

I. OBSERVATION

A. Data Language—Facts

Direct sensory observations which are confirmed by a community of observers tend to become facts. Although there are a number of logical (philosophical) meanings of the term (cf. Cohen & Nagel, 1934), *fact* for our purposes will mean the symbolized representation, usually verbal, of a confirmed sensory observation. This definition best represents the actual usage of the term in ordinary discourse as well as in science. As Guthrie (1946) has ably observed, it is this meaning—the socially accepted verbalized proposition—that we are actually using when we make such statements as "Let's get down to the facts." And it is this kind of generally accepted proposition that is at the heart of the scientific enterprise.

As thus used, the term has several distinguishing characteristics. First, there is the matter of *social consensus*. It is this consensus that produces the factualness in propositions. Second, all facts are *relative*—both in time and place and, especially, in respect to the population of acceptors of the propositions. For instance, it was a fact, several centuries ago, that the world is flat—even though we no longer accept such a statement as a fact. This simply means that it was, at the time, generally accepted as true—and by most if not all of the various classes or populations of people, including scientists. Thus facts are not hard and immutable truisms, but are in actuality quite flexible, as indeed they must be if science is to progress.

Third, the relationship of facts to direct sensory observation is not always apparent. This is so because of the critical element of *belief*, or *trust*, that enters into all facts. Although most facts in science are more closely tied to sensory observations, all are not. Consider, for example, the proposition mentioned above—that the world is flat. Few of us would accept that as fact today, but how many of us, scientists included, can point to direct sensory observation of our own that disconfirms this proposition? Or consider the evidence for the principle of evolution. Few people are in a position to offer observations in support of this proposition, or set of propositions, but to most of us the evolutionary principle has a high degree of factualness. This situation exists because of the fact (for most of us!) that we readily defer to authority in which we place trust. Although these facts may be labeled beliefs, there is no hard and fast line that separates such propositions from those for which we do have direct evidence of observation (such as, the rat turned right at the choice point, or the client wept for five minutes, etc.). As we shall see later, even such apparently simple observations are subject to error, and so there is necessarily a high degree of trust always involved in facts. In this respect scientific facts are on the same continuum as political, economic and religious dogma, although admittedly at somewhat opposite ends in terms of the degree to which direct observation is involved.

In science, data are generally facts that do involve such direct observation. So when we speak of the data language we typically mean the language of empirical observation, as contrasted with reasoning or speculation.

B. Some Problems of Data Gathering

What becomes symbolized as fact, in any science, is a function of those aspects of sensory observation which the community of scientists involved chooses to attend to, to discriminate among, and to count, plot, or measure. Any broad and thorough treatment of this issue relative to psychology would have to deal with the merits and weaknesses of introspective, behavioral, and physiochemical data-gathering techniques. It is my purpose, however, to focus instead on a number of the more specific problems characterizing contemporary psychological research.

Individual vs. Group Functions. Traditionally, in psychological research and theorizing, groups of subjects have been used and conclusions about individuals have been drawn on this basis. Assaults on this practice have been made with increasing vigor within recent years. There have been two major sources of this criticism of group research.

Certain personality theorists, led by Gordon Allport (1937), have criticized research and theory on the ground that it is nomothetic (directed at general laws) rather than idiographic (tailored to the individual person). The rationale for this criticism is that each individual is unique and that he can therefore be understood only through a study of himself, and not by means of nomothetic principles. This has been an influential criticism and has had a particularly strong impact on psychologists who are concerned with the "whole person" as opposed to the specific behavior mechanisms.

Viewing preliminary data, which has the advantage of giving some initial knowledge of results, has the disadvantage of possible biasing of later results, as described in detail by Rosenthal (1966). That is, if one sees some trend in the early data, the expectations thus produced may well bias him in the collection of further data. The safest procedure, generally, is to complete the collection of the data, once the experiment is formally initiated, before attempting to look at any results, even though this does aggravate the problem described above.

Indirect Data. Unlike most biological data, behavioral data need to be viewed abstractly. That is, they cannot ordinarily be looked at directly in the way that one can look through a microscope or observe the growth of a cell, etc. In these situations not only are the data directly obtainable but failure or success is to some degree also immediately evident.

In psychology, operant conditioning has something of an advantage over more traditional methodology in that one can watch a cumulative recorder or observe shaping of behavior directly. In clinical research, especially, behavior modification techniques have these advantages compared with orthodox clinical procedures, such as traditional psychotherapy.

While there does not seem to be any generally applicable ultimate solution to these problems of delayed and indirect behavioral data, they can be alleviated by some of the newer techniques available (e.g., libraries of ready computer programs, use of X by Y computer plotters, etc.). Basically, however, behavioral researchers will need to learn to be more patient and more tolerant of delay and ambiguity than many other scientists. This kind of tolerance needs to be instilled in them, as far as is possible, in their professional training.

Remoteness from Data. It is important that the researcher stay close to his data, that is, that he himself directly observe, as far as feasible, the behavior which makes possible the data. Here there is a very real risk of success corrupting, in the sense that as more and more high-powered technical aids (such as automated controlling and recording devices) are added and various kinds of assistants are employed (made possible by, say, federal largesse in the form of research grants), one tends to spend more time in planning and reporting and less time in actual observations of the kind that probably initiated the research project and that are to some degree necessary for its continued development.

This problem is aggravated by the fact that, in addition to the essential tasks of interpreting and reporting data and planning further observations, the researcher is increasingly committed to various ancillary disciplines. For example, as the scope of his research grows, he may be called upon to be something of an engineer (to understand and make decisions about his equipment, not to mention building or modifying it himself), a mathematician and computer programmer (as data reduction becomes more dependent upon sophisticated computerized procedures), a veterinarian (if he uses animals, in which case he is inevitably faced with problems of disease control), a physicist, chemist, sociologist, etc. (for special knowledge many times required in research, such as the role of sucrose as a reinforcer, personal interactions in small groups, etc.), and finally, a personnel expert for employee selection, and counselor for employee satisfaction, when a research and a research-support staff is assembled.

The increasing use of automated devices poses a special problem for graduate research training. This occurs whenever graduate students work with staff members who have succeeded in obtaining such equipment for their own research programs. If the graduate student is trained exclusively, or nearly so, on such equipment, he is poorly equipped to make do with simpler devices when he moves into his own career without, in all likelihood, the initial advantages he enjoyed in the established laboratory where he was trained. One partial solution to this special problem is for the sponsor to make express provisions for at least some training with simpler devices. This procedure has the added advantage of probably ensuring some experience with direct behavioral observations as well as with the simpler equipment.

Information Retrieval. The psychologist today, and increasingly in the future, has the problem of absorbing a tremendous mass of literature. This publication explosion raises the question of the meaning of scholarship: for example, what does "to know one's field" mean in the light of all this information? A plausible answer to this question is that one must learn guidelines to the literature, and the major principles and procedures; specialization is possible in a progressively narrowing area of knowledge and field of research. While some recent advances in information storage and retrieval may be noted (e.g., use of computer, special indexing systems), these can at best alleviate rather than resolve the fundamental problem, and it is certain that future scholars and researchers will be faced with an increasingly different situation.

As the boundaries of knowledge are enlarged, and the mass of detail within them increased, and as one's specialty becomes relatively more restricted, it therefore becomes increasingly necessary that one learn general principles. But at the same time these principles may be more difficult to learn. Increased concern with the delineation and promulgation of principles and unifying prepositions therefore becomes more important, and indicates the significance of theory development as well as the necessity of more effective publication devices (especially with regard to research reviews and the like).

Significance. Each researcher sooner or later must face up to the problem of the significance of his work. To continue to ignore this issue completely becomes increasingly difficult. This can be evaluated either with regard to real-life or theoretical-interpretative objectives; the former are more often emphasized to the neglect of the latter (pure science pursuit).

In the face of questionable significance on either count, which is by far the most typical situation unless very low standards of significance are used, the scientist must have a strong intrinsic motivation to sustain him through months and years of investigation. Experienced researchers need to reflect upon the common opinion (e.g., Kuhn, 1962), that it is so often the young novice who contributes the significant innovative ideas. Breaking out of old and established patterns of thought, emphasized elsewhere in this chapter, is the major means by which more seasoned investigators can make this kind of contribution.

The ability to tackle the "right" problems as well as tackle them effectively is part of the profile of the successful scientist. This is partly the ability to seize upon techniques that "work" either serendiptiously, as in the case of intracranial stimulation accidentally discovered by Olds and Milner (1954), or purposely, as in the development of the cannula implantation technique for chemical treatment of the brain by Grossman (1960).

II. DISCOVERY AND CONFIRMATION

A. *The Roles of Discovery and Confirmation in Science*

Recognition of these two rather different types of scientific activity—*discovery* of relevant variables and solutions to problems, on the one hand, and *testing* the validity of such solutions, on the other hand—will help to clarify the nature of much of the argumentation both inside and outside scientific circles. Take Freud, for a classic example. Was he a scientist? There seems to be little question but that he was not only an extremely astute observer but also a most insightful thinker, and that he produced ideas as stimulating and provocative as any concerned with personality development. But all of these achievements properly belong within the sphere of discovery, and when confirmation is involved, Freud's scientific weakness quickly appears. Not only was he himself not engaged in what most of us would consider to be adequate scientific testing of his notions, he did not seem to recognize the need for such confirmation, at least on a behavioral level. What is generally called *clinical validation*—repeated observations, made generally under the same (relatively or completely uncontrolled) conditions as those that spawned the original ideas—was apparently all that Freud felt necessary for verification.

Now whether Freud is to be classified as a scientist, on the basis of his great contributions within the context of discovery, or not so classified, on the grounds that he did not act on, or even appreciate, the key necessity for adequate confirmation, is entirely a matter of semantics and one that I will certainly avoid here. Which decision is made is much less important than recognizing the essentially semantic nature of the question, and consequently of the answer.

The complementary character of these two activities, neither of which is sufficient unto itself for science to proceed, should be evident. But this very fact presents us with one of the fundamental dilemmas within psychology: how to maintain scientific rigor, mainly with regard to the adequate testing of hypotheses, and at the same time encourage freshness and innovation in thinking. This dilemma is most critical at the time of research training. It is obvious that most of our graduate training, at least in experimental psychology, consists of procedures that deal with techniques of confirmation. A major reason for this relative neglect of discovery and creativity is that we simply do not know how to teach them—if indeed they can be taught.

B. Creativity Training

Most critics agree that more originality is needed not only in students but also in professionals. As a matter of fact, there has been too little originality in American science generally, at least up to recent times. Most of the major contributions to pure science have come from Europe, or from European-trained scientists who have emigrated to the United States (e.g., Einstein, Fermi, Lewin), while we have excelled in technology.

Our research training procedures in psychology have generally been unrealistic in that they have been disproportionately concentrated on confirmation-type practices at the expense of the encouragement of independent, original thinking (which, in the typical American student, is unfortunately not likely to have been encouraged at *any* stage of his education).

The Apprentice System. The Estes Park conference of a special committee on research training of the American Psychological Association (1959) emphasized the neglect of creativity and opted strongly for the "apprentice system," whereby a student works in close coordination with a senior researcher and his staff, participating in all the phases of on-going research projects. There is no question, I think, but that this is the best overall solution to the problem. However, even this solution has some problems, such as:

1. There are probably not enough senior researchers with sufficiently active and vigorous programs, especially at some of the smaller doctoral training institutions. Furthermore, some of those who do have appropriate

projects may themselves be inhibiting rather than encouraging individuals, and may be more concerned with the efficient completion of their research than with the more time-consuming, and often superficially inefficient, problem of training graduate students to think for themselves. Also, some of the researchers who do have vigorous projects and who would be interested in this kind of training are not in a position to undertake it; for example, many are in governmental laboratories. The increasing popularity of post-doctoral training helps to take care of this problem.

2. Many local problems may intervene to complicate the proper placement of students; for example, politics and jealousies within the department, lack of adequate familiarization devices, premature commitments (such as to clinical or counseling curriculum by a student who turns out to be a better bet for experimental theoretical work but who cannot readily shift without serious loss of time and credit once he is well started on the initial program).

3. Even under ideal conditions, some question may be raised about overconcentration by the student in a single area or laboratory, especially when he starts early in his career (perhaps even as an advanced undergraduate) even though this is the best time from the point of view of optimal advantage being taken of opportunities. An antidote to this problem is the deliberate effort to forge at least small research ties in graduate training in other areas and laboratories, such as by formal requirements in the program.

4. Encouragement of creativity is hindered, throughout our educational system, by two factors that are generally disturbing to teachers: (*a*) allowing students to express original and creative ideas is not only time-consuming but also necessarily produces a great deal of chaff and a relatively small amount of wheat; and (*b*) many such ideas, and especially perhaps the better ones, are threatening to the teacher, both personally and professionally, and so are not always encouraged. Recognition of these problems should help the interested teacher to take steps to overcome them and so facilitate his stimulation of creativity in the student.

Some Reservations. With regard to any attempts to train creativity, two reservations may be mentioned in advance of the discussion.

First, not all scientists need to be equally creative. Much steady, careful work needs to be done in science with a minimum creative component. The consolidation that is necessary after a spate of new ideas is not well or graciously done by those who are interested in what seem to them to be bigger and better ideas. Here a practical problem is the overstimulation of ambition concerning originality and creativity in too many students who are not themselves prime candidates for such achievements, and the consequent ruining of what might otherwise be modest but important careers in science.

Second, it is not possible to force creativity, particularly in many students whose entire background, educational and otherwise, has encouraged conformity rather than independence of thinking. Our educational system, with its dedication to stereotyped problems, solutions, and procedures, simply does not prepare many for a creative career in science.

Some Generalizations. In spite of these cautions, it is important that more emphasis be placed in training on creativity and originality. The following comments are based upon over two decades of laboratory experience and graduate-student advising. The interested reader should also see Mackworth (1965) for an especially provocative discussion, emphasizing the distinction between problem *solving* and problem *finding*.

First, it is important to recognize that creative and original ideas typically come unpredictably, but often in spurts. They mostly come *after* hard work, much preparation, and more or less complete immersion in a problem. Since there is a clear danger that such immersion in a problem tends to fixate sets and rigidify thinking, so as to reduce the likelihood of effective solutions, it is at the same time important for the investigator to take "breaks" from his work and do what he can to encourage fresh points of view. Bringing in "naive" but otherwise qualified consultants for making suggestions as to new starts is a commonly used and often helpful procedure.

Second, typically new ideas look great, at first, but more sober second thoughts and more critical evaluation (by others, if not by oneself) usually reduce the perceived value of them. Some constraints are therefore needed for early screening of ideas but these should not be so severe as to discourage their production. Critical checking of new ideas against reality—preferably experimental data, old or newly obtained—is the ideal procedure. Unfortunately, however, this means hard and detailed work of the kind that is most often put off and avoided.

Third, productive ideas seem most often to be the result of a combination of dreaming and doing, of intuition and observation. They must be close enough to reality to permit testing but enough removed from the ordinary to get out of the ruts, or grooves, of normal thought. Fads and highly and tightly developed systems in psychology seem thus to be among the worst enemies of creativity, since they so clearly tie one down to preconceived notions and well-established patterns of interpretation.

Fourth, productive scientific thinking may be analyzed into two related but empirically separable processes: "inspiration" and "perspiration." Although much more is said of inspiration, or the initial conception of an idea, the development of the idea, involving perspiration, is probably the more important process. This is so because few people have no potentially good ideas—and many people have great numbers of such ideas—but most such ideas are simply not adequately checked out. As suggested above, much more effort is needed to develop an idea than simply to initiate it. Moreover, it is impossible to determine in advance which ideas are the most promising (assuming a reasonable degree of feasibility). The bigness in the idea thus tends to come in the process of development of the idea. Furthermore, new inspirations are much more likely to occur after this kind of perspiration.

Lest the preceding discussion seem to downgrade inspiration too severely, let me say that it plays an obviously essential function in scientific thinking. It seems to depend upon a kind of mental alertness, a readiness to see relationships in a new light, to abstract new variables, etc. It is thus the key factor in the much-emphasized "serendipity," or accidental discovery. It is not the accident per se but rather one's alert noting and interpretation of it that makes the difference.

Helpful in this respect is the ability to notice discrepancies or gaps in raw observations and data as well as theories. It is of course best if the experimenter can take an active role in the process of closing the gaps, that is, make "accidents" occur rather than merely wait for them. But whether active or passive, this ability seems to be dependent upon one's carrying around with him a number of continuing (persistent, if sometimes dormant) *problems* close to the threshold of thinking. And these in turn are dependent upon a high degree of persistent motivation as well as a good fund of information. Great achievements rarely occur in the absence of this kind of strong and persistent motivation and dedication to problems. Kuhn's (1962) influential volume has emphasized the role of revolutionary changes (in so-called scientific "paradigms") in the advance of science, and this kind of development is obviously closely related to the problem of creativity and its encouragement.

Some Positive Suggestions. Finally, a few positive suggestions may be mentioned in the hope that creativity can be encouraged by implementation of them in training. Fundamentally, and most important of all, the student must do research, as often as possible and as soon as possible in his training. The student as experimenter must be free to make his own mistakes, try out his own ideas, etc. Designing experiments is fine, but doing them is better. "Pilot experiments" are especially valuable. The best kind of experience is probably that described above as apprenticeship, where the student participates, as actively as his level of training and local conditions permit, in all phases of an ongoing program, under supervision of more experienced experimenters. Beyond this, the student should:

1. read with research ideas in mind, use research ideas wherever possible in examination papers, term papers, etc.;
2. utilize literature reviews and integrative papers fully (rather than

mechanically in response to course requirements) as these contain much food for effective thought;

3. participate as fully as possible in active research discussions ("bull sessions") as well as more formal research staff meetings and individual conferences.

In addition to these more or less apparent suggestions, there are two particular ways in which the student in training (and the professional psychologist also) can actively search for innovations:

1. He can look for new ways to analyze data, especially when the data have been collected in a routine manner (for example, the goaltime measure that only recently has been included as a separate time in runway studies). Most data analysis tends to be stereotyped and data are seldom sufficiently "milked."

2. He can devise new empirical indicants of critical variables, e.g., anxiety, motivation, implicit goal responses, etc. Only recently, after many years of theorizing, has the first direct, if partial, measure of the latter ($r_g - s_g$) appeared (Deaux & Patten, 1964). The multiplicity of meanings, most without empirical underpinnings, for such gross constructs can not be properly reduced without this kind of innovation.

III. THEORY BUILDING

A. The Role of Theory

Generally speaking, all theory may be viewed as having two major and complementary functions: it serves as a *tool*, to guide observation and so produce new and firmer facts, and it is a *goal* of science in that our ultimate objective is as complete an understanding as possible of the natural world, including, of course, man and his artifacts.

There is some argument as to the utility of theory as a tool, as discussed in more detail below in connection with the inductive, or positivistic, mode of theory construction. Nevertheless, most of us will admit that theory has some utility in this respect, and the general manner in which it so functions is fairly straightforward. The role of theory as an objective (goal) is dual. It has (*a*) summarizing, or descriptive, and (*b*) explanatory functions.

The summarizing function of theory is valuable, because it provides economy of expression. Thus it is simpler to state the "law of gravity," as a kind of general proposition than to state separately the host of discrete observations with regard to falling bodies. Similarly, it is more economical (if sometimes riskier) to use some personality attribute, such as anxiety, to summarize a variety of separate behaviors shown by an individual. Few will argue with this kind of summarizing function, although there is often a danger in premature and overextended summarizing.

The explanatory function of theory takes us one step further. Now we must assume that the ultimate objective of our scientific enterprise is the understanding of the order of nature, and that by use of theoretical constructs and propositions (hypotheses, or guesses at relationships among variables) we are not merely summarizing nature but are also probing, symbolically, its structure. Obviously such probing, by symbolic representations more or less firmly anchored on an empirical basis, entails even greater risks than the use of theory in its summarizing functions.

B. Four Primary Modes

Following the classification and terminology introduced previously (Marx, 1963), we may categorize theories into one of these four paradigmatic classes: model, deductive theory, functional theory, and inductive theory. These four modes are shown schematically in Fig. 1.

Although these paradigmatic modes of theory construction may not often be exactly exemplified, in real theoretical efforts, they are often more or less closely approximated. What is most important is that they do represent focal types of theory construction and do illustrate the major types of interactions between empirical and theoretical levels of discourse.

It will be noted that the fundamental differentiation among these four modes as here treated is the direction of the interaction between the empirical and the theoretical level. Thus in the model there is really no interaction, since no feedback is planned from data to model; exactly the contrary relationship is evident in inductive theory, with no feedback from theory to data planned. True interactions are evident in both deductive and functional modes, with feedback from data to theory emphasized in each case.

The Model. As originally intended, a model is a conceptual analog which is used to suggest how empirical research on a problem might best be pursued. That is, the model is a conceptual framework or structure that has been

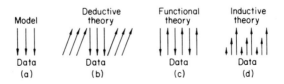

FIG. 1.   Direction of interaction between data and theory in four modes of theory construction (from Marx, 1963).

successfully developed in one field and is now applied, primarily as a guide to research and thinking, in some other, usually less well-developed field. An illustration from the history of psychology would be the use of the telephone switchboard as a model for interpretation of the central nervous system; or, from an even earlier era, the hydraulic system as a model for the nervous system generally. Neither of these two models is seriously entertained today with reference to the nervous system because now we know enough about its functions to see that they are not particularly appropriate; at the time of their initial proposal, however, our ignorance was sufficient to permit their serious consideration. It may also be mentioned that this consideration was more evident with regard to the interpretation of than to the suggestion of empirical research on the nervous system, and in this respect the value of these models was something less than optimal.

The important feature of the model, from the present point of view, relates to the one-way direction of the relationship between theory and data. When a model is used in the manner described, *essentially as a guide to research*, there is no intention that it be modified as a consequence of the results of that research, as is indicated by the direction of the arrows in Fig. 1. The lack of interest in revising the model itself—or its strictly heuristic role, to put it another way—is reflected in the statement that it represents an "as if" type of thinking (Boring, 1957). That is to say, the investigator proceeds "as if" such and such were the case, and is not directly concerned with the validity of his assumptions, only with their practical value in leading him to useful research and interpretation.

Two serious qualifications need to be made to the above description. First, largely as a function of what Koch (1959) has called the "shift in confidence" with regard to formal theorizing, an increasing number of investigators have developed what once might have been called theories but now appear in the guise of "models." In other words, the term model is more and more coming to replace the term theory, mainly perhaps because its use relieves the investigator, or at least may be intended to relieve the investigator, of responsibility for checking the adequacy of his substantive propositions. While there is certainly some justification for much of the current usage of the term "model," it is nevertheless disturbing that the usage has been carried to such an extreme. In addition to erasing what looks like a quite legitimate distinction between the model and the other types of theory construction, the indiscriminate use of what is really theory (at least in our present meaning) in the guise of "model" can too often give the investigator a false sense of security. Ultimately he is going to be called upon to take some responsibility for establishing relationships among the consequences of his interpretative thinking and a good case can be made for the proposition that taking such responsibility should not be too long put off.

Second, there are a number of theoretical endeavors in which a model is used in combination with some other type of theory construction. The best examples here are the recently popular mathematical models in learning theory (Estes, 1959). In these cases a mathematical model, usually fairly simple in form, is taken as an initial framework from which a behavioral theory can be developed. In most cases the theoretical development is of a more or less deductive mode, in that a formal set of propositions is set up and modified in accordance with empirical results. This usage does involve in part what might be called "true" use of the model ("true," that is, to our present definition) because (*a*) the conceptual structure is taken from another discipline, in this case mathematics, and (*b*) there is no intention to modify this conceptual framework, in so far as it applies to mathematics. It is the addition of the behavioral theory, which is intended for empirical test and modification, that complicates this particular use of the model and so can lead to some confusion unless the separation of the total theoretical effort into two (or more) stages is made.

Deductive Theory. As indicated by the diagram in Fig. 1, this kind of theory involves a distinctly two-way relationship with data. It is marked by a more or less formalized set of logically intertwined propositions, well exemplified by the behavior system developed by Hull (1943; 1951; 1952), which are deliberately subjected to a thorough-going empirical attack.

This kind of theoretical effort clearly combines the tool (heuristic) function of theory with the goal (theory as an objective) function. While this is in some ways an advantage it is also a weakness of deductive theory, in that once a formal set of propositions is developed there are certain disadvantages inherent in it. These are well illustrated by the fate of the Hullian system, once serious criticism was directed at it (e.g., Cotton, 1955; Koch, 1954; Seward, 1954). For one thing, there is a strong tendency toward personal involvement which may often interfere with the strictly factual evaluation of the theory itself that is called for, as Skinner (1961) has maintained. Much of the polemic associated with the Hull–Tolman opposition, mentioned above, may be attributed to this personal involvement.

Also, and fundamentally more important, once a theory is formalized and propagated it tends to become invested with more authority than the factual underpinnings merit; the inertia of theory so established may well become a serious detriment to the development of more effective interpretations.

In spite of these difficulties, and those others that will be discussed in connection with functional theory, there is a certain attraction associated with deductive-type theorizing. Part of this is due to its greater elegance, especially in contrast to functional theory, which tends to be messy, like the research to which it is very closely related. All ongoing research is necessarily more untidy in its development than the subsequent account of it. But mostly the attraction of deductive theory is probably due to the fact that it takes the form that we like to think our theory should have—a nicely interrelated network of explanatory propositions all logically tied together. Whether or not the deliberate use of this ultimate type of theory is in practice the best way to *develop* such a theory is an open question; the proponents of functional theory, which we next consider, say no, for reasons which we shall now examine.

Functional Theory. The major distinction between this kind of theory construction and the deductive mode is that the functional mode entails a much more short-term type of theory. That is, nothing as elaborate as the Hullian system is attempted; rather, the emphasis is on much more modest and restricted explanatory propositions, whose development is closely related to a particular experimental problem and the data that can be produced to bear upon this problem. Thus the functional type of theory is not only closer to the data, and therefore much more readily modified, it is also of considerably less scope than the typical deductive theory.

These differences, while important ones, are nonetheless differences of degree rather than of kind, since both types of theory utilize deductive (as well as, less overtly, inductive) reasoning and both types emphasize feedback from research data. Most of the examples of functional theorizing can be drawn, historically, from the functionalism school in psychology (cf. Hilgard & Bower, 1966, Ch. 10; Marx & Hillix, 1963, Ch. 10). Contemporary illustrations are less easy to identify, mainly because by its very nature this kind of modest theorizing is less conspicuous than the other modes. However, it does seem safe to assert that, in various guises, most contemporary theoretical experimental work may be placed in this classification, since the *emphasis more and more tends to be on the problem rather than the theory per se.*

The major criticism that has been generally directed against the functional type of theory concerns its lack of distinctiveness. Much as eclecticism has often been attacked for being nondescript and vapid, as compared with more elegant forms of theoretical doctrine, so functionalism has been accused of a lack of clearcut theoretical substance. Most of this kind of criticism has come from proponents of formal deductive theory, such as Hullian. On the other hand, functional theory is sometimes also attacked from the opposite side, by positivistic psychologists expounding the virtues of inductive theory or no theory at all, for being *too* theoretical. This amenability to attack from either side of the theoretical spectrum reflects the central position of functional theory.

Inductive Theory. As the least overtly "theoretical" mode of interpretation of data, inductive theory is best illustrated in contemporary psychology by the operant-conditioning movement spearheaded by Skinner (1938; 1956; 1961; 1966a; 1966b). This variety of positivism (or ultrapositivism) is marked by an aversion to explicit interpretation of a theoretical sort and by the belief that *once sufficient facts, or data, are accumulated they will speak for themselves.* In other words, summary statements of empirical relationships will be gradually accumulated and will eventually become the kind of generalized explanatory principles which we need. No logical inferences or deductive conclusions are necessary. The strictly inductive procedure—working from individual instances to general conclusions, rather than from hypothesized general conclusions as premises to particular instances, as in the case of the deductive mode—is indicated in Fig. 1, where the inductive mode is shown to involve a strictly one-way relationship of data to theory.

Most of the criticisms of the deductive mode of theory construction, the major ones of which have been mentioned above, have come from the proponents of inductive theory. Besides Skinner himself, these have included Brunswik (1955a; 1955b) and Sidman (1960).

Critics of the strictly inductive mode of theory construction have pointed to the older, and better established, sciences, in which logical (deductive) inferences have constantly played a major role in their development (*in addition to* the primarily inductive activities, or fact-accumulation, the importance of which is not denied). Another argument against the Skinnerian approach is that the positivist is actually using some kind of inference, as in designing his experiments. This activity constitutes in practice a kind of interpretation of prior data and it is better by far that his logic be explicated rather than remain hidden in his own covert (thinking) behavior, or be restricted to those to whom he speaks, as in his laboratory. It is held that the social corrective function of science, by means of which errors of individuals in experiment or theory are corrected when others attempt to repeat observations and interpretations, is best served if such public exposure of the logic behind the data collection is expressly planned and produced.

From the present point of view, it is not necessary to decide which of these various procedures is best, nor to attempt to decide which of the various criticisms has the most merit. It should be mentioned that there does not seem to be an *inherent* weakness in any of the theoretical modes described, although different sorts of weaknesses may develop in the various ways in which the procedures are implemented. All of the modes of theory construction described may therefore be said to have their place in psychology; which we use will be determined partly by our own experimental background, accounting for our own individual styles of research, and partly by the problems we are attacking. But there is plenty of room for each of these procedures and there is greater likelihood of eventual scientific advance if all are used.

C. Key Problems

The following brief statement is intended to outline certain key problems, the resolution of which is necessary before effective research and theory building can proceed.

Parsimony. The principle of parsimony, often called "William of Occam's razor" or "Lloyd Morgan's canon," from early proponents, is concerned, strictly speaking, neither with confirmation nor with discovery. It is a rough guideline to the acceptability of hypotheses and principles. It says that when one selects a proposition as an explanation of some set of events it is safer to choose the alternative that is simplest, in terms of assumptions needed, of those which satisfy all of the data. In this way it is more closely related to confirmation than to discovery, since it emphasizes the fit between data and interpretation. However, its primary function is to guide acceptance, *not testing*, of ideas. In this respect, it is often unfairly maligned, as has been pointed out elsewhere (Marx, 1963, p. 20ff). If anything, parsimony should serve as a spur, not a deterrent, to the creation and testing of new ideas, especially when the proponents of more complex accounts are not satisfied with the simpler accounts.

As hinted above, the applicability of the principle of parsimony is more important in applied science than in pure science. This conclusion follows from the fact that when practitioners or policy makers in government, or education, or industry, or the military must select a new program from among alternatives, there may be enormous practical consequences, for better or worse. Furthermore, there may not be time for extended testing before the decision must be made. Thus it is of critical importance that parsimonious thinking be judiciously applied within these areas.

The basis for the principle of parsimony is partly historical, in terms of our experience in the various sciences, and partly logical. Historically, scientists have learned that the more assumptions there are involved—or the more complex a theory is—the greater likelihood there is of error. And once a serious error creeps in, the whole theoretical superstructure may be fatally weakened. The situation is something like that which obtains when a lie is told; one needs to continue fabrication, in order to support the original misstatement, until a whole new network of falsehood is developed.

Logically, the reason for the greater effectiveness of the simple solution is, in large part, that science mainly consists of a more or less feeble groping towards "truth" (or factualness, as described above) and that most of our original ideas are doomed to extinction. On a probability basis alone, therefore, the fewer the links in the chain the less is the likelihood of serious error.

Apart from practical consequences, such as those mentioned above, the failure to respect the principle of parsimony results in the overloading of relatively untested, and therefore unconfirmed, ideas. Differences of opinion as to the value of such ideas tend to separate experimentally oriented scientists from others, such as some personality theorists within psychology, who have basically different interests. The student should keep in mind, however, that the argument revolves around the *present* acceptability of relatively untested ideas and not their potential utility.

The principle of parsimony is, itself, deceptively simple. This follows from the fact that there are a number of different ways in which parsimony can be applied. The number of premises, mentioned above, is perhaps the most prominent of these and perhaps the most important. However, one can also consider the degree of abstractness (the more abstract notions being generally considered the less parsimonious) or, as in the case of animal behavior, the level of function (that is, reasoning presumed in a dog that shows the trick of returning with a newspaper as compared with a more "mechanistic" or a stimulus–response type of conditioning presumed). But, however it may be implemented, the basic generalization remains the same: one *accepts* the simpler principle, of the principles that are consistent with the available data, if one wishes the least risk of eventual error.

Operationism. Initially expressed by the physicist Bridgman (1927), the principle of operationism is simply a formal statement of a very basic rule in scientific communication: that the empirical basis for each term used, and especially for each theoretical construct, be clear. Fundamentally, this principle merely asks for *clarity in communication*: tell me what you mean, by your language, in terms of operations I can make or observe. Thus viewed, it is logically unassailable. Moreover, it obviously has its greatest impact in those areas of psychology where it is most difficult to apply, for example, in clinical and personality theory.

If the principle of operationism is fundamentally so secure, why has there been so much dispute concerning it, especially in psychology? One answer to this question is suggested by the comment concerning its difficulty of application in certain areas of psychology. Proponents of theoretical propositions which are not based upon operationally clear concepts have consistently argued against the principle, largely on the ground that it discourages creativity and the like. More basically, however, the resistance to operationism has come very largely from the fact that *in practice* this fundamentally simple rule quickly becomes more complicated. That is, its implementation is far more difficult than its fundamental expression. I shall not attempt to deal with the variety of objections that have been raised, but shall instead merely point out that, whatever merit these have (and some of course do have considerable merit), it is more important that we recognize the principle of operationism as an objective in scientific communication, as an *ultimate* requirement rather than as one that needs to be perfectly satisfied here and now, in every facet of scientific communication. But it is also important that progress in intelligibility be made, and that each investigator attempt to improve the operational clarity of his language. Failure to do this can be criticized, particularly when it is evidenced by those who vehemently oppose the fundamental principle.

The Intervening Variable. As a special case of the dispute concerning operationism in psychological theory construction, the role of the intervening variable may be more closely examined. Initially proposed by Tolman (1932) but developed most extensively by Hull (1943) and Spence (1956, 1960), the intervening variable was intended to permit the formal representation of intraorganismic processes. The operational issue was introduced by MacCorquodale and Meehl (1948) when they distinguished between two types of theoretical constructs. What they called the "hypothetical construct" was essentially nonoperational while their "true intervening variable" was said to be operational, that is, a purely descriptive representation of some particular stimulus–response relationship.

Although the intervening variable technique has certainly not led to the immediate success in theoretical endeavors that some of its early proponents may have expected, it is by the same token hardly the complete failure that others have assumed (e.g., Koch, 1959). As in the case of operationism generally, it is necessary to recognize that the intervening variables which have been proposed vary in the degree to which they satisfy the operational requirement and that continuing attempts to improve them in this regard are necessary.

What I have elsewhere (Marx, 1951) called the experimental/control (E/C) type of intervening variable may be cited as an illustration of the kind of use in theory construction that is possible with this technique. Essentially, this kind of variable relates directly to the independent variable that differentiates the experimental (E) from the control (C) group, and is assumed to represent *whatever* intraorganismic functions are necessary to account for the observed S–R relationship (the responses observed to occur in a particular stimulus situation).

As an illustration of the possibilities inherent in this kind of theoretical procedure, the interesting experiment by Mowrer and Viek (1948) and the conceptually similar experiment by Marx and Van Spanckeren (1952) were offered (Marx, 1951). In the former experiment, food-deprived rats were trained to eat mash from a stick presented through the metal bars of a shock-grid floor. All animals were shocked ten seconds after they started to eat (or following a set time interval if no eating occurred). The experimental-control difference concerned whether or not the rat was able to control the shock himself. Experimental subjects were able to turn the shock off immediately by jumping off the grid; each control subject received exactly the same amount of shock on each trial as its matched experimental partner but was unable to influence the duration of the shock by anything it did. An important behavioral difference emerged under these conditions: experimental subjects ate reliably more quickly and more often than control subjects.

In the Marx and Van Spanckeren (1952) study an experimental group of audiogenic-seizure sensitive subjects was allowed to turn off the noxious, seizure-producing stimulus (high intensity, high frequency sound) and showed reliably fewer seizures than matched controls that received exactly the same amount of noxious stimulation but were unable to effect it by their behavior.

In each of these experiments the behavioral difference may be attributed to some difference, within the two groups, that is directly attributable to the difference between the experimental and control treatments and hence is labeled an E/C intervening variable. Several comments may be made concerning this kind of informal theoretical usage.

First, the E/C intervening variable is not a spectacular, attention-attracting type of construct. Rather it represents the kind of workday procedure that is commonly used, without fanfare, mostly in the functional type of theory construction.

Second, a major advantage it offers is that it permits one to strike a balance between two extreme positions, the emphasis on highly formal theory (as represented by Hull, Spence, Tolman), and the ultrapositivistic rejection of all overt theory (as advocated by Skinner and his adherents).

Thirdly, the E/C technique has the further advantage of emphasizing, and thereby helping to open up to public scrutiny, the critical but too often ignored problem of identification of variables. There has been an unfortunate tendency to gloss over this important and necessary process and emphasize instead either theoretical solutions, often in the absence of adequate empirical implementation, or empirical procedures per se. The E/C procedure forces attention on the interfacing problem, the relationship between empirical and theoretical procedures, and thus goes to the heart of the problem of theory construction.

IV. THE BANDWAGON EFFECT

Faddishness and Conformity in Research. Although there are promising signs of a much improved situation, the problem of faddishness has been especially acute within psychology. Currently "hot" research topics—

whether Hullian theory, as in the 1940's, or problems associated with intra-cranial brain stimulation, as is true today—seem to receive all too much attention from professional psychologists, as well as from graduate students. Any researcher is likely to have the problem of adapting and modifying both his experimental procedures and his theoretical guidelines to the needs of his research, rather than sticking blindly to a single experimental procedure or theoretical account (either or both of which he may have learned in graduate training). Against the need for adaptation one must always of course weigh the value of continued single-minded investigation, as both procedures have merit and utility, but on balance the need for adaptation seems best to fit the kind of problems that science faces.

There are many illustrations of situations where some stagnation in research has occurred and seems to have been at least partly produced by the failure to broaden the range of experimental and theoretical attacks on critical problems. To take one example, Thorndike's (1933) spread-of-effect technique, which consisted of having the subject guess numbers to match words or nonsense syllable stimuli in a serial multiple-choice learning task, came to be fixed as *the* procedure used (cf. Marx, 1956; Postman, 1962) and has only occasionally been varied. [For recent developments on this problem, see Greenwald (1966) who attempted to reopen these issues by stimulating reconsideration of Nuttin's (1949) important variation in procedure and theory, and also retorts by Postman (1966) and Marx (1967) as well as the more recent and complete account by Nuttin and Greenwald (1968).] This sticking so closely to a single procedure probably accounts in large part for the paucity of recent effective data on this particular problem.

The recent modifications of Skinner's free-response operant-conditioning technique to apply to discrete-trial (or controlled-operant) methodology (Atkinson & Calfee, 1964; Gonzales, Bainbridge, & Bitterman, 1966; Marx, Tombaugh, Hatch, & Tombaugh, 1965) are an encouraging sign that experimental procedures are becoming freer.

Emotional Involvements. With regard to theoretical issues, we have already discussed some of the problems associated with monolithic theories, such as Hull's, or systems, such as Skinner's. One special problem should be elaborated. This is the extreme emotional reaction, and counter-reaction, that is so often associated with overly zealous attachment to or reaction against some particular systematic position. Just as the most extreme anti-communist is likely to have been at one time an avid communist, or the outspoken atheist at one time a religious devotee, so the polemicist in psychology may swing from one emotional extreme to the other. Two illustrations from the recent history of psychology suggest how this phenomenon, albeit in somewhat milder form, may operate to influence attitudes.

Consider these two contrasting views of Hull's theoretical efforts:

If the earlier publications gave any reason for doubting the fruitfulness of Hull's constructs, *Principles of Behavior* should go far toward dissipating such doubt. Hull's previous work left no room for questioning the methodological maturity of his *general* approach; the present work makes it no longer possible to question the value and richness of his *specific* theoretical assumptions.

and

Under close scrutiny, not a single member of a single class of such [Hull's] theoretical components satisfied the requirements for rigorous scientific theory of the sort envisaged within the theorist's explicit objectives. More importantly, many of the detailed solutions embodied in the theory of major problems in the methodology of psychological theory construction—e.g., the techniques employed for the "measurement" of independent and dependent variables, the techniques for the construction of quantitative, or even qualitative function forms—proved to have little merit within their concrete theoretical context, however suggestive certain of them may be in defining the problems that behavior theorists must face.

Unlikely as it may seem, at least at first glance, these two excerpts were written by the same critic (Koch, 1944, p. 270; Koch, 1954, pp. 159–160). What a difference a decade makes! It is quite apparent that the "close scrutiny" that intervened between the two statements produced a marked turnabout in evaluation, and it also seems quite possible that the extremely negative tone of the second evaluation might be in part a function of the overly optimistic tone of the initial evaluation.

Another illustration of this kind of phenomenon may be seen in the present situation regarding the mechanism of language and language development. Stimulated by Skinner's (1957) interpretation of language, behavioristically inclined psychologists have for some time tended to regard language as a prime example of operant behavior that can be nicely incorporated within an empirical conditioning framework. This view, however, has come under increasing attack from the new linguists, spearheaded by Chomsky (1959), and as a result has been slowly giving way. For example, in a recent paper Bem and Bem (1968, p. 498) comment as follows:

. . . it is not biological considerations which are prompting an increasing number of psychologists to accept some of the extraordinary conclusions about the innate character of linguistic competence, but the apparent failure of any current notions about learning to account for the new linguistic observations in even a remotely satisfying way. Some well-known psychologists (e.g., Jenkins, 1968) have made public "mea culpa's" as mediational models of language have withered under the attack, while others, more discretely, are privately following suit. And, even though one of us has found Skinner's approach to verbal behavior heuristically valuable for illuminating certain non-linguistic phenomena (Bem, 1965), we, too, are among the persuaded.

Again, it is highly probable that such defections would be much less radical had not the early acceptance of the learning viewpoint been less enthusiastic and unguarded. As Bem and Bem point out, this acceptance was often on a strictly programmatic basis, in the absence of empirical data.

A dangerous consequence of this kind of phenomenon, and one that needs to be carefully guarded against, is that once the prematurely accepted point of view is discarded there will not be an adequate effort to salvage potentially valuable parts of it. Thus there has been a tendency to reject all of Hull's system, since it has not lived up to its early promise, and there may well be a similar tendency to disregard the potentially significant role that learning may well play in language development, even granted that nativistic factors are also critical. Adoption of more qualified endorsements of theoretical positions from their inception may help to prevent the occurrence of these kinds of situations in the future.

V. COMMON FALLACIES CONCERNING THEORY CONSTRUCTION

Because of the prominence, among students as well as laymen, of certain fallacious notions concerning science and theory building, it is important that we briefly consider some of the most common fallacies. Our discussion will state a number of these, in positive form, and then in each case indicate why the statement is false.

Science proceeds in a direct line to laws and theories. Nothing could be further from the real situation. In point of fact, science is an extremely messy and untidy business, with errors and false starts much more common than successes. This important point has been elaborated earlier in our discussion.

Science is strictly logical, in a formal sense, as well as straightforward. In fact, formal logic, while potentially useful in some respects, is seldom used in theory building. Its prominence in descriptions and explanations of theories is therefore quite misleading. Deductive logic may be used in a very informal and quite unplanned manner, as suggested above. Watson's (1968) recent account of the "breaking" of the genetic code is a realistic if perhaps extremely frank account of the kind of work that actually goes into scientific successes.

Unless relatively complete success is attained by a particular method or theory, the procedure is not fruitful and should be discarded. Quite on the contrary, approximation (and very incomplete success) is characteristic of all science, and the spectacular theoretical successes described in the popular press and the textbooks are mostly the product of hindsight. That is to say, if one could look more closely at the actual development of an ultimately successful theory he would find that its course was erratic and irregular, with the final success resulting from the cumulative advances made possible by a good number of partial successes and approximations. These are ignored or minimized in later accounts. With the zigs and zags thus eliminated the straight line appears but is not truly representative of the work.

This point has many ramifications. To mention but one illustration, Israel and Goldstein's (1944) early rejection of operationism in psychology was largely, and in my opinion erroneously, based on their conviction that it was a procedure which could not be applied perfectly and completely to scientific work from the very beginning.

Single and generally simple theories must account for all data of a certain class (say, learning). While this is a much more arguable and uncertain point than the preceding, nevertheless it does seem more probable that as more is learned about the interactions of variables (commonly ignored in the early theoretical efforts), complexities will develop even in the simple theories. And while certain monolithic theories, such as Hull's behavior system, can be strongly defended on heuristic grounds alone—that is, in terms of their vigorous promotion of research and their thoroughgoing test of a particular principle or set of principles—there is nonetheless a clear theoretical danger involved. This is the risk that more effective principles will be overlooked when zealous attention to one's own ideas overrides the ideal of scientific impartiality.

It should be noted that many proponents of the simple theory do not propose it in the belief that it will account for all of the data of a certain class but rather on the grounds (again, heuristic) that an effective procedure is to push a simple account as far as one can. While this is a popular and quite defensible notion, it may also be pointed out that it is equally feasible to attempt to work toward simple and monolithic theory in the other direction: that is, to start with the assumption that, say, the various diverse phenomena of learning are explicable on different principles, rather than being expressions of a single principle, and then see how closely these different principles can be brought together through successive researches. This procedure would have the important advantage of letting research success, rather than initial inferences, dictate the direction of the theory development.

Laws and theories must be directly tested, preferably in crucial experiments where alternative accounts are clearly contradicted. While this procedure may be valuable, it is by no means the only, or even the most commonly effective, procedure by which scientific laws and theories are developed. An alternative procedure is to attack specific problems, or experimental-theoretical issues, rather than test specific theories, directly, and then to use the data to throw light on theories, indirectly, in the sense that the problem rather than the theory was the central objective of the research. This will be recognized as a form of the functional mode of theory construction described above.

A good example of the limitations of the direct-test procedure occurred during the 1940's and 1950's when Hullian and Tolmanian learning theories were being opposed. The net result of many (almost countless) experiments directed toward determining which of these two theories is correct is that there was not only no clear resolution of this question but also that there is today little concern with the issue. Inconsistent data (that is, data inconsistent with one or the other of the two theories as initially posed) forced such changes and compromises as to leave little of the original accounts intact. The use of such constructs as $r_g - s_g$ (a Hull–Spence mechanism, referring to implicit goal responses, and one that is close to Tolman's expectancy construct) helps to close the gap between the central notions of what were once apparently quite distinct theoretical positions.

VI. Current Study of Psychology

We may separate all psychological research into three broad, and at least partially separable, categories: behavioral, physiological, and inferential or theoretical. In its narrow, present usage, behavioral research, well exemplified by operant conditioning, utilizes a minimum of inference, as emphasized previously in this chapter, and builds toward theory inductively. Physiological research is directed, reductively, toward an interpretation of behavior in terms of underlying physiological events. Each of these major types of research has recently achieved remarkable successes; cf. the movement called behavior modification, largely utilizing operant conditioning techniques, and all of the spectacular "breakthroughs" of the physiological psychologist, such as the use of minute electrical or chemical stimulations of the brain as a means of identifying the brain bases for behavioral processes.

In contrast to the behavioral and physiological procedures, which either look at behavior directly or look for underlying bodily mechanisms, the inferential approach attempts to build theory, and understanding, by discovery of the psychological mechanisms underlying behavior processes. As we have seen, the older theoretical questions and classical systems are now generally seen to be unfruitful, and there has been an emphasis on a more functional type of approach to particular problems. All areas of psychology are being actively researched as the diversification of both empirical and theoretical effort continues. With regard to payoff in improved theory, there have been some recent successes—for example, the development of new ways of looking at the processing of information—but many more should be forthcoming within the next few decades. Among the more important problem areas in which advances should be made are developmental psychology and psychology of motivation, each rather long neglected but ripe now for empirical and theoretical analysis.

As for the more global or holistic understanding (of the "whole man"), this more difficult problem will probably need to wait somewhat longer for even partial solution. Here the holistic approach, looking at the "whole man" directly, and gaining sufficient understanding for at least some application in practice, will probably need to be complemented by the integration of the more particularistic behavior theories of the sort described above as inferential. Achievement of the understanding of personality, say, by this more indirect method may be slower but in the long run turn out to be a surer and more promising approach.

Finally, what are the prospects for the eventual development of a single, unifying theory for all of behavior? As far as I can see, if this sort of fully integrating principle is ever achieved, it will almost certainly be basically neurophysiological in nature, with parallel development of inferential theory. But the prospects of any such development within the foreseeable future are remote indeed, and for some time in the future we shall need to be satisfied with such less ambitious but more realistic theoretical successes as can be wrung from an ever reluctant, yet exciting, subject matter.

REFERENCES

Allport, G. W. *Personality: A psychological interpretation.* New York: Holt, 1937.

Atkinson, R. C., & Calfee, R. C. An automated system for discrete-trial research with animals. *Psychological Reports*, 1964, **14**, 424–426.

Bakan, D. A generalization of Sidman's results on group and individual functions, and a criterion. *Psychological Bulletin*, 1954, **51**, 63–64.

Bem, D. J. An experimental analysis of self-persuasion. *Journal of Experimental Social Behavior*, 1965, **1**, 199–218.

Bem, D. J., & Bem, S. L. Nativism revisited. A review of E. H. Lenneberg's biological foundations of language. *Journal of the Experimental Analysis of Behavior*, 1968, **11**, 497–501.

Boring, E. G. When is human behavior predetermined? *Scientific Monthly*, 1957, **84**, 189–196.

Bridgman, P. W. *The logic of modern physics.* New York: Macmillan, 1927.

Brunswik, E. Representative design and probabilistic theory in a functional psychology. *Psychological Review*, 1955, **62**, 193–217. (a)

Brunswik, E. In defense of probabilistic functionalism: A reply. *Psychological Review*, 1955, 62, 236–242. (b)

Chomsky, N. Review of B. F. Skinner's *Verbal behavior. Language*, 1959, **35**, 26–58.

Cohen, M. R., & Nagel, E. *Introduction to logic and scientific method.* New York: Harcourt, 1934.

Cotton, J. W. On making predictions from Hull's theory. *Psychological Review*, 1955, **62**, 303–314.

Deaux, E. B., & Patten, R. L. Measurement of the anticipatory goal response in instrumental runway conditioning. *Psychonomic Science*, 1964, **1**, 357–358.

Estes, W. K. Learning. *Annual Review of Psychology*, 1956, **7**, 1–38.

Estes, W. K. The statistical approach to learning theory. In S. Koch (Ed.), *Psychology: A study of a science.* New York: McGraw-Hill, 1959.

Gonzales, R. C., Bainbridge, P., & Bitterman, M. E. Discrete-trials lever-pressing in the rat as a function of pattern of reinforcement, effortfulness of response, and amount of reward. *Journal of Comparative and Physiological Psychology,* 1966, **61**, 110–122.

Greenwald, A. G. Nuttin's neglected critique of the law of effect. *Psychological Bulletin,* 1966, **65**, 199–205.

Grossman, S. P. Eating or drinking elicited by direct adrenergic or cholinergic stimulation of hypothalamus. *Science,* 1960, **132**, 301–302.

Guthrie, E. R. Psychological facts and psychological theory. *Psychological Bulletin,* 1946, **43**, 1–20.

Hearst, E. Resistance to extinction functions in the single organism. *Journal of the Experimental Analysis of Behavior,* 1961, **4**, 133–144.

Hilgard, E. R., & Bower, G. H. *Theories of learning.* (3rd ed.) New York: Appleton, 1966.

Hull, C. L. *Principles of behavior.* New York: Appleton, 1943.

Hull, C. L. *Essentials of behavior.* New Haven: Yale University Press, 1951.

Hull, C. L. *A behavior system.* New Haven: Yale University Press, 1952.

Israel, H. E., & Goldstein, B. Operationism in psychology. *Psychological Review,* 1944, **51**, 177–188.

Jenkins, J. J. The challenge to psychological theorists. In T. R. Dixon and D. L. Horton (Eds.), *Verbal behavior and general behavior theory.* Englewood Cliffs, N. J.: Prentice-Hall, 1968. Pp. 538–549.

Koch, S. Review of Hull's Principles of behavior. *Psychological Bulletin,* 1944, **41**, 269–286.

Koch, S. Clark L. Hull. In W. K. Estes *et al.* (Eds.), *Modern learning theory.* New York: Appleton, 1954. Pp. 1–176.

Koch, S. Epilogue. In S. Koch (Ed.), *Psychology: A study of a science.* Vol. 3. New York: McGraw-Hill, 1959. Pp. 729–788.

Kuhn, T. S. *The structure of scientific revolutions.* Chicago: University of Chicago Press, 1962.

MacCorquodale, K., & Meehl, P. E. On a distinction between hypothetical constructs and intervening variables. *Psychological Review,* 1948, **55**, 95–107.

Mackworth, N. H. Originality. *American Psychologist,* 1965, **20**, 51–66.

Marx, M. H. Intervening variable or hypothetical construct. *Psychological Review,* 1951, **58**, 235–247.

Marx, M. H. Spread of effect: A critical review. *Genetics Psychological Monograph,* 1956, **53**, 119–186.

Marx, M. H. (Ed.) *Theories in contemporary psychology.* New York: Macmillan, 1963.

Marx, M. H. Analysis of the spread of effect: A comparison of Thorndike and Nuttin. *Psychological Bulletin,* 1967, **67**, 413–415.

Marx, M. H., & Hillix, W. A. *Systems and theories in psychology.* New York: McGraw-Hill, 1963.

Marx, M. H., Tombaugh, T. N., Hatch, R. S., & Tombaugh, J. W. Controlled operant conditioning boxes with discrete-trial programming for multiple experimental use. *Perceptual and Motor Skills,* 1965, **21**, 247–254.

Marx, M. H., & Van Spanckeren, W. J. Control of the audiogenic seizure by the rat. *Journal of Comparative and Physiological Psychology,* 1952, **45**, 170–179.

Mowrer, O. H., & Viek, P. An experimental analogue of fear from a sense of helplessness. *Journal of Abnormal and Social Psychology,* 1948, **43**, 193–200.

Nuttin, J. "Spread" in recalling failure and success. *Journal of Experimental Psychology,* 1949, **39**, 690–699.

Nuttin, J., & Greenwald, A. G. *Reward and punishment in human learning.* New York: Academic Press, 1968.

Olds, J., & Milner, D. Positive reinforcement produced by electrical stimulation of septal area and other regions of the rat brain. *Journal of Comparative and Physiological Psychology,* 1954, **47**, 419–427.

Postman, L. Rewards and punishments in human learning. In L. Postman (Ed.), *Psychology in the making.* New York: Knopf, 1962.

Postman, L. Reply to Greenwald. *Psychological Bulletin,* 1966, **65**, 383–388.

Rosenthal, R. *Experimenter effects in behavioral research.* New York: Appleton, 1966.

Seward, J. P. Hull's system of behavior: An evaluation. *Psychological Review,* 1954, **61**, 145–159.

Sidman, M. A note on functional relations obtained from group data. *Psychological Bulletin,* 1952, **49**, 263–269.

Sidman, M. *Tactics of scientific research.* New York: Basic Books, 1960.

Skinner, B. F. *The behavior of organisms: An experimental analysis.* New York: Appleton. 1938.

Skinner, B. F. A case history in scientific method. *American Psychologist,* 1956, **11**, 221–233,

Skinner, B. F. *Verbal behavior.* New York: Appleton, 1957.

Skinner, B. F. *Cumulative record.* (Rev. ed.) New York: Appleton, 1961.

Skinner, B. F. Operant behavior. In W. K. Honig (Ed.), *Operant behavior: Areas of research and application.* New York: Appleton, 1966. (a)

Skinner, B. F. What is the experimental analysis of behavior? *Journal of the Experimental Analysis of Behavior,* 1966, **9**, 213–218. (b)

Spence, K. W. *Behavior theory and conditioning.* New Haven: Yale University Press, 1956.

Spence, K. W. *Behavior theory and learning.* Englewood Cliffs, N. J.: Prentice-Hall, 1960.

Thorndike, E. L., An experimental study of rewards. *Teachers College Contributions to Education,* 1933, No. 580.

Tolman, E. C. *Purposive behavior in animals and man.* New York: Appleton, 1932.

Watson, J. *Double helix.* Bonn, Germany: Atheneum Press, 1968.

Part II

THE RESEARCH AREAS

The Biology of Mind:
Neurobehavioral Foundations[1]

KARL H. PRIBRAM

DEPARTMENTS OF PSYCHIATRY AND PSYCHOLOGY
STANFORD UNIVERSITY
STANFORD, CALIFORNIA

I. WHAT PSYCHOLOGY CAN BE ABOUT

I have been asked to describe here my systematic approach to problems in psychology. At first this seemed a reasonable request, easily met since my experimental work has progressed in a fairly systematic fashion and my lectures to students of psychology seemed not unduly chaotic. A closer review provoked by an undergraduate student who asked simply "what is

[1] This paper was presented in part as the Presidential Address to the Division of Physiological and Comparative Psychology, American Psychological Association, San Francisco, September, 1968. The research was supported by NIMH Grant MH 12970 and USPHS Career Award MH 15,214.

the basic tenet of your system?," made me realize that my approach was not nearly as rigidly forethought as I had suspected. I had not cooly fashioned a model—on the contrary, much healthy intuition, guesswork, groping, and fortuitous circumstance went into what might be called "my position." In fact I was hard put to come up with any one central tenet. What I can present, however, is a central tenet at each level of inquiry to which my interests are directed. Let me begin at the top, the most general level of scientific inquiry, then illustrate the operations by which I implement this approach, and finally present some of my views of brain function and of the psychological process which have resulted from such implementation.

I believe that psychology must concern itself with the problems of mind, i.e., with the contents and processes which become subjectively experienced, verbally and instrumentally communicated, and validated through social concensus. In this I differ from most of my contemporaries who talk and write about psychology as the science of behavior, i.e., they are behaviorists. Behaviorism is usually concerned with some form of stimulus–response relationship, some sort of correlation between an input to the organism and the output generated by this organism consequent to that input. Sophisticated variants of behaviorism include such formulations as Estes (1959) who describes stimuli as mathematical sets of events whose partitions are the responses of the organism. Skinner (1968) recently has clarified his response-oriented views by stating that he is interested in detailing all the environmental events necessary to produce reinforcement, i.e., the increased probability that a particular response will recur. Note that behaviorists are primarily concerned with correlations among environmental events; both stimuli and *responses* are so conceived, e.g., in an operant situation responses are the marks on the cumulative record which, at the end of an experiment, can be taken home for study and analysis. One learns about the organism indirectly from these environmental relationships. The organism is mediator, a black box containing the intervening variables or constructs which give rise to the relationships.

My own approach from its inception has critically departed from behaviorism (Pribram, 1954a). I treat the organism directly as a class of independent variables to be manipulated, not as an intermediate between environmental happenings. Thus I publish the anatomical reconstructions of brain resections I have made as part of the method of my experiments and not, as is the vogue among behaviorists, as a part of the results section of the report. In such experiments behavior becomes the dependent variable which is used to tease out organism–environment (in my experiments brain–environment) relationships. Behavior is used much as is litmus paper by the biochemist studying the interactions of acids and bases.

The results of experiments made within this mold, i.e.,

Organism–Environment
\/
Behavior

can be applied in a variety of ways. They can be used to gain behaviorally relevant knowledge about organismic variables; in my experiments to enhance understanding of the frontal lobes of the brain or of its hippocampus. Or the results can be made party to a further analysis of the behaviorally relevant environmental variables and thus be used as would the behaviorist to study the problem of what constitutes reinforcement. But, in addition, the results can be applied to the formulation of the behaviorally relevant organism–environment *relationship*, and I feel free to apply mental language to describe the terms of such a relationship. In this way an objective, operationally sound study of mind becomes possible.

II. Minding Brain Facts

I do not for a moment underestimate the power which behaviorism has brought to the study of psychological processes. I have exercised seriously in behavioristic research—for a decade I managed a neurobehavioral laboratory devoted to the analysis of brain function by the use of operant conditioning techniques. During this period Lashley was wont to note that every good psychologist must go through a behavioristic phase—Lashley's own experience in behavorism came when he worked intensively with Watson. But, in time, his data and his interests forced Lashley to abandon behaviorism and he once assured me affectionately that I too would some day "grow up." Lashley (1952) never was able to formulate how psychology was to accomplish this growing up but he did indicate, as he so often did, the directions that must be taken. His most explicit statement on this subject was destined to be his last:

Today I shall discuss a subject which, like our Oedipus complexes, has probably troubled many of us but has been suppressed, especially in scientific meetings. Suppression, is a sign of conflict, and I hope that I may be able to contribute something to lessen the tension. I refer to the problem of how the brain knows that it knows; what characteristics of neural activity constitute mind. The pioneers in neurology were not troubled by this problem. They accepted the metaphysics of their day, which regarded the brain only as the agent of mind. Mind was for them a little man, seated in the head, who did all the thinking and willed all the actions for the brain. The brain was really only an impediment to him since, by the doctrine of survival, he could get along even better without it. (No one seems to have noted that this concept involved an infinite regression, like puppy dogs and little fleas.) When Fritsch and Hitzig reported the excitability of the cortex. they readily interpreted the excitable areas as "the place of entry of single psychic functions into material." And students of cerebral localization, even when they did not subscribe to mind-brain interaction, were content to ascribe mental functions to specific areas, without inquiring how the areas carry out the functions. Even today this mixing of the mental and physical retards analysis of the actual functions of specialized parts of the nervous system.

In 1881 Bubnoff and Heidenhain wrote, "It seems to us absolutely necessary that investigations of the physiology of the brain be kept as distinct as possible from the accompanying psychological processes." Pavlov, who studied for a time with Heidenhain and was much influenced by him, developed this attitude still further in his attempt to construct a complete account of behavior in terms of conditioned reflexes without reference to mental phenomena. Bechterev, who anticipated Pavlov in the formulation of behavior in terms of associative reflexes, accepted a psychophysical parallelism. Pavlov was less explicit but came to regard mental phenomena as of no concern to the physiologist; a fit subject only for psychologists and philosophers, whom he held in slight esteem. The behaviorist school in America has carried this conception to its logical conclusion, not only denying that mental phenomena are relevant in the study of behavior, but asserting that they do not provide a basis for any scientific study whatever. Their position, however, still leaves them with the problem of how man ever developed the delusion that he is conscious.

Students of neurology might well be content to leave the problem in such hands, although it is certain that no solution will come from those sources. Mind, for psychologists since Watson, has become a naughty word. Metaphysicians and theologians have spent so many years weaving fairy tales about it that they have come to believe one another's phantasies.

There are indications, however, of an increasing interest in the problem of mind among neurologists. I would not intrude the question here, in what I am sure will otherwise be a serious scientific discussion, save that, within the past few years, three leaders in neurology, specialists in different fields, have asserted that mind cannot be explained by the activities of the brain and have sought to reseat the little man on his throne in the pineal gland.

Sherrington, after demonstrating that mind is not a special form of energy, wrote:

The sun's energy is part of the closed energy cycle. What leverage can it have on the mind? Yet through my retina and brain, it seems able to act on my mind. The theoretically impossible happens. In mine, I assert that it does act on my mind. Conversely my thinking "self" thinks that it can bend my arm. Physics tells me that my arm cannot be bent without disturbing the sun. My mind then does not bend my arm. Or, the theoretically impossible happens. Let me prefer to think that the theoretically impossible does happen.

Eccles accepts Sherrington's conclusion that the mind is not a form of energy. then evolves an elaborate theory as to how non-energy mind can act on matter, appealing to telepathy as supporting evidence. He accepts Eddington's misrepresentation of Heisenberg's principle of uncertainty and makes elaborate calculations to show that a minute "influence," within the limits which Eddington sets to the uncertainty principle can act upon a synaptic junction and modify behavior. As Heisenberg himself has told me, the principle of uncertainty is entirely irrelevant to the question of causal determination. It is a principle of unobservability, and as a basis for doctrines of will it is in a class with the belief that the invisible face of the moon is made of green cheese. Also, I still consider the gambling house odds more reliable than Rhine's statistics.

Walshe bases his argument for reviving the soul chiefly upon the assertion that man is more wonderful and more dignified than the earwig. I cannot quote the earwig but can quote Archy, the cockroach, in reply (Don Marquis). "A man thinks he amounts to a great deal but to a mosquito he is only something good to eat."

I am not ready to accept these doctrines of scientific despair and Christian hope. They are based upon a thorough misconception of the facts of consciousness. They fail to analyze the problem and show no conception of what phenomena are to be explained, or cannot be explained, by the action of the brain. The problem requires an entirely different approach; a thorough analysis of the phenomena of consciousness, oriented with reference to the phenomena of neural activity. Only when such an analysis has been made, will it be possible to test the correlation of mental states and processes with the brain's activity. I am confident that when the questions which are now held to be unanswerable are properly formulated, they will turn out to be capable of translation into physiological terms and will fall within the competence of present methods of physiological research.

As Lashley notes, the class of organismic independent variables which has most to do with organizing the psychological process is brain. Thus, my career has been devoted to the study of brain mechanisms. But I believe Lashley leaves unsaid a most important aspect of the problem—that brain research without the proper environmental–behavioral analysis will lead nowhere. There are those, mostly physiologists, who feel strongly that we will come to an understanding of mind when we have researched the physiology of the brain completely. My view is that a considerable number of brain facts may be irrelevant to an understanding of mind and that an understanding of brain alone will not give rise to an understanding of mind. A good analogy to use here is provided by present-day computers. Complete knowledge of their hardware, their machinery, does not completely specify their power. Only when software, the multitude of ways the machinery can be programmed to behave, is taken into account can we know what these devices are capable of.

At the most general level, therefore, my tenet is that we gain access to mind through the use of both brain and environmental-behavioral analyses. Since the latter include observations of verbal as well as of instrumental behavior, the question is raised as to the relation between consciousness and other psychological states. What of those determinants of behavior which do not have easy access to awareness? There is, of course, the likelihood that awareness accompanies only some and not all states of the neural apparatus. Kamiya and his students (1968) have shown that by using ordinary operant techniques awareness of certain neural states can be learned. Whether all central states are subject to such training remains to be seen. But there is another set of neural happenings which are not readily accessible to awareness. These are the neural processes which compose the *structure* of mind. Again an example: The grammatical rules by which we speak and write are not readily accessible to awareness, but linguistic analysis has shown, not only the possibility of coming to grips with the structure of language but the importance of doing so. The study of mind does not exclude unconscious determinants.

Today the surge both of cognitive and of physiological psychology has made some aspects of my position reasonably respectable with each group although neither has as yet accepted, to any considerable extent, the researches performed and conclusions reached by the other. But the situation has not always been even this favorable.

As a practicing neurosurgeon I attended my first American Psychological Association convention twenty years ago. The occasion was the presentation of a paper prepared jointly with Blum and Semmes, both graduate students in psychology at the time. The experiment to be reported was an important one. It related to the then-popular therapeutic procedure of frontal lobotomy (or leukotomy). This surgical operation, though producing marked changes in the personality of patients, was said to leave intellect intact. Hebb had just published his well-received study which showed no detectable deterioration in IQ, etc., after bilateral frontal lobe resection in man (Hebb, 1945; Hebb & Penfield, 1940).

Working with Lashley, we were interested in preparing animal "models" of clinical neurological conditions so that we could examine the brain-behavior relationship experimentally. Monkeys had brains ideally suited for the purpose. However, removals of monkey frontal lobes produced a characteristic problem-solving difficulty: tests of short-term memory such as delayed response and alternation had been shown by Jacobsen (1936), Nissen (Jacobsen & Nissen, 1937), Malmo (1942), Finan (1942), and a few others to be selectively impaired by the frontal lesions—in monkey.

Thus a major discrepancy stood in the way of letting us make the rhesus monkey our experimental model. We turned to the chimpanzee for help. And indeed we found that the ape could perform the delay task but did so by giving himself external reminders such as tapping the side of the cage during the delay interval.

I found also that human lobotomy patients could perform the delay tasks—the delay could even stretch through the surgical procedure—provided they coded the task verbally. Many years later, I was to show that a major problem-solving deficit does, in fact, result from lobotomy when the verbal mode of solution is precluded (Poppen, Pribram & Robinson, 1965; Pribram, Ahumada, Hartog, & Roos, 1964).

But twenty years ago we came to the American Psychological Association eagerly to present our chimpanzee data. It was our good fortune to have Jacobsen in the chair for our session—so we introduced ourselves en masse— i.e., all three of us. Jacobsen was moderately interested in the results of our experiments but had to excuse himself because of a committee meeting. This posed the dilemma which is the point of this anecdote. What should we do—three authors of an important study on the frontal lobes of the brain, a vital subject both in the clinic and in the laboratory? Our Chairman had deserted us, and with his departure went our audience. *For no one else came to the brain function session and ours was the only paper scheduled.*

It was the heyday of behaviorism. The Division of Physiological and Comparative Psychology had been dissolved and absorbed into the Division of Experimental Psychology. The organism had become a black box. The search for the engram in the brain had shown that no mechanism existed whereby learning and remembering could possibly occur (Lashley, 1950).

Twenty years later—now—the situation has changed. There is an audience, estimated to be well above the 500 mark for each of the major papers sponsored by the division. The division has been reconstituted, and knowledge about brain function is accumulating rapidly. Every paper presented tells us of the functions of some nucleus in the brain, of some part of the cortex, of some autonomic neural mechanism, of this or that endocrine substance. Physiological psychologists have become, as they should, hard scientists. But they have taken this to mean that they should devote themselves exclusively to learning more and more about less and less. And so they have not changed the image of psychology. Members in good standing in this division herald, as did their forebears twenty years ago, their texts by the unfortunate title "Psychology, The Study of Behavior."

So again I must declare: psychology is and has been, except during the excesses of the behaviorist revolution, the study of mind. We who deal with brain should be the first to realize that the study of behavior and the study of brain complement each other: we do not just use behavior to determine brain function; nor do we work with brain just to find out how we behave. It is the psychological process, mind, we wish to understand. My proposal is that the time is ripe for an objective study of mind and that the study of brain function coupled with that of behavior must lead the way to this more mature psychology.

III. THE EXPERIMENTAL ANALYSIS OF MIND

Presented in such global terms, this proposal sounds heretical and visionary. But in practical fact a growing number of researchers are already engaged in shaping psychology to this image. Let me illustrate: could the strict behaviorist legitimately study the process of attention? He could not, because he limited himself to studying observing responses, and attention is not observable in behavior. But we, the brain people, can objectively measure what is going on inside the organism. The pioneering work of Lindsley in this area of research is familiar (Haider, Spong, & Lindsley, 1964). Let me here provide an example from my own laboratory. We have been pursuing the functions of the inferior part of the temporal lobes of primates. This part of the brain is usually called an "association" area but it is better termed "intrinsic" since its functions are specifically visual and not in any sense associative (Pribram, 1960a). Our problem has been that we could not trace any direct input from the visual system to this part of the brain. In fact, neither radical disconnections of the cortico-cortical (Chow, 1951; Pribram, Spinelli, & Reitz, 1969), nor complete destructions of the thalamocortical pathways (Chow, 1954) result in the visual deficit obtained when the inferior temporal gyrus is ablated. I therefore suggested that perhaps the influence of this part of the cortex works downstream, via a pathway leading from the brain and terminating in the visual system (Pribram, 1958) (see Fig. 1). Thus the functions in vision of the so-called association cortex would be ascribable to the control exerted over the visual mechanism.

A number of experimental results have supported this hypothesis.

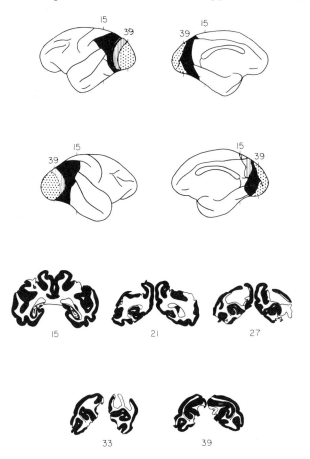

FIG. 1. Reconstruction of prestriate lesion in S 283.

Nauta and Whitlock anatomically demonstrated the efferent pathways from the inferior temporal gyrus (Nauta & Whitlock, 1954). Using electro-physiological techniques, we have confirmed these results and extended them to show that these effects of electrical stimulation of the cortex extend far into the periphery of the visual system. About 8–10% of the fibers in the optic nerve of cats have been shown by electrophysiological techniques to be efferent to the retina (Spinelli & Weingarten, 1966). Changes in the shape and extent of the visual receptive field of units in the optic nerve are produced when these efferent fibers are centrally activated (Spinelli & Pribram, 1966, 1967). (See Fig. 2.)

But what has all this to do with "attention?" One of the experiments we performed showed that we could change the "excitability" of the visual mechanism by electrical stimulation of the inferior temporal cortex (Spinelli & Pribram, 1966) (see Fig. 3). This result was especially welcome since it gave us a clue as to the neurological mechanisms by which the inferior temporal cortex exerts its control over vision. We thus wanted to explore further this mechanism. Successive groups of graduate and postdoctoral students came to the laboratory fired with enthusiasm by our finding. But alas, as so often occurs when a really new result is obtained, we could not replicate. At least not consistently enough to begin a study in depth. Yet the problem was sufficiently important to warrant persistence. We needed a more stable indicator of excitability in the visual system so we abandoned, for the moment, the paired flash paradigm. Bypassing the retina, stimulating electrically within the system itself, should provide the stability we needed. It might also bypass the lability necessary to obtain the effect we were interested in, but we had to take this chance. And indeed, at first, electrical stimulation of the inferior temporal cortex failed to have an effect.

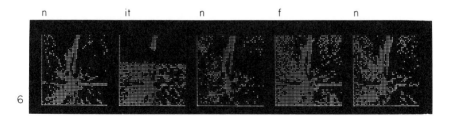

FIG. 2. Effects of stimulation of the posterior "association" cortex of a cat on a visual receptive field recorded from a neural unit in the optic tract. (These records are made by moving a spot with an X-Y plotter controlled by a small general purpose computer, PDP-8, which also records the number of impulses emitted by the unit at every location of the spot. The record shown is a section parallel to and 2 SD above the background firing level of the unit. Note the dramatic change in the configuration of the receptive field, especially after stimulation of the posterior "association" cortex, IT, inferotemporal.)

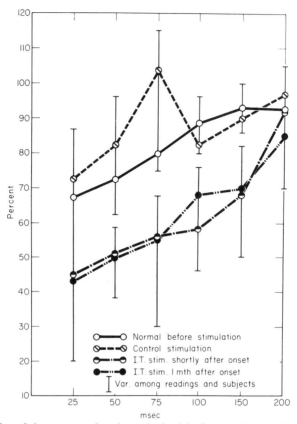

FIG. 3. A plot of the recovery functions obtained in five monkeys before and during chronic cortical stimulation.

Persistence and ingenuity were not to be permanently denied a harvest, however. Gerbrandt, a postdoctoral fellow, solved the dilemma with a simple observation. He showed that the amplitude of the responses evoked by electrical probe stimulations within the visual system was a function of the attentiveness of the monkey during the experiment. When the monkey was enclosed in a box, the response evoked was small. When the box was opened and the monkey was looking around, the response evoked was large. Further, inferior temporal cortex stimulation could make the small response obtained in the closed box into a large response, but had no influence on the large response. Finally, using the size of this probe-evoked response as a monitor, he could predict in the closed-box situation whether inferior temporal cortex stimulation would or would not affect the recovery function of the visual system (Gerbrandt, Spinelli, & Pribram, 1970). (See Fig. 4.)

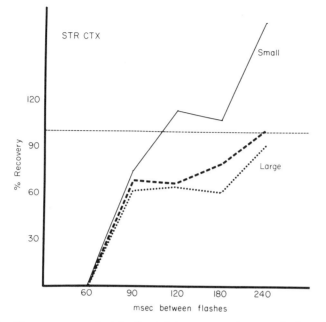

FIG. 4. The response evoked in the striate cortex to the second of a pair of flashes is compared with the response to the first flash. Solid line indicates the recovery function when the flash response pair is preceded by a probe response which is small. Dotted line indicates the recovery function when the flash pair is preceded by a probe response which is large. The dashed line indicates the paired-flash recovery function when no probe is given. A probe response is produced in the striate cortex by electrical stimulation of the lateral geniculate nucleus.

Thus whenever the monkey was attentive, the effects we had earlier obtained were not observed. When, however, the monkey became "bored," tended to nod into sleep, etc., the effect on the recovery function was clear-cut. In our initial experiments we had daily performed a long routine of procedures: paired flashes, paired clicks, click-flash and flash-click combinations, patterned flashes, etc., were presented in regular order, day in, day out, week in, week out. Not only the monkeys, but Spinelli and I, who were performing the experiments, became disenchanted with the routine. One of us was delegated to keep watch on the other two to see to it that sleep would not intervene. The monkey was watched through a peephole and when he nodded the enclosure was tapped gently. A small displacement of the stool of the nodding investigator accomplished the same end. In short, we got our results because the monkeys were not attentive. Subsequent teams testing monkeys only on the recovery cycle phenomenon, working with monkeys fresh to the situation and apparently interested in the goings-on of the experiment, obtained different results. Only when, through repetition, the situation became boring to us and the monkey, did the recovery-cycle effects again emerge.

This is not all there is to the neural mechanism of attention. These experiments deal more with the vigilance aspect of the attentive process than with selective or focal attention. We are now engaged in exploring these dimensions. Mackworth has developed a superb instrument to study visual observing behavior (Mackworth, 1968). Using eyeball photography, it is possible to measure the sequence of visual fixations on a stimulus pattern. Monkeys with removal of the inferior temporal gyrus show disturbances of their fixation durations and sequences. But we are still in the process of analyzing results and so cannot report the full meaning of the observed disturbances.

I have presented in detail the explorations of attention for a purpose. It is my view that once there is sufficient specification of *the environmental, the organismic, and the behavioral* variables that go into the description of a mental term, the term loses its mystical aura, and stigma, and becomes scientifically respectable. Few of you raise an eyebrow when the term visual field or its derivative, visual receptive field, is used. The definition of visual field is "that part of the environment responded to by an organism using one eye without moving that eye." The receptive field of a neural unit is defined in a like fashion—in fact, we often talk colloquially about the field "seen" by the cell. These terms are acceptable because we know so much about the physical and the sensory neural events that make up vision. In short: the mental terms "vision," "to see," "to look," are objectively respectable.

The term "expectancy" is going through a similar scientific legitimization by physiologically oriented experimentalists. The work of Sokolov (1960) has shown that behavioral habituation was not a simple fatigue-phenomenon but the construction of, as he calls it, a neuronal model against which input must be matched. The work of John, Zubin, and Sutton (Sutton, Tueting, Zubin, & John, 1967) and that of Lindsley (Haider *et al.*, 1964) has shown that the components of responses evoked by visual stimuli vary with the expectations of organisms (including man). The work of Walter (1964) and of Lacey (Lacey, 1969; Lacey & Lacey, 1958) has shown that a wave of negative electrical potential sweeps the brain from front to back as organisms (including man) prepare to perform a task. This last observation is perhaps more relevant to the process of intention than to that of expectancy, but "intention" has as yet not been sufficiently investigated to attain objective respectability. Within a few years I am sure this will have been remedied and clear-cut neurological as well as behavioral distinctions will make it possible to talk objectively about both expectancy and intention.

"Voluntary" is another such term. Clinical neurologists have never given up its use. But the defining operations, behavioral and neurological, have never been adequate to the subtleties demanded by the full meaning of the process. Now, however, beginnings are being made. MacKay (1966) and Mittlestaedt (1968) talk of feed-forward mechanisms and Teuber (1960) searches for corrollary discharges to account for the differences between the results perceived when movement is passive and when it is voluntary.

Obviously we are at the beginning of an era during which a biologically based, objective study of mind will redress the extreme provincialism produced in experimental psychology by the behaviorist revolution.

IV. A Difference That Makes a Difference

Most physiologically oriented psychologists and brain scientists are first and foremost experimentalists exploring the universe with the tools and techniques they have labored to forge. They are not all that seriously concerned whether someone wishes to call a particular performance a voluntary action or a piece of operant behavior—*unless it makes a difference to their explorations.*

I believe, seriously and strongly, that it *does* make a difference which language is used (and by this I don't mean just the words in that language) to describe one's interests and the results of pursuing those interests. Again let me turn to an example from research in my laboratory to illustrate how this difference comes about.

Some years ago we showed that the effects of temporal lobectomy on changes in temperament and personality resulted from the removal of the amygdala, one of the limbic system structures contained within the temporal lobe (Pribram & Bagshaw, 1953; Pribram, 1954). Further analysis showed that these limbic formations were involved in a variety of behaviors labeled as the four F's, an extension of Cannon's "fight and flight" label for sympathetic neural function (Pribram, 1960b). Our four F's included, in addition to Cannon's, feeding and sexual behavior. The close anatomical linkage between the limbic and hypothalamic structures made this result a reasonable one. The problem arose when I became dissatisfied with just a descriptive correlation between brain anatomy and behavior and tried to understand the mechanism of operation of this relationship.

Had I been satisfied to pursue behavior per se I should have next asked, as others have, whether different parts of the amygdala served feeding, fighting, fleeing, and sexual behavior. Just for the record, a negative answer appears to have been given when experiments (whether ablation or stimulation) have been addressed to this question. But what I wanted to know had to do with the psychological process, the commonality, that characterized the four F's, so that a single lesion (even of a somewhat complex anatomical formation) could alter, at one stroke all of these diverse behaviors. The concept, "instinct" (Beach, 1955) though plausible, failed to satisfy for a number of reasons as did a variety of forms of the concept "drive," which would have been a natural because of the strong connections between amygdala and hypothalamic mechanisms. As will be noted later, such drive concepts have also failed to account for the effects of hypothalamic damage and stimulation. I therefore decided to take an opposite approach to the problem and ask whether behaviors which in no apparent way were innately based or drive controlled, would be affected by amygdalectomy.

The experiments performed therefore went far afield from the proverbial four F's. In collaboration with Schwartzbaum (Schwartzbaum & Pribram, 1960), with Bagshaw (Bagshaw & Pribram, 1965) and with Hearst (Hearst & Pribram, 1964a, b), transfer of training experiments were undertaken. In one procedure transposition behavior was studied, in the other the reaction to stimulus equivalences. Stimulus generalization was analyzed as a control measure. The tasks were chosen because they seemed to us reasonably remote from hypothalamic influence.

Amygdalectomy affected performance in both transposition experiments but not in those testing stimulus generalization. My conclusion was therefore that the amygdala, at least, influences processes other than those ordinarily ascribed to the hypothalamus.

A clue to what this process might be came from an observation made while testing the monkeys on the transposition task. The amygdalectomized subjects neither transposed nor did they choose the absolute cue. Instead they treated the test trials as a completely novel situation, performing initially at chance (Douglas, 1966; Schwartzbaum & Pribram, 1960).

Pursuing this observation, Bagshaw and her collaborators in my laboratory (Bagshaw & Benzies, 1968; Bagshaw & Coppock, 1968; Bagshaw, Kimble, & Pribram, 1965; Bagshaw & J. Pribram, 1968, Kimble, Bagshaw, & Pribram, 1965), showed that amygdalectomy did indeed alter monkeys' reactions to novelty. Behavioral (and some components of EEG) habituation to novelty were markedly prolonged. On the other hand, the viscero-autonomic indicators (GSR, changes in heart and respiratory rates) of orienting to novelty were wiped out by the lesions (without impairing the response mechanisms per se). These results led me to suggest that orienting to novelty proceeds through two hypothetical stages. The first, characterized by behavioral orienting reactions, "samples," scans the novelty. The second, characterized by viscero-autonomic reactions, leads to the "registration" of experiencing the novelty and so to its habituation (Pribram, 1969, a, b). Without such registration the temporal organization of behavior cannot occur, thus fighting, fleeing, feeding, and sexual behavior, as well as delayed alternation behavior (Pribram, Lim, Poppen, & Bagshaw, 1966), etc., become impaired.

Thus a much greater span of data regarding amygdala function are encompassed. And this is not all. Reference to the psychological process of registration helped explain an, until then, inexplicable observation I made many years ago (Miller, Galanter, & Pribram, 1960, Ch. 14). A patient on whom a bilateral amygdalectomy had been performed a year earlier had gained much weight. She seemed to present a golden opportunity to find out directly what she experienced to make her eat so much. Her answer was always that she experienced little—she did *not* feel, i.e., register that she was inordinately hungry. Such a lack of registration is a commonplace in clinical epileptic seizures originating from abnormalities around the amygdala, abnormalities which also produce the famous deja vu and jamais vu phenomena.

As noted earlier, the type of analysis of limbic system function of the amygdala which I have presented here does not stand alone. For hypothalamic function a similar route has been forced on physiologically oriented psychologists. The paradoxical finding of Miller, Bailey, and Stevenson (1950)—that rats with ventromedial lesions will eat more but work less for food—remained unexplainable in drive, i.e., behavioristic terms. The impasse remained until some sense was made of the data by Teitlebaum (1955) and by Grossman (1966) who invoked mental concepts such as "finickiness" and "affect." Immediately new meaningful experiments and new analyses were generated.

Again I have dwelt on detail because the terms used by the experimentalists working in the field are mental ones. To give them objective as well as subjective substance takes a great deal of careful observation, experimentation, and scientific analysis, both at the environmental-behavioral and at the neurobehavioral level. Neither level by itself has the explanatory power nor serves as well the generation of meaningful experiments. Thus the challenge to psychologists today, it seems to me, stems from the very fact that the study of brain added to the study of behavior appears to make psychology whole again.

The fascinating problems which behaviorism had to exclude not only *can*, but *must*, be tackled when neurobehavioral techniques are brought into play.

V. OF INTERDISCIPLINARY ENDEAVORS

Laboratory experiences such as these have led me to try to formulate the process by which my brand of scientific inquiry procedes. This is difficult to do thoroughly without altering the process and thus chancing damage to a successful operation. Some formulation has been possible, however. First, my experiments are conducted as interdisciplinary efforts. Any single discipline centers on a technique such as the use of microelectrodes, of operant behavior, of mathematics, or of paper chromatography. As long as only one technique is used, the results can be codified only in descriptive terms. When several techniques are brought to bear on a problem, the resultant interdisciplinary data allow the structure of the problem to be explored more fully: the processes and mechanisms involved can be approached. Further, the data obtained in *intra*disciplinary programs tend to generate technique-oriented variations on those data. What was found on the mouse is looked for in the rat; the description of the visual receptive field of a unit in the optic nerve leads to an experiment detailing the visual receptive field at the lateral geniculate level of the visual system. By contrast, *inter*disciplinary programs tend to be problem oriented: the process of pattern perception is studied by simulation on computers, by the use of microelectrode recordings in cats, in monkeys and in man, by a variety of behavioral techniques and by a combination of any or all of these if possible. Since the problems are never completely solved, new technology is continuously recruited and older methods abandoned. Thus interdisciplinary programs are never seen by outsiders as very original: the problems were posed centuries ago and have been reframed in ever more precise form since; the techniques are usually borrowed from technologies which, as a whole, are far more advanced than those aspects adapted to the program. What intrigues those of us inside the interdisciplinary endeavor is the enduring nature of the issues, the fact that they are fundamental and that any progress in sharpening our views of them will be equally enduring and fundamental.

Second, and related, my brand of scientific inquiry makes abundant use of analogy and metaphor. I am not afraid to view the brain as a computer nor the cortex as a hologram. The attributes of the mechanical artifacts are more accessible to manipulation than is the biological organism and so we can sharpen issues more quickly and then test them more precisely in the biological world. The biochemist performs many such in vitro (in glass) experiments before relating them to what is going on in vivo. Note however, that I said view the brain as a computer, I did not say the brain is a computer. I do not for a moment think the brain works just as does a present-day computer. But some parts do, and some aspects of brain functioning and computer functioning are remarkably similar. It is our job, and fun to boot, to find out just where the similarities and differences lie.

Finally, my brand of scientific inquiry is systematic. It aims at comprehending large issues not trivial ones; at the interrelations among many sets of variables, not just a few. I want a view of the brain and of the psychological process, not just a theory of the functions of the reticular formation or of fixed-interval behavior. This may seem grandiose but my experience is quite the contrary. As Ashby notes (1960) the job of any experimenter is to produce results; as he calls it, to obtain straight-line behavior. In multivariate systems such as all brain and behavior experiments are, straight-line behavior can be managed in a variety of ways. The experimenter may be fooled into thinking that the way he has done it is relevant to the biological universe. He therefore is tempted to generalize his limited but highly predictable result into a more meaningful context. The behavior of pigeons in an operant situation too readily becomes a theory for understanding language. The reactions of rats to 24-hour food deprivation and to shock too easily become gradients of approach and avoidance explaining conflicts experienced by man. When one takes the larger view from the beginning, the irrelevancies spewed as data by our technology can relatively quickly come to be seen as such.

A penalty entailed by approaching one's subject matter from a wider scope is that focus on any particular is attained more slowly. This is, of course, a virtue as well as a penalty. But even the whole takes shape reluctantly and keeps changing contours. Contrary to the image many of my colleagues currently hold of me, only recently, and after much laboratory experimentation and laborious analysis of the results obtained, have I been able to formulate in words some reasonably satisfactory statements of my own views.

VI. The Language of the Brain

Many of these statements are contained in a forthcoming book entitled *The Language of the Brain* (Pribram, in press). In this book, the brain is considered to be a device which codes the information provided to it, and then recodes and recodes and recodes it. In short, the brain is conceived as a producer of languages.

The coding operations take place at various levels. At the most basic, a solution must be sought for the fact that the brain must both process and store information. This double task is accomplished not so much by virtue of neurons, the anatomical units of the nervous system which relay signals from one location to another, but by a microstructure, a set of patterns, organized of the events which occur at the junctions among neurons. These junctional microstructures (constituted of patterns of postsynaptic electrical potentials) (Stevens, 1966) are in the first instance more or less temporary but steady neuroelectric *states* with which inputs from sensory receptors must interact. Second, they provide the matrix in which more permanent chemical and histological residues of experience, memory traces, can develop.

These basic operations are combined into logic elements which form the building blocks of the nervous system. Interactions among junctional patterns of activity compose the logic. These interactions are of two sorts, excitatory and inhibitory. It is the inhibitory interactions which give form to the logic.

Inhibitory interactions can be classified according to the functions they perform. One class of inhibition enhances contrast among the elements making up the pattern. Contrast is enhanced because each neuron inhibits its neighbors, thus emphasizing the neuroelectric differences between the fields of excited and nonexcited neighboring neurons. As detailed earlier in this paper, this contrast-enhancing mechanism is assumed the basis for reactions to novelty (orienting responses) and therefore to what is to constitute information for further processing.

The other class of inhibition acts on the excited neuron itself, damping its activity over time. This self-inhibition takes place because of the negative feedbacks present everywhere in the central nervous system. The ubiquity of such negative feedback has made it necessary to view the organization of reflexes not as stimulus–response chains or reflex arcs, but as servomechanisms, thermostat-like devices, controlling behavior via changes in biases, the tuning of receptors to accept or reject as information the signals introducing perturbation—a process somewhat like adjusting the wheel of a thermostat to indicate the temperature to which one wants to set the heating system. Inhibition among neighboring neurons which enhances contrast is critically involved in the setting of the servo; the mechanism of self-inhibition, of feedback, is basic to its stability of operaton. The biasable servoprocess, or as it is often called, the homeostat, is thus conceived as the basic logic element of the nervous system.

Logic elements must in turn be combined if they are to be effectively functioning structures. In the brain, one way in which logic elements appear to be composed is into "screens" which process signals in stations all along the sensory and motor systems. As already noted, the neuroelectric events (the configurations of postsynaptic potentials) which are generated at neural junctions, enhanced and given stability by neural inhibitory interactions, form a screen in which a microstructure of interfering wavefronts develops. The effects of these neuroelectric events can be stored as changes in conformation of macromolecules such as proteins along synaptic and dendritic networks, and thus influence subsequent synaptic and postsynaptic activity. By way of analogy with the powerful use of interference effects in the field of optical information processing, the microstructures derived from interference effects are called neural holograms (Pribram, 1966). Just as in the optical hologram, the assumption is made that when appropriately activated by either a reference mechanism or by an input similar to that which originally composed it, perceived "images" are produced from neural holograms.

Images are of different kinds. Perceptual images are "images-of-events." The images involved in feelings are of a somewhat different nature. The distinction between perceptions and feelings, between our knowledge of the world-out-there and the world-within, is based both on differences in the organization of the neural mechanisms controlling the receptors and on what it is they receive. The images involved in feelings turn out to be "monitor-images," monitoring hungers and thirsts, the variety of moods, as well as the motivational and emotional feelings of interest, tranquility, or upset.

The core parts of the brain stem, including the hypothalamic regions and reticular formations contain the receptors which monitor the chemicals which compose the stimuli for the world-within. The limbic formations of the forebrain are, as detailed earlier, the neural systems critical to the continuing, i.e., temporal organization of the monitoring process. Though this neuro-behavioral relationship is reasonably well established, we remain almost totally ignorant of the details of the mechanism by which monitor-images might be constructed.

A third type of image is involved when the organism acts. One of the major puzzles in the study of behavior has been that though behavior is effected by the use of moving muscles, a great variety of patterns of movement may in actuality be used to accomplish any particular behavioral result. How can consistent action develop in the face of the organism's variability? How can a nest be built of sticks and stones, or shreds of leaves or newspapers, with beak or claw or both? How can the selfsame manuscript be produced in handwriting, type, or as a tape recording? A step toward an answer is given when it is recognized that the brain may generate what I have called "images-of-achievement." The fact is that most movement is controlled not by any direct excitation or inhibition of muscles but by a change in the bias or tuning of the *receptors* attached to muscles (the muscle spindles, etc.) which inform the central nervous system of the forces acting on the muscle. Thus, even the generation of behavior, the control of movement, is effected by the tuning of muscle receptors, and thus turns out to be primarily the problem of managing receptors and only secondarily that of controlling effectors (Held, 1968).

In fact, microelectrode recordings from the motor cortex indicate that the critical stimulus dimensions of which images-of-achievement become constructed are the forces which impinge on the receptors of the muscles carrying out the task (Evarts, 1967). The consistency of actions is due there-fore to consistencies in the field of environmental forces necessary to accomplish the act. These consistencies are processed to make up the image-of-achievement.

From what has been already stated it is clear that the screens from which images are constructed must be continually modified by experience. How this occurs constitutes the set of problems usually handled under the rubric "reinforcement." Reinforcement is conceived as a mechanism by which the consequences of behavior interact with the organism's already developed competences (the logic elements composing screens) to produce new ones. Perception, feeling, and action all undergo such modifications by experience. The neural mechanisms involved follow a course similar to that described in embryogenesis by the process of induction, and the possibility is posed that reinforcers induce neural changes (by way of RNA) which lead to growth of connections in the brain much as growth of a structure (e.g., an optic cup) is induced (e.g., by RNA) in the appropriate site of an embryo (Pribram, 1966).

The process of reinforcement entails the interactions between consequences and competences within an image-mode; interactions between image-modes also occur. The primary interimage interactions are between images-of-achievement and the other two types. Thus, images-of-achievement interact with images-of-events in the construction of "signs" and with monitor-images in the construction of "symbols." Signs are produced by making discriminative choices, actions on events to classify them. Signs are attributive. Symbols are generated when acts are monitored and thus made relevant to the world of feelings. Symbols are arbitrarily assigned on the basis of usefulness. Much of my own brain-behavior research with monkeys has been occupied with specification of the neural processes involved in sign and symbolic behavior. The so-called association cortex of the brain is especially involved in accomplishing this mix among images. However, as we saw earlier in this chapter, the mix is not performed within this cortex per se but by controlling and tuning the electrical events occurring in the more primary sensory and motor systems.

At the highest level of neurobehavioral organization are thought and talk. Here the neurological evidence is harder to come by since it must come almost exclusively from clinical studies of man. These, however, can be evaluated as part of the systematic approach developed here and some realistic interpretations can be made. Thought is viewed as the processing of symbols into signs; the logical operations of choice and classification are brought to bear on symbolic content. Talk is the obverse; language makes arbitrary symbolic use of signs and thus provides flexibility to the linguistic process. Thought and talk build on one another, each new level constructed of the complexity of the language achieved by the previous level.

The major requirement which must be met to bring these operations to fruition is reversibility in coding, i.e., the transformations involved in processing one code into another must allow the reverse transformation to occur without undue distortion. This can be done by keeping track of the transformations employed, as is done in the cultural use of language or more easily in the central nervous system by using a transformation which when used again will generate a reasonable replica of the original. The type of transformations which involve the holographic process of image construction have this replicating characteristic. This is thus another powerful attribute of the holographic hypothesis of brain function.

VII. The Emergence of a Biological Rationalism

These then are the powers of the brain. Being the recoding device that it is, generating languages to describe the signals it begets and receives, man's brain solves the philosophical bind of describing itself. This is accomplished by applying over and over again in rapid juxtaposition that old and ubiquitous biological trick of replicating its essential structure in different form. Biology is thus the key to the brain's power and as such it is the key to understanding the psychological process.

I have already shown that a biologically based objective study of mind can cope with such concepts as attention, relevance, expectancy, intention, volition, finickiness, and affect. The challenge continues. We must take the step which goes beyond even that radical empiricism which provides much insight into the nature of experience. In the mind–brain–behavior area of investigation, empiricism, applied to its pragmatic purpose with the usual scientific controls, generates a new dimension in the understanding of psychological processes—a new biological rationalism. This, as I see it, is the departure which the work and workers interested in the biology of mind can bring to psychology. The message before us is clear, its voice compelling: are we willing to think as psychologists and not just as physiologists and behaviorists and will we speak out unashamedly so as to make the intellectual community listen?

For more is at stake than the direction taken by scientific psychology. The mind–brain–behavior relationship is, as it has always been, an important focus of how man views himself. An outmoded neurology based on a horizontal analysis of brain function once proclaimed that primitive spinal and brain stem functions come in evolutionary history progressively under the control of higher, i.e., upstairs, cortical mechanisms. Though in part correct, more recent vertical analysis of the nervous system such as those detailed earlier in this chapter and also in my article in Koch's, *The Study of a Science* (Pribram, 1962), have shown that each neural structure has its primitive components overlayed by new accretions which may alter its system properties considerably. The old and inadequate data led to a popularly held view of man, initiated by psychoanalysis and today promulgated by such lay "spokesmen for science" as Ardrey (1966) and Koestler (1967): the view that man

behaves as beast because at base he is beast. Cortical control expressed as
language and culture is, according to this view, a veneer which is either thin
and easily and dangerously cracked, or else so thick that it constrains the
inner man, shackling self-expression and communication with his fellow men.

By contrast, today's neurological data find no unaltered primitives, no
beast within the shell. Phylogenetic comparisons show neurological systems
enriched and altered, not superceded. It is a fallacy, for instance to think of
dogs as macrosmatic and man as microsmatic. True, the dog's olfactory
brain is sizable and he can track odors we barely discern. But man's olfactory
brain is made larger yet by developments not present in subhuman mammals
and by virtue of these developments man can appreciate the culinary artistry
of a Tour D'Argent which is well beyond the ken of any dog.

Aggression is a topic currently so important to us that it must be seriously
looked at in this light. Much is being said these days of the territorial imperative
and much of what is said rings true. However, what is fiendish about man is
not that he shares with other mammals the fact of territorial needs, i.e., the
need to be himself, to isolate a part of his universe from the unbounded
complexities that assail him. What makes man fiendish is his rational capacity
to formulate and codify his territorial claims conceptually and so to proclaim
them religiously right. It is the rational in man—the new neurology, not the
primitive—which gives rise to his problems. Man's wars are not bestial.
As has been pointed out repeatedly, *intra*species annihilation is a rarity in
nature. *Man's wars are rational* and any hope we may have of staying war
is through understanding man's rationality and not his bestiality. At present
we tend to equate the rational with equable reasonableness. Biological studies
of mind show it to be otherwise. The neural mechanisms serving motivation
and emotion are those, which when they become more differentiated, become
the substrate of rational action (Pribram, 1967; Pribram, 1970; Pribram
& Melges, 1969). When action is blocked, rationality becomes fierce with
emotion and in defense of its motives. The rational becomes dysrational in
its fierceness, especially when it becomes institutionalized and its various
aspects can be distributed among a number of individuals. Only by recognizing
this fierce dysrationality for what it can do to us will we be able to come to
grips with it, and therein lies our hope.

And so I have come full circle. A behaviorist looking at aggression sees
agonistic behavior and studies its presumed environmental antecedents and
consequences. The physiologist looks for a neurochemical substrate he hopes
he can correlate with anger. The biologically oriented student of mind also
does these things but he is clearly aware that agonistic behavior is merely
one expression of anger and that there may be a variety of nonangry *reasons*
for a display of agonistic behavior. The total mental process (anger and/or
reason) to be studied must be approached through an analysis of brain

function, of observations of relevant environmental (in this case cultural) determinants and of behavior.

So far, what research undertaken in this spirit has taught me is that the brain is the unique instrument which through the coding and recoding of information produces languages and through languages the culture by which we live. Thus it is man's linguistic rationality that provides both the culprit and the hope, both rigid reason for enduring and flexible reasonableness for creating.

REFERENCES

Ardrey, R. *The Territorial Imperative.* New York: Atheneum, 1966.

Ashby, W. R. *Design for a brain: The origin of adaptive behavior.* (2nd ed.) New York: Wiley, 1960.

Bagshaw, M. H., & Benzies, S. Multiple measures of the orienting reaction and their dissociation after amygdalectomy in monkeys. *Experimental Neurology,* 1968, **20,** 175–187.

Bagshaw, M. H., & Coppock, H. W. Galvanic skin response conditioning deficit in amygdalectomized monkeys. *Experimental Neurology,* 1968, **20,** 188–196.

Bagshaw, M. H., Kimble, D. P., & Pribram, K. H. The GSR of monkeys during orienting and habituation and after ablation of the amygdala, hippocampus and inferotemporal cortex. *Neuropsychologia,* 1965, **3,** 111–119.

Bagshaw, M. H., & Pribram, J. D. Effect of amygdalectomy on stimulus threshold of the monkey. *Experimental Neurology,* 1968, **20,** 197–202.

Bagshaw, M. H., & Pribram, K. H. Effect of amygdalectomy on transfer of training in monkeys. *Journal of Comparative and Physiological Psychology,* 1965, **59,** 118–121.

Beach, F. A. The descent of instinct. Presidential address, Eastern Psychological Association, 1952. *Psychological Review,* 1955, **62,** 401–410.

Chow, K. L. Effects of partial extirpations of the posterior association cortex on visually mediated behavior in monkeys. *Comparative Psychology Monographs,* 1951, **20,** 187–217.

Chow, K. L. Lack of behavioral effects following destruction of some thalamic association nuclei in monkey. *AMA Archives of Neurology and Psychiatry,* 1954, **71,** 762–771.

Douglas, R. J. Transposition, novelty and limbic lesions. *Journal of Comparative and Physiological Psychology,* 1966, **62,** 345–357.

Estes, W. K. The statistical approach to learning theory. In S. Koch (Ed.), *Psychology: A study of a science II.* New York: McGraw-Hill, 1959. Pp. 380–491.

Evarts, E. V. Representation of movements and muscles by pyramidal tract neurons of the precentral motor cortex. In M. D. Yahr & D. P. Purpura (Eds.), *Neurophysiological basis of normal and abnormal motor activities.* Hewlett, New York: Raven Press, 1967. Pp. 215–254.

Finan, J. L. Delayed response with pre-delay reinforcement in monkeys after removal of the frontal lobes. *American Journal of Psychology,* 1942, **55,** 202–214.

Gerbrandt, L. K., Spinelli, D. N., & Pribram, K. H. Recovery cycles and evoked response measures of excitability in primate striate cortex. *Electroencephalography and Clinical Neurophysiology,* 1970, **29,** 146–155.

Grossman, S. P. The VMH: A center for affective reactions, satiety, or both? *Physiology & Behavior*, 1966, **1**, 1–10.

Haider, M., Spong, P., & Lindsley, D. B. Attention, vigilance and cortical evoked-potential in humans. *Science*, 1964, **145**, 180.

Hearst, E., & Pribram, K. H. Appetitive and aversive generalization gradients in amygdalectomized monkeys. *Journal of Comparative and Physiological Psychology*, 1964, **58**, 296–298. (a)

Hearst, E., & Pribram, K. H. Facilitation of avoidance behavior by unavoidable shocks in normal and amygdalectomized monkeys. *Psychological Reports*, 1964, **14**, 39–42. (b)

Hebb, D. O. Man's frontal lobes: A critical review. *Archives of Neurology and Psychiatry*, 1945, **54**, 10–24.

Hebb, D. O., & Penfield, W. Human behavior after extensive bilateral removal from the frontal lobes. *Archives of Neurology and Psychiatry*, 1940, **44**, 421–438.

Held, R. Experience and capacity. In D. P. Kimble (Ed.), Fourth Conference on Learning, Remembering and Forgetting. Washington: New York Academy of Sciences Interdisciplinary Communications Program, 1968.

Jacobsen, C. F. Studies of cerebral function in primates. I. The function of the frontal association areas in monkeys. *Comparative Psychology Monographs*, 1936, **13**, 3–60.

Jacobsen, C. F., & Nissen, H. W. Studies of cerebral function in primates. IV. The effects of frontal lobe lesions on the delayed alternation habit in monkeys. *Journal of Comparative Psychology*, 1937, **23**, 101–112.

Kamiya, J. Operant Control of the EEG alpha rhythm and some of its effects on consciousness. In C. Tart (Ed.), *Altered states of consciousness*. New York: Wiley, 1968.

Kimble, D. P., Bagshaw, M. H., & Pribram, K. H. The GSR of monkeys during orienting and habituation after selective partial ablations of the cingulate and frontal cortex. *Neuropsychologia*, 1965, **3**, 121–128.

Koestler, A. *The Ghost in the Machine*. London: Hutchinson & Co., Ltd., 1967.

Kohler, I. *The formation and transformation of the perceptual world*. New York: International Univer. Press, 1964.

Lacey, J. I. Readiness to remember. In D. P. Kimble (Ed.), Third Conference on Learning, Remembering and Forgetting. New York: Gordon & Breach, 1969, vol. 2. pp. 573–574. 1970, pp. 41–53.

Lacey, J. I., & Lacey, B. C. The relationship of resting autonomic cyclic activity to motor impulsivity. In C. Soloman, S. Cobb, & W. Penfield (Eds.), *The brain and human behavior*. Baltimore: Williams & Wilkins, 1958. Pp. 144–209.

Lashley, K. S. In search of the engram. In *Physiological mechanisms in animal behavior*, New York: Academic Press, 1950. Pp. 454–482.

Lashley, K. S. Functional interpretation of anatomic patterns. *Research Publication, Association for Research in Nervous and Mental Disease*, **1952, 30**, 537–539.

MacKay, D. M. Cerebral organization and the conscious control of action. In J. C. Eccles (Ed.), *Brain and conscious experience*. New York: Springer, 1966. Pp. 422–445.

Mackworth, N. H. The wide-angle reflection eye camera for visual choice and pupil size. *Perception and Psychophysics*, 1968, **3**, 32–34.

Malmo, R. B. Interference factors in delayed response in monkeys after removal of frontal lobes. *Journal of Neurophysiology*, 1942, **5**, 295–308.

Miller, G. A., Galanter, E., & Pribram, K. H. *Plans and the structure of behavior*. New York: Holt, 1960.

Miller, N. E., Bailey, C. J., & Stevenson, J. A. Decreased "hunger" but increased food intake resulting from hypothalamic lesions. *Science*, 1950, **112**, 256–259.

Mittlestaedt, H. Experience and capacity. In D. P. Kimble (Ed.), Fourth Conference on Learning, Remembering and Forgetting. Washington: New York Academy of Sciences Interdisciplinary Communications Program, 1968.

Nauta, W. J. H., & Whitlock, D. G. An anatomical analysis of the non-specific thalamic projection system. In J. F. Delafresnay (Ed.), *Brain mechanisms and consciousness.* Springfield, Ill.: Charles C. Thomas, 1954.

Poppen, R. L., Pribram, K. H., & Robinson, R. S. Effects of frontal lobotomy in man on the performance of a multiple choice task. *Experimental Neurology,* 1965, **11**, 217–229.

Pribram, K. H. Toward a science of neuropsychology: Method and data. In R. A. Patton (Ed.), *Current trends in psychology and the behavioral sciences.* Pittsburgh: Univer. of Pittsburgh Press, 1954. Pp. 115–142. (a)

Pribram, K. H. Concerning three rhinencephalic systems. *Electroencephalography and Clinical Neurophysiology,* 1954, **6**, 708–709. (b)

Pribram, K. H. Neocortical function in behavior. In H. F. Harlow (Ed.), *Biological and biochemical bases of behavior.* Madison: Univer. of Wisconsin Press, 1958. Pp. 151–172.

Pribram, K. H. The intrinsic systems of the forebrain. In J. Field & H. W. Magoun (Eds.), *Handbook of physiology.* Vol. II. *Neurophysiology.* Washington: American Physiological Society, 1960. Pp. 1323–1344. (a)

Pribram, K. H. A review of theory in physiological psychology. *Annual Review of Psychology.* 1960, **11**, 1–40. (b)

Pribram, K. H. Interrelations of psychology and the neurological disciplines. In S. Koch (Ed.), *Psychology: A study of a science.* Vol. 4. *Biologically oriented fields: Their place in psychology and in biological sciences.* New York: McGraw-Hill, 1962.

Pribram, K. H. Some dimensions of remembering: Steps toward a neuropsychological model of memory. In J. Gaito (Ed.), *Macromolecules and behavior.* New York: Academic Press, 1966. Pp. 165–187.

Pribram, K. H. The new neurology and the biology of emotion: A structural approach. *American Psychologist,* 1967, **22**, 830–838.

Pribram, K. H. Four R's of remembering. In K. H. Pribram (Ed.), *On the biology of learning.* New York: Harcourt, Brace and World, 1969. (a)

Pribram, K. H. The neurophysiology of remembering. *Scientific American,* 1969, **220**, 73–86 (b)

Pribram, K. H. Feelings as monitors. In M. Arnold (Ed.), Third International Symposium on Feelings and Emotions. Loyola University, 1968. New York: Academic Press, 1970, Pp. 41–53.

Pribram, K. H. *The Language of the Brain.* Englewood Cliffs, N.J.: Prentice Hall (in press).

Pribram, K. H., Ahumada, A., Hartog, J., & Roos, L. A progress report on the neurological processes disturbed by frontal lesions in primates. In J. M. Warren & K. Akert (Eds.), *The frontal granular cortex and behavior.* New York: McGraw-Hill, 1964. Pp. 28–55.

Pribram, K. H., & Bagshaw. M. H. Further analysis of the temporal lobe syndrome utilizing fronto-temporal ablations. *Journal of Comparative Neurology,* 1953, **99**, 347–375.

Pribram, K. H., Lim, H., Poppen, R., & Bagshaw, M. H. Limbic lesions and the temporal structure of redundancy. *Journal of Comparative and Physiological Psychology,* 1966, **61**, 368–373.

Pribram, K. H., & Melges, F. T. Psychophysiological Basis of Emotion. In P. J. Vinken & G. S. Bruyn (Eds.), *Handbook of Clinical Neurology.* Amsterdam, North Holland Publ., 1969. Pp. 317–372.

Pribram, K. H., Spinelli, D. N., & Reitz, S. L. The effect of radical disconnection of occipital and temporal cortex on visual behavior of monkeys. *Brain*, 1969, **92** 301–312.

Schwartzbaum, J. S., & Pribram, K. H. The effects of amygdalectomy in monkeys on transposition along a brightness continuum. *Journal of Comparative and Physiological Psychology*, 1960, **53**, 396–399.

Skinner, B. F. In C. Chagas (Ed.), Proceedings of the IBRO/Unesco Symposium on Brain Research and Human Behavior. Paris, March 1968. New York: Springer, 1968.

Sokolov, E. N. Neuronal models and the orienting reflex. In M. A. B. Brazier (Ed.), *The central nervous system and behavior*. New York: Josiah Macy, Jr. Foundation, 1960. Pp. 187–276.

Spinelli, D. N., & Pribram, K. H. Changes in visual recovery functions produced by temporal lobe stimulation in monkeys. *Electroencephalography and Clinical Neurophysiology*, 1966, **20**, 44–49.

Spinelli, D. N., & Pribram, K. H. Changes in visual recovery function and unit activity produced by frontal cortex stimulation. *Electroencephalography and Clinical Neurophysiology*, 1967, **22**, 143–149.

Spinelli, D. N., & Weingarten, M. Afferent and efferent activity in single units of the cat's optic nerve. *Experimental Neurology*, 1966, **3**, 347–361.

Stevens, C. F. *Neurophysiology: A primer*. New York: Wiley, 1966, Pp. 182.

Sutton, S., Tueting, P., Zubin, J., & John, E. R. Information delivery and the sensory evoked potential. *Science*, 1967, **155**, 1426–1439.

Teitelbaum, P. Sensory control of hypothalamic hyperphagia. *Journal of Comparative and Physiological Psychology*, 1955, **48**, 156–163.

Teuber, H. L. Perception. In J. Field, H. W. Magoun & V. E. Hall (Eds.), *Handbook of Physiology*. Vol. III. *Neurophysiology*. Washington: American Physiological Society, 1960. Pp. 1595–1668.

Walter, W. G. Slow potential waves in the human brain associated with expectancy, attention and decision. *Archiv fur Psychiatrie und Zeitschrift f. d. ges. Neulroogie*, 1964, **206**, 309–322.

Philosophy and Method in
Behavior Genetics: Its Relation to Biology[1]

D. D. THIESSEN

DEPARTMENT OF PSYCHOLOGY
UNIVERSITY OF TEXAS
AUSTIN, TEXAS

Behavior genetics is only in part concerned with correlating classes of genotypes with classes of behavior (see especially definitions and reviews by Broadhurst, 1960; Fuller & Thompson, 1960; Hall, 1951). Recently behavior genetics has aligned itself with ethology and other biological studies, and is

[1] This research was supported by NIMH Grant MH 14076-02 and NIMH Research Development Award MH-11, 174-02 to D. Thiessen. (Drs. John C. Loehlin and Jan H. Bruell kindly gave valuable comments on the manuscript.)

71

more concerned with "pathways" of genetic expression and adaptive mechanisms. It has also become a working tool to be used by any behaviorist, much like statistical techniques are used to buttress many disciplines. These changes have been rapid and extensive; therefore, the distinguishing features of the discipline are only beginning to take form.

This chapter has as its goals the setting forth of the basic tenets of behavior genetics and the specification of new directions of inquiry into the biological sciences. It is not heavily concerned with specific analytic techniques, although basic methods are included within the body of the paper. Rather, emphases are on the nature of the field, its philosophical assumptions, and its biological relevance. Attention is first given to the overwhelming and complicating fact of individual variation in behavioral processes, and to the possibility of abstracting general laws from this welter of differences. Following this is a description of animal forms that are suitable for behavior genetic investigations and which give the greatest hope of elucidating general principles. The third section discusses mechanisms intervening between genes and behavior. In it are references to the recent advances in molecular biology that are beginning to be applied to the decoding of complex processes of behavior. Finally, the chapter takes up the problem of adaptive qualities of behavior and their relation to natural selection in constant and changing environments.

While it is admitted throughout that individual variation is widespread at all levels of inquiry, from the genetic and physiological to the behavioral and evolutionary, it is a basic argument of this paper that individual variation is only important to the degree that it leads to principles that extend beyond unique characteristics. Before such principles evolve, however, it is necessary to determine the extent of individual differences and place them in a more general context.

I. The Extent of Individual Differences

Perhaps the widest theoretical cleavage between general psychologists and behavior geneticists has occurred over the view of fundamental biological processes underlying behavior. Psychologists, in the main, have held tenaciously to the notion that *all* species and populations, especially mammalian, are put together in basically the same way, and that species and individual parts are interchangeable, at least conceptually. There is credibility in the notion that to some degree at least behavior is managed in the same way at all species and population levels. A neuron, regardless of species, conducts impulses on the background of membrane changes involving potassium and sodium; a reflex is a stimulus–response arc whose form is virtually invariant for all neurologically wired organisms; and an endocrine organ and its chemical secretions are pretty much alike regardless of phylogenetic status. Variations often seem to be quantitative oscillations around the same theme, and, accordingly, add little to basic knowledge.

Considerable data have now been amassed against this extreme premise in the form of individual and species variations on almost all conceivable behaviors and physiological processes. Behaviors and mechanisms simply are not always the same in different genetic forms. With the possible exception of monozygous twins, all individuals are genetically unique. One source of variation is alternative forms of the same gene (allele) which may appear at the same chromosome site (locus). If only one chromosome locus with two allelic alternatives is considered, say A and a, three genetic classes are possible: AA, Aa, and aa. With three alternative alleles, say A, A', and a, the recombiant possibilities leap to six: AA, A'A, A'A', Aa, A'a, and aa. In general, for n alleles at a locus the population potential is $n(n + 1)/2$ genotypic classes. Now, the number of human loci may be the order of 10^4 of which perhaps the majority possess alternate forms of the same gene. Even if each locus has only two alternatives, the number of resultant genotypes is 3^n, where n is the number of independently segregating gene pairs. Only four loci, each with two gene possibilities provides 81 genotypes. The inherent variability of single and multiple loci is illustrated in Table 1. Clearly the genetic potential for variability is fantastic.

When the genomes are considered, much variation can be detected among the diploid (paired) chromosomes. For n pairs of chromosomes, there exists the possibility of 2^n genomes. The 23 pairs of chromosomes in man could lead to 2^{23} genomes, a tremendous potential for individuality. Added to these potentials are mutations, gene crossovers between chromosomes, chromosome abnormalities, mosaicisms, and, of course, unique gene–environment interactions, all of which add variability. In total it can be judged that the number of phenotypic outcomes is a function of the number of genotypes involved (G), the number of environments specified (E), and the number of interactions that are possible in each environment (G × E).

Mammalian species clearly differ in their behavior under a wide range of environments. Genetic selection for particular characters has demonstrated this point many times. Individuals and populations that are known to vary genetically are also known to differ in learning ability (e.g., Bovet-Nitti, Oliverio, & Bovet, 1968; Fabric, 1965; Tryon, 1940), preference for sucrose and alcohol (e.g., Levine, 1968; Rodgers, 1966), reaction to drugs (e.g., McGaugh & Petrinovitch, 1965), to noxious stimuli (e.g., Thiessen & Rodgers, 1965), to maternal deprivation (Newell, 1967), and to early experiences and handling (e.g., LaBarba, 1967). In short, nearly every behavior of current interest to psychologists shows genetic variation (the extensive literature is

TABLE 1

GENETIC AND PHENOTYPIC EXPECTATIONS FOR DIFFERENT NUMBERS OF GENE PAIRS

No. of segregating gene pairs	Intercross ($F_1 \times F_1$)							Backcross ($F_1 \times$ recessive P):
	No. of gametes	No. of recombinants	No. of genotypes	No. of phenotypes[a]	Occurrence of most frequent genotype	Occurrence of most frequent phenotype[a]	Occurrence of least frequent genotype[b] and phenotype	No. of genotypes and phenotypes
1 (Aa)	2	4	3	2	1/2	3/4	1/4	2
2 (Aa,Bb)	4	16	9	4	1/4 (Aa,Bb)	9/16 (A-,B-)	1/16	4
3 (Aa,Bb,Cc)	8	64	27	8	1/8 (Aa,Bb,Cc)	27/64 (A-,B-,C-)	1/64	8
4 (Aa,Bb,Cc,Dd)	16	256	81	16	1/16 (Aa,Bb,Cc,Dd)	81/256 (A-,B-,C-,D-)	1/256	16
n (General case)	$(2)^n$	$(4)^n$	$(3)^n$	$(2)^n$	$(1/2)^n$	$(3/4)^n$	$(1/4)^n$	$(2)^n$

[a] Dominance assumed at each locus.
[b] Homozygotes.

summarized in reviews by Fuller & Thompson, 1960; Hirsch, 1967; Manosevitz, Lindzey, & Thiessen, 1969; McClearn, 1962; Parsons, 1967; Thiessen, 1970, in press; Vandenberg, 1965; Vandenberg, 1968). In some cases the greatest part of the observed variance can be understood with reference to genotype.

It is necessary, therefore, that individual variation be studied before general principles can have meaning or encompass exceptions. Many species, subspecies, strains, and individuals must be investigated before we can become familiar with their differences and similarities under a number of environmental conditions. Beach (1950) pointed out that approximately 50% of all behavioral experiments have been conducted on 1/1000 of 1% of all extant species (primarily the albino rat) and the situation has not improved much since (Bitterman, 1965; Lockard, 1968). A study of a single species or population can be misleading.

Given the fact of individuality, how are general principles to be constructed? There is, of course, no complete solution at this moment. Individuality at all levels from the genotype to the actualization of that genotype in a phenotype will always put a strain on those hypotheses that assume that any animal can become the prototype of any other. However, much of the potential or actual genetic variation never reaches the phenotype, offering hope that all possible variation need not be considered. Gametes do not always pair randomly, accounting for the predominance of some chromosome units over others; some genetic combinations are inviable and hence never appear; and other variability is never expressed because of dominance of some alleles or the canalization of development by ontogenetic pressures. Moreover, there may be a great many organisms sharing common behaviors and mechanisms regardless of species or population. In some cases we might even entertain the proposition that individual variation around a core property of genotype or behavior is no more important than is the uniqueness of cloud formation to the basic principle of condensation. Increased knowledge of physiological processes and adaptive properties of behaviors, such as those discussed in the following sections, will clarify the relation of individual differences to more general descriptions of behavior. Yet almost as a matter of definition, generalities of behavioral organization will emerge only *after* a detailed survey of individual and species variations, and not *before*.

II. The Search for Genotypes

Behavior geneticists have an almost unlimited source of variation for study. The number of extant species approaches one million, and if only mammals are considered, about 4300 separate species exist (Morris, 1965).

Obviously not all species can be considered as subjects for detailed investigation. Each would require a lifetime of study. In fact we can be virtually certain that only a small fraction of the possible genotypes within any one species will ever be thoroughly studied. Behavior geneticists have therefore had to search for "appropriate" species to investigate, species that are amenable to genetic manipulation and still represent widely distributed organisms. This section presents a general picture of the species search and its resultant influence on the structure of behavior genetics.

The problem of deciding on appropriate species for study may not be as terrifying as it first seems, and does not imply an inability to arrive at general conclusions about animal behavior. Fortunately many factors contrive to limit genetic and phenotypic diversity and hence reduce the range of possible variation between species. It is just such factors that reduce analytical difficulties and permit the construction of general laws of behavior. At the molecular level, identical DNA and RNA structures shared by nearly all animals presuppose identical biochemical schemes that have relevance for behavior. Sturtevant (1965) has pointed out that: "The more recent comparative biochemical data . . . favor the idea of the great stability of genetic systems, since they show essential identity of some of the gene-controlled basic biochemical pathways in bacteria, fungi, and vertebrates" [p. 115]. Stable genetic systems and identical biochemical pathways, like those discussed by Sturtevant, set restrictions on phenotypic (behavioral) diversity and certainly limit the number of controlling mechanisms. A wider discussion of this appears in subsequent sections.

There are other important stabilizing features in the environment, aside from limits of expression imposed by the biochemical nature of the organism. All living organisms regardless of origin and ecology have had to cope with some of the same environmental pressures and consequently have evolved functions in common. Nearly all animals must contend with light and heat periodicities, restricted ranges of humidity and atmospheric pressure, processes of ingestion, metabolism, and excretion, and necessities of perception, locomotion, and reproduction. To be sure there are a myriad of ways in which the details of these requirements are met, but the general themes of adaptation are often similar across phylogenetic lines and offer some hope that fundamental laws will emerge and that some species may be generally representative of many.

The selection of representative species, however, presents some difficulties, and is nowhere near complete. To date, emphases have centered on mammalian prototypes: the domestic and wild mouse, the rat, and occasionally other rodents. These are probably reasonable choices if the desire is to learn something general about mammalian species. Rodents, as it turns out, comprise the greatest proportion of the 4237 mammalian species; namely, 1729 (41 %). Moreover, they are the only terrestrial species found in all areas of the world, with the exception of bats, and can be found in the wild or domesticated state. Thus, the range of adaptation which can be scrutinized is broader than for any other mammalian group. Coupled with the advantages of species representation and availability of rodents are the ease of maintenance and short generation time.

Drosophila have provided an entirely different source of genetic material for behavioral studies. Although these *Diptera* do not mimic the physiology of mammalian systems, they possess many important advantages not shared by rodents and still may be representative of general genetic systems. First, at least 479 loci have been located and mapped on chromosomes (Altman & Dittmer, 1964), more than in any other species. Second, much cytological data are available for reference (Lindsley & Grell, 1968). Third, crossbreeding is easily accomplished, and the generation time is so short that a year's study can sometimes accomplish as much as ten to fifteen years of work with most rodent species (e.g., Hirsch, 1967). *Drosophila* will clearly remain the species of choice for some time with those investigators interested in extending classical Mendelian genetics to behavioral phenotypes.

Other species have been observed in behavior genetic experiments and may eventually become favorites (see Fuller & Thompson, 1960; McClearn, 1962), but for now they remain rather limited in prospect. Many species are difficult to maintain and breed in the laboratory, while others have such long breeding generations that classical genetic experiments are nearly impossible. Special experimental and observational techniques are being devised to handle these difficulties and more can be expected. Man, of course, is being studied with profit, especially in situations where pedigrees can be mapped and isolated genes followed in their biochemical influence (McKusick, 1966).

The remainder of this section describes the most commonly used species for basic behavior genetic experiments. Data for man and other species can be found in Manosevitz *et al.* (1969) and Vandenberg (1965, 1966, 1968). Other species will be mentioned that are likely to be of analytic advantage in the near future. From this brief outline the reader can judge the relative merits of the organisms for use in experiments designed to generalize across genotypes.

A. Inbred Strains of Mice as Research Instruments

The mouse, *Mus musculus*, is and probably will remain the principle species for investigation of gene-behavior relations. It is small, easily adapted to the laboratory, in some cases "genetically pure," and resembles other mammalian species including man in many physiological ways.

The mouse has traveled the world with man and inhabits every niche common to mammalian species. Man and mouse easily coexist in each other's world of commerce and in some instances are highly dependent upon each other. The mouse may live opportunistically off man, but man has also enriched his own position by delving into the life style of the mouse. The relationship between man and mouse is one of the oldest adaptations ever evolved.

Man's earliest use of the mouse can be traced to pet fanciers and breeders in antiquity (Keeler, 1931; Grüneberg, 1952). The waltzing mouse with its exaggerated circling motions was one of the first behavioral mutants to reach recorded history. It can be traced to its origin in China as early as 80 B.C. The historical chain extends to the present time. If five generations are assumed to arise each year, then approximately 10,245 generations have passed since the waltzing mouse was first described. This amounts to the equivalent of 204,900 years of human life—truly an impressive pedigree.

It is even said (Sturtevant, 1965) that Gregor Mendel originally worked out laws of genetic segregation and recombination with the mouse but suppressed the mammalian work for fear of antagonizing the Church. He, of course, eventually published his monumental paper in 1865 using common garden peas. Nevertheless, von Guaita (see Grüneberg, 1952) and others demonstrated regularities of inheritance in the mouse at the close of the 19th century that, after the rediscovery of Mendel's work in 1900, could clearly be interpreted along the same lawful lines as the pea experiments. In fact, von Guaita published data on the inheritance of waltzing in mice that nicely demonstrated that circling was the result of a single recessive genetic unit. This experiment is perhaps the first systematic study in behavior genetics. The universal application of Mendel's insights set the tone for all genetic investigations to follow.

Behavior genetics is one of the beneficiaries of this knowledge, and the mouse has become a primary prototype of mammalian systems. The use of *Mus* is a logical outgrowth of the need for a variety of genetic populations convenient to manipulate, an organism resembling man biologically, and experimental animals that are readily available. Many specially bred domestic as well as wild mouse lines ably serve these purposes.

Taxonomically *Mus musculus* is in the order Rodentia, the family Muridae, and the subfamily Maurinae (Simpson, 1945). Within *Mus musculus* many domestic and aboriginal forms exist. All these genetic groups provide important sources of experimental materials for evaluating intrinsic laws of behavior and evaluating the adaptation of man.

Much behavior genetic work has concentrated on highly inbred strains originally developed for differential susceptibility to neoplastic diseases. The major strains and their lineage are shown in Fig. 1. The first inbred line, now known as DBA, was begun at Harvard in 1909 by Clarence Cook Little. Within 15 years after the origin of the first inbred line most of the other strains used in cancer research had been established. In 1921 at Cold Spring

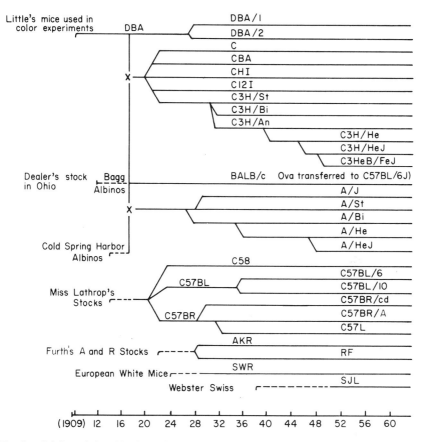

Fig. 1. Origins of the older inbred strains of mice (from Staats, 1966). (Used with permission of McGraw-Hill, New York.)

Harbor, Leonell C. Strong mated an albino mouse obtained from Halsey J. Bagg with one from an albino stock from Little's colony and began inbreeding. The A strain, now an important line in behavior genetic investigations, resulted. In 1920 Strong made a series of crosses between Bagg's albinos and the DBA line and developed the C3H, CBA, C, CHI, and C121 inbred strains. The C3H line was later separated into several sublines.

Another strain often used in behavioral research, the C57, also dates from 1921. Little obtained two litter mates from Miss A. E. C. Lathrop, a mouse fancier in Granby, Massachusetts, and mated these. The offspring segregated as black and brown, which, with inbreeding, led to the C57BL and C57BR strains. J. M. Murray later developed the C57L strain from a coat color mutant found in the C57BR subline.

Charleton MacDowell, also at Cold Spring Harbor, originated the C58 line from descendants of Miss Lathrop's progenitors of the C57 lines. MacDowell also inbred the Bagg albino stock to develop the well-known BALB/c inbred strain.

Other strains were soon to follow. Jacob Furth of the Henry Phipps Institute in Philadelphia began inbreeding mice in 1928 to yield the AK and RF strains. Clara J. Lynch of the Rockefeller Institute inbred within the common Swiss albino mice to obtain such lines as the SWR/J and SJL/J. Altogether, over 200 lines have appeared (Staats, 1966), each inbred, usually by brother–sister matings. In addition, special stocks are maintained that carry single genes of interest (Lane, 1964), and at least 80 neurological mutants, ideal for investigations of relations between brain function and behavior, are available (Sidman, Green, & Appel, 1965).

A great deal of information about special strains of mice can be found in edited volumes of the *Federation Proceedings* (see Guide 1960, 1963), a *Catalogue of Uniform Strains of Laboratory Animals Maintained in Great Britain* (1958), *Biology Data Book* (Altman & Dittmer, 1964), general reference texts (Green, 1966; Lane-Petter, 1963), and a privately circulated periodical devoted to the mouse (*Mouse News Letter*, edited by Mary F. Lyon). Standardized nomenclature of inbred mice can be found in a publication edited by Staats (1964), and bibliographies of behavioral studies using inbred mice are also found in publications by Staats (1958, 1963).

The extraordinary value of inbred mice in behavior genetic analyses is due to the extreme genetic homogeneity among individuals of the same strain and divergence among individuals of different strains. In brief, inbreeding is the assortive mating of individuals sharing genes in common. Outbreeding, conversely, is the mating of individuals sharing fewer genes in common than expected from a random assortment of genes. Inbreeding, therefore, increases the number of homozygous (identical) loci and outbreeding increases the number of heterozygous (nonidentical) loci. Inbred mice are generally obtained by brother × sister mating for a minimum of 20 generations (heterozygosity is reduced by approximately 19% in each generation using this system of breeding). Animals within an inbred strain are isogenic; that is, they are considered genetically alike, homozygous at all loci. All animals within a strain are as identical as monozygous twins in humans (twins derived from the splitting of a single fertilized egg). Therefore, genetic variation within an isogenic line is at a minimum. The within-strain phenotypic variation, and there is always a great deal, must derive from two environmental sources: (*a*) more or less permanent influences (long-term environmental effects), and (*b*) special influences of short duration (short-term environmental effects). Long-term influences are often ascribed to developmental and nutritional causes, whereas short-term influences can be due to any number of temporary living conditions. The former environmental effect is difficult to untangle from genetic influences, while the latter is usually assumed to be error variance randomly distributed around the mean value of the genotype.

The key to several methods of behavior analysis lies in the theoretical assumption of absence of genetic variability in nonsegregating groups (e.g., parental and first generation groups, F_1). Nonsegregating groups, as a result, constitute our best estimate of environmental influences on a trait. When several separate inbred lines are observed under identical conditions the differences must be ascribed to genotypic variations since environmental effects are held constant and assumed to be the same for any genetic line. The method is simple to the extreme: a number of strains thought to be different inbred samples of a larger gene pool are housed identically and tested for a behavioral characteristic. The differences found are due to the genetic variations between strains.

This particular methodology has been used in behavior genetics to the point of monotony; and it is not an exaggeration to say that every behavior sampled shows a genetic effect. We might simply enumerate a few: learning ability, general activity, negative geotaxis, emotionality, brightness discriminations, alcohol preference, audiogenic seizure susceptibility, and response to population stress (consult earlier references). Often strain differences are so wide that there is absolutely no overlap between distributions.

An important attribute of inbred lines is their consistency over generations. Excluding random mutations and "genetic drift," strains remain uniform as long as an appropriate inbreeding system is followed. The repeatability of genetic differences offers the investigator stable biological material with which to judge behavioral effects. The material, and hope of replication, is available to any interested investigator. Little by little, a great number of behavioral differences are being described for scores of strains. Once a catalog of strain variations is assembled individual strains can be selected for any behavioral characteristic imaginable. Several strains are beginning to approach this level of utility.

A natural extension to the description of strain differences is to ask what the ratio is between the strain variance (Vb) and the total variance (Vt). This simple ratio is called the intraclass correlation (t) and provides a rough estimate of the genetic influence on a behavior. The entire variance can be divided into between group (strain) variance and within group variance (Vw). According to the arguments offered above, the between group variance for inbred lines is genetically determined and the within group variance is entirely environmentally determined, Thus:

$$t = \frac{Vb}{Vt} \quad \text{or} \quad \frac{Vb}{Vb + Vw}$$

describes the amount of the total variance due to a genetic influence. The variance components are computed in the usual way as for any analysis of variance model.

Genetic lines can be used in another way to estimate the major variance components of the total phenotype. The total phenotypic variance, Vt, is considered to be composed of a genetic component, Vg, and environmental component, Ve, and interaction component between the two, Vi,

$$Vt = Vg + Ve + Vi.$$

Either by definition or because the interaction term in fact sums to zero, the two most relevant terms are Vg and Ve. The use of inbred lines to estimate these two components becomes a powerful tool. An inbred line is one of the best estimates of environmental variance we have. The F_1 cross between lines is also nonvarying genetically, as all animals are isogenic and heterozygous at many loci depending upon the gene differences in the original parents. An F_2 cross between two strains (a segregating population), on the other hand, is a population in which genetic variance is present along with environmental variance. Thus the P_1, P_2, and F_1 groups offer three separate estimates of environmental variance, and the F_2 population offers an estimate of combined genetic and environmental variance. Subtracting the mean environmental components from the F_2 variance leaves a component of genetic variance relatively free of environmental influence. The ratio of genetic variance to the total variance gives the genetic determination of the trait. In summary:

$$\frac{VF_2 - (\bar{X}VP_1, VP_2, VF_1)}{VF_2} = \frac{Vg}{Vt},$$

or the *coefficient of genetic determination*. The coefficient expresses the relative importance of the genetic variance to the total variance. The coefficient of determination has been called heritability in the broad sense. It does not perfectly describe the amount of genetic variation which is additive (heritability in the narrow sense, h^2). Additive variance is free of dominant and epistatic effects that cannot be used to predict the breeding value of the population. We will not describe the methods of computing heritability in the narrow sense (see Falconer, 1960, for details). For many traits the two measures, heritability in the broad and narrow sense do not differ much. In such cases, of course, either may be used. In any event both measures are highly susceptible to the genotypes involved, the particular testing conditions used and the behavior observed.

A minimum estimate of the number of genes controlling a trait is approximated by:

$$\frac{(m_1 - m_2)^2}{8(VF_2 - VF_1)}$$

where m_1 and m_2 are the means of the parental populations and the other symbols remain as described (see Falconer, 1960, for an introduction to this rationale).

There are numerous other uses of inbred and cross lines in behavior genetics. One extremely valuable use is to observe single gene variations on an otherwise invariant genetic backgroup. Usually a single gene is back-crossed onto an isogenic line and left as the only segregating allele. Whenever a difference between litter mates occurs due to the substitution of one allele, that difference must be ascribed to only that locus allowed to vary. Other methods of interest include regression analyses of parents on offspring (essentially genetic correlations) in highly heterogeneous groups, factor analyses of traits in genetically diverse groups, diallel crosses among several inbred lines, and complex variance analyses using components derived from numerous familial relationships. These techniques have been applied to the problem of describing the genetic, environmental, and interaction components for behaviors of interest. Many are discussed in a publication by Manosevitz *et al.* (1969).

In summary, the major uses of inbred strains in behavior genetics are (*a*) the cataloging of repeatable genetic differences for behaviors of major interest, (*b*) the stabilizing of physiological variations of possible significance to behavior, (*c*) the partitioning of phenotypic variance into genetic and environmental components, and (*d*) the study of single genes against uniform genetic backgrounds, In addition, the degree of inbreeding depression for various traits can be studied by examining hybrid vigor upon crossing inbred lines. Hybrid vigor (heterosis), where the offspring outscore either parent, is the direct opposite of inbreeding depression. Whenever it is found by crossing inbred lines, a likely hypothesis is that the trait originally suffered from inbreeding depression. Traits related to evolutionary fitness should show inbreeding depression and hence heterosis. This use of inbred lines is therefore a method of attacking some aspects of behavioral evolution.

There are limitations to the use of inbred strains. Any particular strain is a minute sample of all possible available strains. We must acknowledge the ensuing restrictions on our generalizations about the gene pool at large. Moreover, an inbred animal is far different from any animal found in the wild. It lacks heterozygosity and lethal and semilethal recessives. Deleterious genes in the homozygous state often depress reproductive fitness or lead to "genetic death." Hence, strains carrying such genes cannot be developed or maintained. And coadaptive gene sysems related to reproductive fitness are probably at a suboptimal level. Virtually no inbred strain could survive in

the wild, as it carries the great weight of inbreeding depression. In all probability the most important behaviors of selective significance are attenuated
in scope and efficiency; some may be lacking altogether. The animals are
therefore unique, artificially contrived, and lacking in vitality. Still, these
disadvantages do not preclude basic behavior genetic studies or work where
it is necessary to preset the genotype or physiology. Generality can be
improved by investigating many strains under specified conditions, by using
genetically heterogeneous offspring obtained by crossing many diverse lines,
and by comparing measured variation with natural populations of *Mus
musculus*.

B. *Other Types of Mice Important for Behavioral Research*

Wild, commensal, and domesticated mice are only beginning to appear
attractive to researchers in behavior genetics. Their heritage is without
the systematic control found in inbred lines; because of this, however, their
diversity and adaptation to natural environments can offer insights into the
evolutionary history of behavior.

According to Schwarz and Schwarz (1943) wild or aboriginal mice form
four separate subsepecies: *Mus musculus wagneri*, *Mus musculus spicilegus*,
Mus musculus manchu, and *Mus musculus spretus*. All four lack direct communication with man; hence the populations offer gene pools for study that
are not affected by human activities. In addition, the first three species have
developed commensal populations that have followed man around the world
and have, consequently, diverged genetically. The range of dispersal is wide,
especially for *M. m. wagneri*, giving groups of mice specifically adapted to
local ecologies. The three main centers of dispersal are shown in Table 2.

Wild mice are classified into genetic groups on the basis of origin, distribution, body weight, and tail length, head size, coat color, and interbreeding
capacity. The biological separation between stocks is not always complete,
giving gradations such as in Iran where areas of *wagneri*, *bactrianus*, and
praetextus meet, and hybrids such as in Kenya where ranges of *bactrianus*
and *castaneus* overlap, and the whole of the Norwegian coast where *domesticus*
meets *M. m. musculus*.

Intrapopulation variation prevents the subspecies from being accurately
classified. On the other hand, differences in gene frequency, polymorphisms,
and continuous phenotypic variation provide the raw material for the study
of adaptation to specific locales. Inbred strains, with their redundant and
restricted genotypes, offer few of these advantages.

Few behavioral studies have been conducted on wild mice and their
common derivative, although some progress is being made in this direction.
Bruell (1970) has proposed designs for evaluating the effects of inbreeding

TABLE 2

MAJOR COMMENSAL RADIATION OF THREE
STOCKS OF WILD *Mus musculus*

First center of dispersal

Mus musculus wagneri
(Russian Turkestan)

M. m. bactrianus → Africa	*M. m. praetextus*
(India)	(Iraq)
↓	↓
M. m. hormourus	*M. m. brevirostris* → Latin America
(China)	(Italy and Spain) and Southern U.S.
	↓
M.m. urbanus M.m. castaneus → Africa	*M. m. domesticus* → Canada
(N.E. India) (Peninsular India)	(W. Europe) and Northern U.S.

Second center of dispersal	Third center of dispersal
Mus musculus spicilegus	*Mus musculus manchu*
(Southern Russia)	(Japan)
↓	↓
M. m. musculus	*M. m. molossinus*
(Into Siberia)	(Japan and Korea)

on wild populations which combine observations of animals in the wild and systematic studies in the laboratory. A major interest of his is to contrast the adaptive differences between inbred and outbred populations Selander (Selander and Yang, 1970) has studied several rural populations of domestic mice using blood esterases and hemoglobin as genetic markers to study geographic variations in polymorphisms. Significantly, Selander finds that even within single barns without physical barriers, "demes" and other subgroups of mice are "isolated breeding populations" with characteristic gene frequencies. Territorial and aggressive behavior, especially by the male, are potent isolating devices.

Studies like those designed and implemented by Bruell and Selander are likely to extend our knowledge of natural influences on genes and behavior, complement the more restricted uses of inbred strains of mice, and extend our notions of biological populations.

C. *The Genus* Peromyscus *as a Tool in Behavior Genetics*

Peromyscus species (deer mice) have been less thoroughly exploited as significant animals for research in behavior genetics. They combine many of the advantages inherent among inbred and wild strains of *Mus musculus*.

Peromyscus are numerous, spread widely over geographic areas of North and Central America, have been selectively adapted to local habitats, and are relatively easy to maintain in the laboratory. The genus *Peromyscus* contains 56 species, 23 of which are polytypic and 33 of which are monotypic. The polytypic species have from 2 to 63 subspecies with a median of 4 each. The widely distributed species, *maniculatus*, ranges over most of North America, and diverges into many subspecies. The narrowly distributed species, such as *floridanus* which is limited to peninsular Florida, are monotypic.

According to King (1961) the genus is separated into five subgenera, two subgenera with one species each, one subgenus with four species, another with 11 species, and another with the remaining 39 species. The classification based primarily on tooth structure is given in Table 3.

Maniculatus once ranged over southeastern United States. Apparently the inundation of the Gulf Coastal Plains isolated outlying populations of *maniculatus*, which subsequently diverged into the species *polionotus*. Other genetic divergencies apparently occurred between populations connected only by a narrow range. *P. t. truei* and *P. t. gilberti* which intergrade only in a limited area across Walker Pass in California apparently diverged in this fashion.

King (1961) provides evidence that the morphological and behavioral responses of various species and populations to the environment have been adaptive and relatively uniform within taxonomic groups. Grassland forms tend to be small with short tails and small ears. Forest forms usually are larger mice with long tails and large ears. The longer tails of the forest mice aid them in climbing and balancing. The pale coat color of arid forms is cryptic on the light soils of the desert and hence offers protection from predators. Variation in ear size may be related to differences in the need for acoustical concentration related to the detection of predators or for social communication. The large hind feet characteristic of forest dwellers and sand-dune forms have been related to climbing ability in the first case and snowshoe effect in the second.

Other traits tend to confirm the relationship of behavior to ecological requirements. *Peromyscus leucopus* occupies upland forests throughout much of its range, while the closely related *P. gossypinus* occupies lowland forests. When both species were offered a choice between these two habitats in an isolated woodlot, each species tended to migrate to its preferred habitat (McCarley, 1954).

Harris in 1952, published the first report of habitat preference in prairie and woodland deer mice. Each type of mouse displayed a clear preference for an artificial habitat matching closely that of its natural environment. Even laboratory-reared mice exhibited the "correct" artificial choices of

TABLE 3

CLASSIFICATION OF THE GENUS *Peromyscus*[a]

Subgenus	Species group	Species	Subspecies
HAPLOMYLOMYS		*crinitus*	8
		californicus	5
		eremicus	14
	Maniculatus	*maniculatus*	63
		polionotus	8
		melanotis	1
	Leucopus	*leucopus*	16
		gossypinus	7
	Boylei	*boylei*	13
		perfulvus	1
		oaxacinsis	1
		hylocetes	1
		pectoralis	4
PEROMYSCUS	Truei	*truei*	13
		nasutus	3
		difficilis	3
	Melanophrys	*melanophrys*	6
	Lepturus	*furvus*	1
		lepturus	1
		lophurus	1
		guatemalensis	2
	Mexicanus	*mexicanus*	7
		banderanus	3
		yucatanicus	2
	Megalops	*megalops*	3
MEGADONTOMYS		*thomasi*	1
PODOMYS		*floridanus*	1
OCHROTOMYS		*nuttalli*	4

[a] From King (1961).

environments, strongly suggesting that genotype rather than experience determines the choice.

A most interesting study by King, Maas, and Weisman (1964) lends additional support to the notion that genetic selection facilitates the formation of behaviors. In Canada and the United States the north–south distribution of stocks of deer mice is *P. m. gracilis, P. m. bairdii, P. polionotus,* and *P. floridanus.* Interestingly this is nearly the same rank order difference in the amount of nest material used by these stocks in the laboratory to construct nests. *Gracilis* use more nest material than *bairdii* and both use more material than either *polionotus* or *floridanus.* Only *P. polionotus* and *P. floridanus* build nests of equal size. It would appear that northern forms build larger nests to provide insulation as a protection from colder weather. Equally large nests are unnecessary in warmer climates. Since all stocks tested were descendants of laboratory-reared mice, the differences are clearly genetic in origin, and seem to conform to past behavioral requirements and selection results. Other references to habitat selection, reproductive and developmental processes could be made to emphasize the point that the genetic and phenotypic variation found in *Peromyscus* is conditioned by the environment (e.g., Blair, 1953; Dice, 1947; Kavanau, 1967; King, Price, & Weber, 1968; Moore, 1965; Ogilvie & Stinson, 1966; Smith, 1965).

Studies of this kind will reveal much about the interplay between the gene pool and the demands imposed by the environment. Eventually some of these adaptations may be reduced to relevant biochemical factors, thus suggesting generalities at this level. It seems more apparent, however, that many generalities will appear at the *functional* level, independent of specific genotypes or biochemical correlates. Phenotypes only survive if they meet environmental requirements and this can be done in numerous genetic and biochemical ways. This argument is extended in a later section.

D. Drosophila *in Behavior Genetic Experiments*

Much of the progress in classical genetics would not have been possible without the benefit of many stocks of *Drosophila* (Carlson, 1966; Dunn, 1965; Sturtevant, 1965). The *Diptera* fly offers an organism that breeds rapidly and shows evidence of almost every classic genetic response known to man. With this simple organism as a tool many general concepts unfolded. Genes as units of inheritance became apparent. The relation of genes to chromosomes was found, and linkage maps of genes on chromosomes were established. Experimental mutations were first accomplished in *Drosophila*. Cytological studies confirmed the earlier work and led to classic studies of gene action and biochemical differentiation. The mass of knowledge accumulated on various forms of *Drosophila* is of unparalleled value to anyone interested in the basic relations between genes and behavior.

William F. Castle introduced *Drosophila* into genetics in 1905, actually one year before William Bateson coined the term "genetics" and only five years after Gregor Mendel's classic experimental report of 1865 was rediscovered by Hugo de Vries, Carl Correns, and Erich von Tschermak. This led very quickly to a surge of research, led by T. H. Morgan, C. B. Bridges, and A. H. Sturtevant all at Columbia, and W. Bateson at Cambridge, that placed Mendelian genetics on a solid foundation and suggested the notion that *all* traits in *all* organisms are at least partially under the biological control of gene particles.

TABLE 4

Wild Type Stocks[a]

Austin
Started at the University of Texas before 1929. Viability and fertility good

Canton-S: Canton-Special
Derived from wild flies collected in Canton, Ohio. Selected by Bridges. Contains a recessive for multiple thoracic and scutellar bristles, which overlaps wild type in most flies but appears sporadically in strains partly derived from Canton-S. Bridges found that salivary chromosomes were normal

Lausanne-S: Lausanne-Special
Stock derived from wild flies collected in 1938 by Bridges at Lausanne, Wisconsin. Has short posterior scutellar bristles. Salivary chromosomes normal, according to Bridges

Oregon-R
Stock derived from wild flies collected in 1925 or earlier by D. E. Lancefield at Roseburg, Oregon. Stock contains a slight ebony allele, a branching of the posterior crossvein (in chromosome 2), and an occasional scooped wing. Salivary chromosomes homozygous for $Df(2R)Ore-R$

Oregon-R-C
Selected by Bridges in 1938 from Oregon-R. Body color not so dark as that of Oregon-R. Homozygous for $Df(2R)Ore-R$

Samarkand
Stock derived from wild flies captured in 1936 at Samarkand, Uzbek Republic in Asiatic USSR. Original stock contained a low frequency of inversions in $3R$; chromosomes probably are now all of standard sequence. Ives reports that females of his lines of Samarkand are distinguishable from Oregon-R females in that they have no faint trident on the thorax and there is always a well-defined black band on seventh (most posterior) dorsolateral abdominal segment

Stephenville
Derived from wild flies captured at Stephenville, Texas in 1935. Salivary chromosomes probably normal. Fertility and viability good

Swedish-b
Stock established by Bridges from flies collected near Stockholm in 1923. Slight abnormality of abdominal banding and position of scutellar bristles. Salivary chromosomes homozygous for $Df(2R)Sw-R$

Swedish-c
Derived by Bridges from Swedish-b in 1928. Body color lighter than that of Swedish-b. Homozygous for deficiencies in tips of $2L$ and $2R$

Urbana-S: Urbana-Special
Selected by Bridges from flies collected at Urbana, Illinois. Body color somewhat lighter than standard wild type. Salivary chromosomes normal

---

[a]From Lindsley and Grell (1968).

The most common wild type stocks are listed in Table 4, although many more forms are found in laboratories all over the world and are often commercially available (e.g., Carolina Biological Supply Co., Burlington, North Carolina). It is not difficult or time consuming to inbreed or select divergent lines; hence a nearly complete nomenclature is available, as is true for inbred strains of *Mus musculus*.

As already mentioned, at least 479 loci have been mapped for *Drosophila*. Fewer than 20 of these have been studied with a view toward elucidating behavioral features (see Thiessen, Owen, & Whitsett, 1970, for a review). Far more impressive is the recent surge of work dealing with quantitative features of behavior, initiated and performed primarily by Hirsch (1967) and his colleagues at the University of Illinois. These investigators in almost tour de force fashion have demonstrated genetic effects on a number of behaviors including phototaxis and geotaxis. Strains have been deliberately selected for high and low values of these traits in the shortest possible time using mass screening techniques not possible with other organisms. Dobzhansky and his associates (e.g., Dobzhansky & Spassky, 1962) have duplicated these results in all essential features.

Hirsch has extended his earlier findings by ingenious techniques of chromosome substitution that denote the relative contribution of three of the four *Drosophila* chromosome pairs to negative and positive geotaxis. None of this work would be possible in conventional species used by psychologists. Moreover, as he and others have demonstrated, replicate designs are not only feasible but justifiable in terms of time and effort (that is, multiple replications of the experiment can be run simultaneously). Other important landmarks in *Drosophila* behavior genetics are reviewed by Parsons (1967) and include reference to the thorough analyses of reproduction by Manning (1965) and Spieth (1952). For both laboratory and field studies, such as those discussed in relation to rodents, *Drosophila* can extend our knowledge into the genetic components of ecological and behavioral adaptation. The advantages of working with a small organism with a short generation time are obvious.

The species and strains discussed represent a very small proportion of those species available for study. Rodents do, however, have the merit of being psysiologically similar to man and other mammalian species and are readily available for field and laboratory work. *Drosophila* give the advantages associated with genetic manipulation. Together these species will doubtlessly provide a wealth of basic information about genetic variation and general pathways of genetic expression.

Other species should not be neglected. Rats, of course, have been studied extensively by psychologists and will continue to be of interest. Several inbred lines are available which could serve the experimentalist in some cases as well as inbred mice (Institute of Laboratory Animal Resources, 1964). Fish, with all their diversity, and in some cases reproductive advantages, should be included in the arsenal of the behavior geneticist. Likewise avian species such as pigeons (already selected for divergent behaviors and morphologies) and canaries, which occur in abundance and about which much information is already available, should be carefully studied. Eventually it will be necessary to survey a range of reptile and amphibian species; otherwise it will be impossible to describe the degree to which generalities occur across wide taxonomic groups and the cases in which species-specific and individual-specific "laws" must apply.

III. Mechanism-Specific Approaches in Behavior Genetics

Technically behavior is not inherited; only DNA molecules are inherited. From that point on behavioral formation is a problem of a constant interplay between genetic potential and environmental shaping. The contribution of the genes is, of course, substantial, but their expression is a matter of developmental opportunity. In some sense then, the more direct effects on behavior, and certainly those developmentally closer to behavior, are biochemical, physiological, and morphological in nature (as an aggregate these will be referred to as structural or mechanistic effects). In other words, the cause and effect relations between variables will be more directly expressed between mechanism and behavior than between gene and behavior, and our focus of attention should be directed there.

Moreover, environmental effects may produce an exact duplicate of a genetic condition (a phenocopy). Clearly the understanding of both the phenocopy and genetic effect rests on knowledge of the mechanisms altered by the environment or the genetic equivalent, and much less on knowledge of the organism's particular genotype. For example, ingestion of food in several mammalian species can be caused in numerous ways which involve the same "common pathway" (Rosenzweig, 1962). The easiest way to establish eating behavior is to deprive the animal of food for several hours. It can also be done by substituting genes for obesity, injecting insulin, or goldthioglucose, stimulating the dorsal-lateral aspects of the hypothalamus, or by lesioning the ventral-medial nucleus of the hypothalamus. There is no obvious reason why all these techniques should lead to the same behavior. However, when mechanisms are compared they appear quite similar if not identical. Food deprivation and insulin lower blood sugar levels in critical hypothalamic areas and in this fashion activate feeding. Goldthioglucose damages a hypothalamus inhibiting mechanism as does a lesion to the ventral-medial nucleus. Stimulation of the dorsal-lateral areas apparently overrides the inhibitory control. Thus it appears that the final common neurological mechanism lies at least in part at the hypothalmic level. Many diverse methods of inducing eating behavior share this common substrate. The method involved, whether it be genetic, pharmacological, or surgical, is of lesser concern and of more peripheral interest than the nature of the mechanism. The structure-function link is not limited to particular individuals or populations, or even to single species. It is not, in other words, gene specific, population specific, or species specific. The relation is *mechanism specific* and is conceptually independent of specific genes or environments.

The implication is not that genes can be overlooked, but only that their action must be understood. Genes act in sequence and compound their effects. They are repeatedly inactive, active, and inactive.

Hence, the temporal regulation of gene action on mechanisms and the variation of structure in regard to function must form the basis for the understanding of much of behavior. Correlations between genes and behavior at a particular point in time are insufficient for the understanding of any structure-function relation. It is often easier to see the biological basis of a behavior if it can be viewed during development. In some cases the factors that "induce" new lines of development can facilitate the task of relating mechanisms to behavior. These may be embryological in nature, like "biochemical triggers," or specific internal or external events that influence development during critical periods. It is evident that if behavior is to be completely understood one must know what affects the course of development and what factors stimulate and inhibit gene response. Simply correlating gene aggregates with behavioral traits is insufficient.

The mechanistic approach in behavior genetics is relatively new (Rodgers, 1967; Thiessen & Rodgers, 1967), but is being seen more and more in studies aimed at elucidating behavior and arriving at principles that are not gene specific. The rest of this section discusses the dimensions of this new movement and suggests how classical behavior genetics can break from the traditionalism of overparticularizing the behavior into genetic units. The examples illustrate how important it is to understand structure-function relations and their ontogeny. New concepts now in the process of formation in other biological disciplines are drawn upon as necessary for incorporation into behavior genetics.

A. Parsimony in Behavior Genetics: Structure-Function Relations

Genetic analyses outline the diversity of behavior but do not offer explanations for its organization. Physiological analyses can sometimes provide needed explanations, and at times give simple descriptions of otherwise obscure phenotypes. An example of how knowledge of structure-function relations have apparently explained a wide difference in learning ability concerns the C3H inbred strain of mouse. This strain differs from other strains (e.g., A, DBA, C57) in its ability to learn maze problems (Lindzey & Winston, 1962). Superficial examination of this strain in any number of situations strongly suggests the C3H animals are intellectually deficient. A recent examination of several strains by Bovet, Bovet-Nitti, and Oliverio (1969) points up the difficulty that this strain has in shock-avoidance shuttle responses using the onset of light as a conditioning stimulus. Relative to DBA, BALB, A, and some Swiss mice, C3H mice never perform above chance, and are often below chance. The CBA strain studied and some other Swiss mice are equally poor learners.

Bovet and his colleagues build a differential consolidation hypothesis based on these and similar data to indicate different cognitive processes in the good and poor learners. The fact which they note but deemphasize as important is that nearly all C3H strains examined, at least one form of CBA mouse, and several Swiss mice (all "cognitively" deficient in regard to avoidance conditioning) suffer from retinal degeneration (*rd/rd*) and probably cannot see the light stimulus that precedes the onset of shock (Sidman & Green, 1965). It is known that the response threshold to light intensity in *rd/rd* mice is 10^5 greater than normal mice (Fuller & Wimer, 1966), and even the light that is perceived may bypass usual visual channels and enter the visual system directly through the skull (Ganong, Shepherd, Wall, Van Brunt, & Clegg, 1963). Moreover, the visual deficiency of *rd/rd*, regardless of the genetic background, is apparent in depth discrimination (Frank & Kenton, 1966). It is hardly surprising, therefore, that some strains do relatively poorly when a discrimination depends on the perception of light.

Even if performance difficulties are found in nonvisual problems for the C3H strain and other lines with *rd/rd*, retinal degeneration may be implicated, for degeneration of the rods in mice is followed by transsynaptic neural degeneration up to and including the visual cortex (Terry, Roland, & Race, 1962). Any task dependent on the integrity of cortical units would be affected. Parenthetically, for problems in which visual sensitivity is not a prerequisite of learning and in which the cortex plays little or no part (e.g., water escape), the C3H mouse performs as well as or better than other strains (Winston, 1964).

A second example, also involving the visual system likewise shows how unintelligible findings may quickly reduce to obvious explanations when the underlying mechanism is known. Albino rats of various strains are deficient in transferring visual input from one hemisphere to another. That is, learning a task with one eye occluded will not be readily displayed when the opposite eye is exposed to the same task (Sheridan, 1965). Pigmented rats, on the other hand, show significant interocular transfer. The reason for the genetic variation remained obscure until it was pointed out by Lund (1965) that albino rats have only a few optic fibers that cross between hemispheres. Thus the loss of information because of a deficiency of crossover routes precludes much interocular transfer among albino strains.

Certainly the genetic difference now has a sufficient explanation at the structural level and will generalize to situations wherever the optic differences appear.

Another behavioral problem that has been partially solved by attending to structure-function relations is the abrupt decline in audiogenic seizure susceptibility found with DBA/2 mice as they reach maturity. DBA/2 mice begin to respond to high frequency sounds with severe tonic–clonic seizures at about the time they are able to locomote, around 14 days of age. As they become older the frequency of seizures decreases until it disappears altogether around 30–40 days of age.

The explanation for the seizure susceptibility may depend upon specific ratios of biochemicals (Schlesinger & Griek, 1970), although the exact mechanisms are unknown. The decline in susceptibility to noise, however, may have a much simpler explanation. Ralls (1967) has recently demonstrated that some inbred strains of mice, including the seizure-prone DBA/2 strain, lose their hearing at the same time that they lose their tendency to convulse. Clearly, mice cannot seize when they cannot hear the exciting stimulus. The explanation is probably that clear cut.

Obviously not all explanations will be as simple as those described above, and even these are doubtlessly incomplete. Many effects should be easily described, however, and we might as well account for as many as possible before proceeding to more difficult problems. A solid beginning would be to account for as much variation as possible by looking first at receptor mechanisms. One of the first steps in adjusting to environmental demands is the adequate processing of sensory information. Thus many genotypic differences among individuals and species are probably mediated by structure-function relations in sensory systems long under natural selection.

The identification of genetic differences in behavior is only a beginning to the further demonstration of mediating mechanisms. Genes, whether in single or multiple doses, provide variations in structures that lead to clues for explaining variations in function. Behavior genetics is particularly well suited to specify the details of structure-function relations because it can manipulate the structure through direct breeding experiments in its search for correlated functions. The results can then be compared with those obtained with other methodologies, such as brain stimulation and recording, brain lesions and hormonal manipulations.

B. Behavior Genetics without Segregation

The analysis of genetic factors underlying behavior does not necessarily depend upon special breeding techniques when the goal is to understand structure-function relations. Organisms within a single generation can sometimes provide information ranging from the description of the relevant genes to the actual behavioral response. Genetic crosses used to establish recombination of genes may be in special cases superfluous to the understanding of mechanisms of behavior.

In this section three newer approaches are described. None will be recognized as classical methods in behavior genetics. The first rests on the assumption that gene action, and thus behavior, is regulated in systematic ways by biochemical changes either initiated by the genes themselves or through environmental stimulation. The second method emphasizes the environmental control over DNA-controlled RNA and protein synthesis which underlie behavioral processes. The third suggests how amino acid substitutions in hormones or other proteins can provide information about the gene structure and mechanisms of behavior control. In combination, the three methods depend upon the assumption that genes are dynamic contributors to behavioral organization and are sensitive to feedback systems from the internal and external environment.

Gene Regulation. Recent developments in microbiology and developmental genetics are offering behavior genetics its greatest challenge. These basic disciplines are shifting emphases from the transmission qualities of the gene to its biochemical action and environmental sensitivity. The relevant findings are that (*a*) deoxyribonucleic acid (DNA) specifies the kind of ribonucleic acid (RNA) produced in the nucleus which in the cytoplasm determines amino acid sequences in structural proteins and enzymes (Watson, 1965), and (*b*) the observation that only about 10% of the available genes are active at any one time, the active number depending upon the tissue and environment considered (Beerman, 1965). Cytoplasmic constituents appear to regulate the dynamic discharge of genetic messages. The implications for behavior genetics are that genes engage themselves with behavior through long chains of active biochemical interactions, and that environmental factors acting through metabolic intermediates specify the kinds of genes which function as well as their consequences.

Jacob and Monod (1961) early in this decade discovered that some genes direct protein formation (*structural genes* that we ordinarily consider as typical genes), while others act as switches to turn these genes off and on (*operator genes*), and still other genes act to repress or derepress the switch genes (*regulator genes*). Regulator genes are controlled by cytoplasmic material and are thus open to environmental influences. Almost all we know about this interaction was determined from the bacterium *Escherichia coli*. One of the first observations was that the synthesis of galactosidase by a structural gene was under the control of a single regulator gene which was responsive to the amount of galactose in the cytoplasm. Since then other evidence has accumulated to warrant the conclusion that there is a precise interaction between the operator-structural unit (the operon) and the regulator gene with its cytoplasmic involvement (Meissner, 1965). Behavior may be under the control of similar dynamic interaction.

The regulatory mechanism perhaps best known in biological processes is the molting patterns of *Diptera* and midge (*Chironomus*). The metamorphosis of these insects is from the larva to the pupa and the molting of the pupa to the imago, or adult. The life history of the organism changes abruptly in metamorphosis from a worm-like animal to a fully developed fly. The sequence is dependent on the producton of the molting hormone, ecdysone, and its effect on certain loci of Chromosomes I and IV. The differentiation of morphology and behavior is directly related to the pattern of gene action on these two chromosomes released by ecdysone. The neuro-endocrine pathways are known in some detail, and the effects of ecdysone on the genome have been described in broad outline (Beerman, 1965; Scharrer & Scharrer, 1963).

Hormones, like ecdysone in insects, which act to initiate or modulate responses, may act by "turning" genes on and off at the regulator gene level. Those hormones in mammals which appear to stimulate messenger RNA production are estrogen, testosterone, growth hormone, adrenocorticotropic hormone, thyroxin, and insulin (Davidson, 1965; Hamilton, 1968; Tata, 1966). While these same hormones may act in a variety of ways, there is evidence in every case that they also stimulate RNA and protein synthesis probably by inducing certain segments of DNA (genes) to act. Behavior, which is hormonally controlled could, of course, be influenced in this way.

Not many clear examples of gene induction and behavior are evident, although some indirect evidence does exist. In our laboratory we have found that testosterone, the male sex hormone, when injected directly into the brain can stimulate territorial marking behavior in the Mongolian gerbil (*Meriones unguiculatus*). Marking is normally done by the male rubbing a belly scent gland over objects, and is dependent on the integrity of the testes (Lindzey, Thiessen, & Tucker, 1968; Thiessen, Friend, & Lindzey, 1968). When genes are prevented from templating RNA by adding actinomysin-D to the hormone in the brain, an antibiotic which binds DNA and prevents its action, the hormone is no longer effective in producing the behavior. Our tentative explanation is that testosterone normally acts in the brain by turning on specific genes, probably by acting on regulator genes. The RNA which is formed is involved in the ultimate formation of proteins (enzymes?) which allow the motor response of territorial marking to occur. Later experimentation may show that most hormone-behavior relations are based on this gene-regulator model, and the concept may extend to many chemical-response processes.

RNA and Protein Synthesis. Environmental stimuli can alter the kinds and amounts of RNA and protein formed in the brain (Gaito, 1966). In most cases an increase in stimulation will enhance these biochemical processes and a decrease in stimulation will reduce their activities (however, see Altman, 1966). Neurons demonstrate an increase in RNA content of as much as 30% within one hour, and the supporting glia cells even more (Hydén, 1967). As both RNA and protein are dependent on DNA activity, it would appear that environmental stimuli mediated through neural processes excite DNA.

Alterations in proteins and RNA may be quite specific to the behavioral process under consideration and its associated neural elements. Flexner (1966), for example, has shown that the antibiotic, puromycin, which depresses protein synthesis to a significant degree will disrupt short- and long-term avoidance learning in mice when the antibiotic is injected into fairly specific brain sites. "Recent" memory was lost when puromycin was introduced into the hippocampi and caudal cortices, including the temporal cortices with their associated entorhinal areas. The loss of past memory, on the other hand, required the additional involvement of substantially greater parts of the neocortex. To be effective, inhibition of protein synthesis had to be of the order of 80% for approximately 8–11 hours. The studies of Flexner suggest that learning ability involves the formation of proteins by sequential DNA and RNA activities in specific brain areas.

Hydén (1967) has shown how specific the environmental influence can be. In one experiment "right-handed" rats were induced to use the left forelimb in retrieving food in a narrow tube. The stimulation resulting from the change in hand preference resulted in significant increases in RNA in areas of the motor cortex associated with the change in preference. Even the bases used to form RNA, adenine (A), guanine (G), cytosine (C), and uracil (U), showed unique changes. The $(G + C)/(A + U)$ ratio decreased significantly from 1.72 to 1.51. Moreover, the nuclear RNA formed had a DNA-like base ratio composition. Hence, it would seem that the genes activated are those associated with neural centers appropriate to the behavior involved. The hormone experiment with the gerbil reported above can be interpreted in the same way.

The RNA associated with training procedures has been demonstrated to be unique in other ways. Fjerdingstad and his colleagues (1965) have extracted RNA from the brains of trained rats and injected the extract intracisternally in naive rats. Learning was facilitated in these naive rats compared with rats which received RNA from untrained rats. Gaito and his group (Machlus & Gaito, 1968) have shown in elegant RNA hybridization experiments with trained and untrained rats that the RNA from trained rats is distinctly different from that of untrained rats. A critical review of these and similar studies can be found in a book by John (1967). The tentative conclusion is that unique sites of DNA nucleotides are stimulated by specific cues in the environment. One cannot fail to be impressed at the extent to which genes appear to respond to their environment, and to what degree behavior is related to the dynamic aspects of DNA activity.

Amino Acid Substitutions. Variations in amino acid structure can reflect specific changes in DNA and RNA molecules. When such variations also affect behavior they suggest specific genetic factors at work, and in part account for the behavior in simple biochemical terms.

Little has been done in behavioral investigations with biochemical strata that differs in amino acid numbers or sequences. One series of systematic studies deserves recognition, however. The early work was with adrenocorticotropic hormone (ACTH), a straight-chain polypeptide of 39 amino acid residues. ACTH eminates from the anterior pituitary and is instrumental in the stimulation of the adrenal cortex. There are species variations in the molecules that are confined to the amino acids that occupy positions 25 through 33, although these amino acids do not appear necessary for its biological activity (Turner, 1966). The ACTH-adrenal cortex response is essential during stress and forms a significant component of many behavioral processes.

The early work done with rats (Murphy & Miller, 1956) indicated that ACTH did not alter speed of acquisition of a shock-avoidance conditioning response. It did, however, retard extinction of the response when shock was no longer given to the animals. In a subsequent study (Miller & Ogawa, 1962), the extinction effect was again demonstrated. Inhibition of extinction was evident without the mediation of the adrenals, as their removal had no effect on the extinction. More recently it has been pointed out that the ACTH action on learning is independent of the presence of the thyroid; apart from its behavioral effect ACTH can stimulate the thyroid (de Wied & Pirie, 1968).

As is true with the biological potency of ACTH, not all of the 39 amino acids in ACTH are necessary for its behavioral effect on extinction. de Wied (1966) found that only the first 10 are necessary. In sequence these are: serine, tyrosine, serine, methionine, glutamic acid, histidine, phenylalanine, arginine, tyrosine, and glycine. Even more interesting is the additional finding by Bohus and de Wied (1966) that the substitution of the dextro-rotatory form of phenylalanine (D-Phe) in the 7th position of the ACTH 1-10 molecule reversed the extinction response, so that with the D-form extinction was facilitated over that of control animals receiving only placebo injections. Differences did not appear for other behaviors such as general activity, defecation, or grooming. The significance of a far-reaching change on behavior arising from the substitution of one form of amino acid for another is that this is the type of change that could result from a specific nucleotide change at the DNA level (possibly by mutogenic factors) and become responsible for the evolution of an entirely new system of behavior.

In the above report and others (Bohus & de Wied, 1966, 1967; de Wied, 1966) it was observed that the melanocyte-stimulating hormone which is identical to ACTH in the first 13 amino acids also retards the extinction process in rats. Apparently these particular amino acids are specific to the behavioral effect regardless of their separate hormone implications. There is some possibility that the action of ACTH is directly on the brain, as lesions in the parafascicular nuclei of the thalamus prevent the delay in extinction. The exact mechanism is unknown, but is likely to involve processes related to fear. Recently it was demonstrated that hypophesectomized rats lacking ACTH show less fear than normals in a passive avoidance situation, but the adrenalectomized animals lacking adrenal steroids show greater fear (Weiss, McEwen, Teresa, Silva, & Kalkut, 1969). Perhaps ACTH arouses an animal to respond to fear-provoking stimuli and adrenal steriods act to counteract the response.

Other studies of this kind should begin to point out the particular significance of amino acid sequences on different behaviors and eventually lead us to a greater understanding of the relations between DNA, RNA, polypeptides, and behavior. The neurohormones like oxytocin and vasopressin, should certainly be studied with a view toward deciphering amino acid codes and behavior. These hormones from the posterior pituitary are responsible for contraction of smooth muscles, milk ejection from mammary glands, effects on blood pressure and water metabolism, and release of other pituitary hormones. Only eight amino acids are involved in the following forms of neurohormones: oxytocin, arginine, lysine, vasotocin, isotocin, and 8-isoleucine oxytocin. These forms differ one from the other by only one to three amino acid substitutions in such a manner that many combinations and differences in amino acid chains could be observed for behavioral influences. Other proteins and polypeptide chains, such as thyroxin derivations and blood proteins, could be adapted for testing in the same way. Eventually an "amino acid map" may be established for a variety of behaviors, and our approach to structure-function explanations will be extended from the gene to the behavior.

IV. ADAPTIVE QUALITIES OF BEHAVIOR

Viewing mechanism-specific behaviors is one important approach to the understanding of principles that transcend genotypic barriers. A consistent relation is often found between structures and functions that appear vital to life. Several such systems have been mentioned, including peripheral receptors and their associated activities, mechanisms adapted to hunger, structures related to posture and locomotion, processes extending to endocrine and neural adaptation, and many bodily structures related to the processing of sensory information. Those systems less vital to immediate existence appear to take on local, species, and individual characteristics on both the mechanistic and behavioral levels. This is another way of saying that for absolutely vital functions, selection pressures have been so intense and uncompromising that only limited ways of handling the problems have arisen. Functions of lesser concern in the short run (although of sometimes equal significance for the individual in the long run) have more potential for local variation in style and outcome.

The distinction of "vital" vs. "subvital" adaptations is in part one of recognizing existing variation and determining heritability and environmental requirements. There will be few clear-cut distinctions, but for purposes of discussion the differences will be magnified. Something as vitally important as breathing in mammals can be only accomplished in limited ways and selection will rigidly lock in the relation between lungs, control mechanisms based on blood content of carbon dioxide and oxygen, and the act of breathing. Genetic survival in this case depends on the relative *lack* of phenotypic variability (and low heritability), as only certain concatenations of variables will insure success. Variants lacking the coadapted system will fail. When selection is less intense or more variable due to changeable environments, individuals within populations will differ widely and take on local characters. Phenotypic variability and heritability will be relatively high in this case.

Falconer (1960) arrived at the same conclusion that characters differ inversely in heritability according to their contribution to fitness, using a strict genetic argument. The implications of the above reasoning are several: (*a*) genetic and phenotypic variance of vital functions is minimal and subject to little change under natural and artificial selection: (*b*) vital functions can be explained with mechanism-specific principles that are common to a great many genotypes, while less vital functions lack this explanatory advantage; (*c*) variability at all levels of analysis is greater for less vital characters, and, in contrast to more vital systems, less critical characters are locally adapted to their environment; and (*d*) less vital activities can be described in terms of their utility under unique selection demands, and, in contrast to vital systems, correlate well with their immediate environment.

This section emphasizes the importance of natural selection in the regulation of behavior. Species and populations adapt, first of all, to invariant qualities of their environment. Second, they adjust to specific and sometimes shifting needs. In the case of specialized adjustments, generalizations do not always rest on the invariance of structure-function relations, but rather on the adaptiveness of the response, *regardless of genotype or mechanism*. Classic Mendelian analyses are hardly relevant to the clarification of control mechanisms, as a near infinite sample of genes and gene products can manage the same solution. Evolution is very opportunistic in the sense that it will take advantage of any genetic variance which will satisfy the same environmental requirement. An appropriate analogy is the construction of a building. If all that is required is a shelter, it can be built from wood, brick, or steel. The material used may be chosen because of price, convenience, or availability. The same is true in genetic selection: the only constant in the construction of a trait may be its utility.

Thus, in addition to our concern for mechanism-specific behaviors that appear in the necessary aspects of life, we must extend our investigations in the direction of portraying the interplay of variable environments with the adaptiveness of the response pattern.

Unless otherwise indicated, the discussion of these two emphases that follows is based on references by Cott (1940), Lofts and Murton (1968), Mayr (1965), Rensch (1959), and Wynne-Edwards (1962).

A. Convergent Evolution: Vital Systems and Physiology

It sometimes appears that evolution is a creative principle causing development of certain characteristics in inevitable directions. The vitalists at one time called this process "aristogenesis" (or "hologenesis," or "nomogenesis"). At times this "evolutionary predetermination" almost appears true. Man, for example, has shown a progressive increase in brain size and brain weight relative to body size and spinal cord over millions of years (Thiessen, 1970, in press). The horse, cat, dog, and bear have gotten progressively larger. And many characteristics take on the same structure and form regardless of taxonomy. The vesicular eye with retina, pigment layer, lens, cornea developed in groups of Coelenterata (Charybdaea), Annelida (Vanadis), Echinodermata (Asterias), Onychophora (Peripatus), Gastropoda, Cephalopoda, and Vertebrate. The compound eye of insects developed independently in Anthropoda, Annelida, and Mollusca. Similarly, the structure and shape of jumping grasshoppers, fleas, kangaroos, jumping rodents, and marsupials correspond closely. It is as if evolution has goals and through successive approximations approaches the best solutions.

Aristogenesis, or various forms of the same concept, is a naive view of the mechanisms of evolution. Evolvement of characters is dependent upon the circumstances of the gene pool and environment, and not on guiding forces with predetermined ends. Evolution in its simplest outline is the substitution of one allele for another (Williams, 1966). But it is far more than that, as nearly all allelic possibilities are dependent upon the genetic diversity in the population and the stipulations applied by the environment. Over extended periods of time the gene pool is shaped and reshaped to conform to the demands placed upon it until an aggregate of adaptive structures and functions finally arise. The basic truth is that those organisms whose gene endowment and response patterns happen to fit the environmental demands survive to pass their genes onto the next generations. Organisms lacking the adequate gene-response relations suffer genetic death.

Prepotent selection factors, like climate, food supplies, shelter requirements, predation, and photoperiodicities can act so strongly on a great many gene pools that analogous response systems will evolve. They need not be based on identical genes or biochemicals, but in some cases this may be true. For example, as the climate becomes cooler from the equator to higher latitudes the following general changes occur in morphology, biochemistry, and behavior of mammals and avian species.

1. Body size increases (Bergmann's rule).
2. The tail, ears, bills, and limbs become relatively short (Allen's rule).
3. The relative length of hair increases.
4. Wings become more pointed.
5. The relative size of the heart, pancreas, liver, kidney, stomach, and intestines increase.
6. There is a reduction in the biochemicals phaeomelanins and eumelanins related to pigment formation (Gloger's rule).
7. Migratory instincts become stronger.
8. Larger and warmer nests are constructed (King's rule).
9. Oxygen consumption increases, overall metabolic needs decrease, and general activity diminishes.

Most of these changes are directly related to the need to conserve body heat, compete more successfully for limited or seasonal food supplies, and find protective habitats for parents and their offspring. The fact that so many species exhibit these changes implies a similar need to cope with seasonal variations and not a vital force acting to create the perfect specimen.

The general increase in body size with increasing latitude has considerable bearing on behavioral adjustments. Larger mammals have larger and often flatter lenses and have poor visual accommodation as the lens occupies most of the interior cavity and little space is given over for movements of accommodation. The absolute number of visual cells is greater in larger vertebrates and larger insects: the blowfly *Calliphora vomitoria* has 4585 ommatidia, the small *Drosophila melanogaster* only 688; the large beetle

Carabus coriaceus possesses 4250 ommatidia, while the medium-sized *C. violaceus* has 3200, and the smaller beetle *Bembidium rupestre* has only 400. The specific variations in resolving power for these forms is not known but visual acuity apparently decreases along with the decrease in visual receptors.

Larger animals are also more vigorous and resistant to adverse environments. As weapons for attack and defense grow with marked positive allometry (a rate faster than general growth), a distinct advantage is given to more aggressive and faster-growing animals. Many of these features show coordinated development. Evolution in large running vertebrates includes the lengthening of legs, a reduction in the number of toes, reinforcement of hip and shoulder girdles, strengthened heart and lungs for performance, larger eyes, and the strengthening of flight instincts. In other forms increasing in size, where running is less important, the legs display negative allometry and this leads to their loss and a change in locomotion to serpentine movements. Lizards from *Ophimorus tridactylus* to *Chalcides ocellatus*, and *Eumeces algeriensis* show this progressive change. As the relative length of the legs decreases there is a corresponding increase in the number of presacral vertebrae and a move toward serpentine locomotion. Diversities of morphology and behavior follow critical and pervasive modifications in environments; they show the general principles of organization and integration so vital for the understanding of universal facets of behavior.

Reproductive competence is certainly one of the most important activities of any organism. Here, especially, pervasive environmental demands will preserve salient adaptations and eliminate egregious features. Climate again serves as a classic force of natural selection so intense that fundamental relations have evolved in many genetic groups. Avian species provide clear-cut examples of relations between variation in climate, physiology, and reproductive processes (Lofts & Murton, 1968), although other species could serve as well (Marler & Hamilton, 1966).

Many avian species depend on increases in day length for full expression of breeding capability and performance. Usually this means that breeding in temperate climates is correlated with the onset of spring, so that egg laying is timed to produce young when their care and feeding is easiest during the spring and summer months. At least 60 North-Temperate male species in widely separate avian orders have proved to be dependent on photostimulation for gonad recrudescence and mating, while only one, the Feral pigeon *C. livia* appears to proceed through normal reproduction independently of seasonal light changes.

Many modifiers affect the gonad cycle, but the primary stimulus is an increase in the amount of daylight. In British tits, for example, the spring-time response is modified by environmental temperatures so that egg laying and the production of young correspond to the abundance of defoliating caterpillars used as food. The caterpillars in turn increase in numbers because of the same temperature changes which influence the tits. Hawks may respond directly to their food supply and so may be more independent on day-length changes. The short-eared owl *Asio flammeus*, snowy owl *Nyctea scandiaca*, rough-legged buzzard *Buteo lagopus,* and Pomarine skua *Stercovarius pomarinus* which all prey on voles and lemmings in the Arctic fail to breed in poor rodent seasons.

Females display a gonadotropic response to photostimulation, but unlike the testes in males, the ovaries require appropriate psychic stimuli, such as the appearance of a breeding male or nest material, for the final phase of reproductive development (Lehrman, 1961). No single factor will therefore account for the entire regulation of a breeding cycle. However, it is generally the most obvious factors of the ecology that either directly control the cycle or act as significant modifiers.

Tropical and equatorial animals are not faced with annual fluctuations in photostimulation and hence other proximal factors such as rain regulate breeding. In fact, seasonal differences in gonad size in birds are correlated with the latitude, northern species showing a much greater difference between maximum and minimum gonad size. The gonad size of northward migratory birds is greater than in the same or closely related species of tropical resident forms, gonads being bigger in animals receiving the most photostimulation.

Animals that are spaced across an environment that varies in some systematic way will show correlated responses, especially if the environment is crucially involved in the support of life. Often this will hasten the evolvement of functions that are mechanism specific. Radiating out from the equator will be animals with characters that depend more and more on changes in climate, photostimulation, oxygen, and periodic shifts in food supplies, temperature, and humidity. Where the environment is more generally constant, or at least without major clines in life support elements, animals will adapt to more proximal conditions of a less uniform sort. Tropical animals and marine forms exposed to relatively constant environments are more specialized in this sense.

The lesson for the behaviorist concerned with relating genes to physiology and behavior is obvious: experimental payoff depends upon first knowing the most critical environmental factors the organism must cope with, and second on determining the means by which adaptation is accomplished. When the environment varies by degrees in essential ways the mechanisms specific to the adaptation may become obvious. Evolution is basically conservative and will use the same principle whenever possible, rather than devise new methods for every possible contingency. Thus, if reproduction in the tropics depends on gonadal hormones, these same hormones are likely to be used with species that migrate out to new environments. The details will change, and in ways that increase the likelihood of survival. It is essential that many species breed and reproduce in the spring; therefore, seasonal changes in photostimulation will modify the gonadal response so that it is active at the most opportune time. The basic relation between sex hormones and behavior remains invariant and is keyed to systematic changes in photostimulation.

B. Convergent Evolution: Functional Behavior Genetics

Thus far we have been concerned with selective forces of such magnitude that common structures and functions appear across wide phylogenetic groups. The analytic advantages are obvious; these are problem areas in which behavior geneticists can make substantial contributions in working out the most general relations between natural selection, physiological mediators, and adaptive behavior.

It would surely be convenient if evolutionary problems could be solved by single courses of action through natural selection, and that a limited number of solutions would appear as identical in all individuals and in fact all species sharing the same needs. In reality, however, many adaptations are equally suited for the same goal and mechanism-specific rules will not hold for all adaptations. Adjustments made by *Drosophila* to humidity requirements and the adaptation by mice to temperature variations are two examples that have been discussed elsewhere (Thiessen, 1970, in press). Populations of *Drosophila* adjust to the hazard of desiccation by evolving morphological barriers to water loss, or response proclivities to moisture, or negative phototaxes. Mice cope with temperature variation in several ways, including metabolic adjustments, direct manipulation of their thermal environment (e.g., nest building), and migration into a more favorable area. Convergence of evolution is as apparent for behavioral adjustment to photic and thermal stimuli as it is for the streamlining of the morphology of the porpoise and whale.

Selection pressures are rarely identical; neither are gene pools nor environmental opportunities. It is expected, therefore, that diversity of adaptation is the rule rather than the exception. Nevertheless, to the degree that selection is successful, each adaptation will bear a clear relation between environmental demands and behavioral capacities, and in some cases of vital functions clear mechanism-specific relations will appear. The investigator must remain alert to these possibilities and pose his experimental questions accordingly.

Function and not mechanism, however, is the key to the understanding of a great deal of convergent evolution, which implies that our attention must be directed toward the outcome of evolution rather than simply toward the genetic structure underlying a particular phenotype. Behaviors may differ widely and rest on different genetic bases but still share identical functions. For instance, it is essential for most avian species to incubate their eggs or have other species perform the task for them. But it can be accomplished in a variety of ways (Lehrman, 1961; Rensch, 1959). Incubation may be strictly a female task as it is in the wren (*Troglodytes*), bullfinch (*Pyrrhula*), chaffinch (*Fringilla*), crow (*Corvus*), and snipe (*Scolopax*). Or, incubation may be strictly a male job as in the *Tinamidae*, *Casurarius*, and *D. romaeus*; or it may be shared by both sexes as in *Sylvia*, *Picus*, *Columba*, and *Struthio*. Finally, in other cases no incubation occurs at all as in some cuckoos (*Cuculus*, *Clamator*, *Eudunamys*), some starlings (*Molothrus*, *Cassidix*), and weavers (*Vidua*, *Tetranura*).

In other situations major meterological features such as photostimulation determine breeding in North-Temperate birds. In tropical and equatorial animals daily fluctuations in photoperiods are relatively slight or absent, and hence have no obvious advantages as timing devices. In many cases, therefore, seasonal rains and associated changes in the vegetation often act as the proximate environmental synchronizers. Still, the same purpose is served in preserving a breeding synchrony compatible with survival. Many xerophilous species occupying desert or semiarid areas have adapted their reproductive cycle to take advantage of sporadic rainfall that may occur at anytime. When rainfall is plentiful such birds may breed two or three times in quick succession, but in seasons of drought breeding may be suppressed altogether. In the desert areas of Arizona the towhee *Pipilo aberti* will nest within 10–14 days after heavy rains in March and April and continue breeding in a scattered fashion as long as the rains continue.

Convergent evolution of cryptic coloration, form, or behavior due to a similar selection pressure have occurred in innumerable species. The need for green camouflage in areas of dense foliage has occurred in tropical snakes, families of lizards, frogs, and birds, and also in Coleoptera, Lepidoptera, Hemiptera, and Orthoptera. The green coloration may be caused by the ingestion of certain foods or synthesized in different biochemical ways. The only common denominator is the need for camouflage and it occurs regardless of taxonomic affinity, biochemical processing, or anatomy.

Local effects are multiple and serve specific functions of the populations. Ordinarily the color, form, and behavior are well coordinated and match the need in question. Pale-colored mice are found on sandhills and dark forms on black lava beds. If given preferences of typical environments, the distribution of responses for these mice will be compatible with their general habitation (see above). The advantage of color matching and appropriate preference was shown by Dice (1947) who offered predatory owls *Peromyscus* mice that differed in their degree of matching to backgrounds, and found that owls actually captured the less camouflaged mice first. Similarly, Sumner (1934, 1935) in elegant experiments exposed black and white "mosquito fish" *Gambusia patraelis* in black or white tanks to their predators, the Galapagos Penquin, the Night Heron, or Sunfish. In three experiments the results were the same, namely, that predation was greater for fish that were mismatched with their environment. Out of 2672 individuals offered as prey, 66 % of those killed were conspicuous against their environmental background.

The examples could be multiplied. Bark-like moths (Sphingidae, Nocturidae, Notodontidae, Tortricidae, Pyralidae, Geometridae) conform well to their respective environments and are rarely seen apart from the environments they resemble. The ability to approach birds and other animals is closely associated with the degree of concealment and coloring; "closesitters" include Partridges, Ptarmigan, Short-eared Owls, and many dark species— all highly inconspicuous in their nests. More conspicuous species, and those characterized by flight, include Lapwing, Oyster-catcher, Coot, Moorhen, and different gulls and terns. The same principle applies to lizards, snakes, turtles, toads, frogs, spiders, crabs, and other arthropods.

Even in species that assume immobility when approached by possible predators, the stance differs depending upon the environment. In the field the normal habit is crouching, but in "reedy", more vertical environments, freezing may mean assuming an erect posture ("Poor-me-one," *Nyctibicus griseus*, and the Variegated Heron are examples). Snakes like *Pxybelis* in Central and South America, *Thelotornis* in tropical Africa, and *Dryophis* in Southeast Asia appear and even move like slender green vines in the wind with which they are associated.

Aposematic animals (poisonous or dangerous species) appear and act quite differently from the cryptic forms that are under constant threat of predation. They display conspicuous and often frightening effects, and are generally diurnal in behavior, and often sluggish and without fear. In Anura most frogs and toads are more or less cryptic and mainly nocturnal or crepuscular. The more conspicuous species and those that are aposematic (*Atelopus stelzneri, Phrynomantis bifasciata, Dendrobates tinclorius, Hyperolius marmoratus*) are diurnal. Again the principle applies to lizards, caterpillars, butterflies, grasshoppers, and other species.

Communicative signals in a variety of species differ widely depending upon the environmental requirements (Sebeok, 1968). Nocturnal and short-ranging species are likely to evolve auditory and chemical signaling devices while diurnal and wide-ranging species may depend upon visual as well as auditory signaling and deemphasize chemical channels of information processing. Short-ranging species will resemble aspects of their environment more because of their close and constant association; whereas wideranging species are more variable in their resemblances to any particular local features.

Similarly, the ability to process information will differ according to species and habitat demand, and will not faithfully reflect phylogenetic changes in neural complexity. Evolution of intelligence is not necessarily continuous. Rather, there are discontinuities of development that reflect unique species requirements. Brain weight and intelligence show some progressive increase as we ascend the phylogenetic scale, but methods of handling information may be in large measure species-specific. Bitterman (1965) is one of the few investigators who has challenged the dogma of neural continuity on an experimental basis. Species comparisons among fish, rats, turtles, pigeons, and monkeys on visual, spatial, probability learning, and reversal learning reveal many qualitative differences that cannot be explained simply on the basis of differences in brain size or number of neurological elements. On spatial problems involving either reversal or probability learning, the monkey, rat, pigeon, and turtle perform similarly, that is show the same functional relation between stimulus and response. Fish, on the other hand, do not learn in the same way. On visual problems the situation is even more complex. Where the subject is required to reverse its habits, the monkey, rat, and pigeon perform alike, but the turtle and the fish respond differently. Where an animal has to anticipate the probability of reward the monkey and rat are alike and the pigeon, turtle, and fish are similar. The conclusion relevant to evolution is that as we ascend the phylogenetic scale intellectual discontinuity is the rule. Moreover, the adjustment evolved by higher forms appears earlier in spatial than in visual contexts. Interestingly, the removal of significant amounts of cortex in the rat changes its performance on visual and spatial tasks in the directions of the turtle, and not simply in the direction of a dull rat. These cleverly conceived studies suggest that brain structures evolved by higher species do not merely add increments to old functions and modes of intellectual adjustment, but mediate entirely new ones.

V. Conclusion

Like many biological sciences, behavior genetics is altering its character and extending its range of inquiry. The days of merely pointing to genetic influence are over. The demonstrations have been sufficiently frequent and strong to convince everyone but the greatest skeptic. Neither is it necessary to preach the gospel of gene–environmental interaction. Again this has been done sufficiently often for nearly every possible behavior. Similarly, the partitioning of phenotypic variance into genetic and nongenetic components, specifying the degree of heritability and estimating gene number, have sharp limitations for deriving explanatory principles beyond the very restricted circumstances of the measurement itself. Pointing to individual differences, specifying the common-place gene and environmental interaction and quantifying interactions have several illustrative purposes, but have also brought behavior genetics to a *cul de sac*.

One can, of course, detail the genetic and environmental influence and their combined effect on every imaginable behavior with all possible species. Indeed there would be value in cataloging all possible genetic and environmental components in as precise a form as possible. Clearly this would be of advantage in dealing with specific problems (e.g., mental diseases) and add to our ability to control behavior through breeding or by contriving appropriate environments. Such a listing of factors would add specificity to known events and confirm predictions. It would not, it seems to this writer, add new concepts or generalizations beyond the specific problem of interest.

It may be fair to say that classical behavior genetics, that type of behavior genetics which has duplicated Mendelian work with behavioral phenotypes, has destroyed itself because of its own success. Behavior conforms to Mendelian principles as does any other phenotype. The discipline can now benefit from its close association with biology. It must not be lost sight of, however, that the primary aim of behavior genetics is to explain behavior; this distinction gives it the uniqueness of a separate field.

This chapter has set behavior genetics in the larger context of biology by assuming that the task at hand is the understanding of behavior from the DNA molecule through the complexities of ontogeny to the full expression in a functioning organism. The union of behavior genetics with biology seems most appropriate since each adds vigor to the other and allows work to proceed at various levels without artificial lines of demarcation between disciplines. The study of hormones and behavior can only add to the understanding of genetic processes; the investigation of selective forces on behavior can advance the notions of mechanism-specific behaviors and functional adaptations; and the study of brain action will forward our understanding of ontogeny, information processing, and the relations between gene action and environmental modification.

To arrive at generalities investigators must (*a*) focus on species and populations that appear to be representative of wide taxonomic groups, (*b*) emphasize structure-function relations that transcend gene differences, and (*c*) seek the adaptive characteristics of behavior and relate these to major and minor features of the environment. Not all behaviors will yield to these treatments. Unique variation and species-specific behaviors are facts of nature and must be analyzed. Yet, before idiosyncratic factors can take on importance, more general features of structure and function must be analyzed.

REFERENCES

Altman, J. Autoradiographic examination of behaviorally induced changes in the protein and nucleic acid metabolism of the brain. In J. Gaito (Ed.), *Macromolecules and behavior*. New York: Appleton, 1966. Pp. 103–128.

Altman, P., & Dittmer, D. S. *Biology data book*. Washington: Federation of American Societies for Experimental Biology, 1964.

Beach, F. A. The snark was a boojum. *American Psychologist*, 1950, **5**, 115–124.

Beerman, W. Cytological aspects of information transfer in cellular differentiation. In E. Bell (Ed.), *Molecular and cellular aspects of development*. New York: Harper, 1965. Pp. 204–212.

Bitterman, M. E. Phyletic differences in learning. *American Psychologist*, 1965, **20**, 396–410.

Blair, W. F. Population dynamics of rodents and other small mammals. *Advances in Genetics*, 1953, **5**, 1–41.

Bohus, B., & de Wied, D. Inhibitory and facilitatory effect of two related peptides on extinction of avoidance behavior. *Science*, 1966, **153**, 318–320.

Bohus, B., & de Wied, D. Failure of α-MSH to delay extinction of conditioned avoidance behavior in rats with lesions in the parafascicular nuclei of the thalamus. *Physiology & Behavior*, 1967, **2**, 221–223.

Bovet, D., Bovet-Nitti, F., & Oliverio, A. Genetic aspects of learning and memory in mice. *Science*, 1969, **163**, 139–149.

Bovet-Nitti, F., Oliverio, A., & Bovet, D. Effects of cross-fostering on avoidance learning and freezing behavior of DBA_2J and C3H/He inbred mice. *Life Sciences*, 1968, **7**, 791–797.

Broadhurst, P. L. Experiments in psychogenetics: Applications of biometrical genetics to the inheritance of behavior. In H. J. Eysenck (Ed.), *Experiments in personality*. London: Routledge and Kegan Paul, 1960. Pp. 3–102.

Bruell, J. H. Behavioral population genetics and wild Mus musculus. In G. Lindzey and D. D. Thiessen (Eds.), *Contributions to behavior-genetic analysis: The mouse as a prototype*. New York: Appleton, 1970. Pp. 261–291.

Carlson, E. A. *The gene: A critical history*. Philadelphia: Saunders, 1966.

Catalogue of Uniform Strains of Laboratory Animals Maintained in Great Britain. Charshalton, Surrey, England: Laboratory Animal Centre, M.R.C. Laboratories, 1958.

Cott, H. B. *Adaptive coloration in animals*. London: Methuen, 1940.

Davidson, E. H. Hormones and genes. *Scientific American*, 1965, **212**, 36–45.

de Wied, D. Inhibitory effect of ACTH and related peptides on extinction of conditioned avoidance behavior in rats. *Proceedings of the Society for Experimental Biology and Medicine*, 1966, **122**, 28–32.

de Wied, D., & Pirie, G. The inhibitory effect of ACTH 1-10 on extinction of a conditioned avoidance response: Its independence of thyroid function. *Physiology & Behavior*, 1968, **3**, 355–358.

Dice, L. R. Effectiveness of selection by owls of deer-mice (Peromyscus maniculatus) which contrast in color with their background. *Contributions from the Laboratory of Veterinary Biology*, 1947, **34**, 1–20.

Dobzhansky, T., & Spassky, B. Selection for geotaxis in monomorphic and polymorphic populations of Drosophila pseudoobscura. *Proceedings of the National Academy of Sciences of the United States of America*, 1962, **48**, 1704–1712.

Dunn, L. C. *A short history of genetics*. New York: McGraw-Hill, 1965.

Fabric, S. I. Emotional behavior of Long-Evans and Hall-Spence rats on walled and unwalled runways. Unpublished thesis, Univer. of Florida, 1965.

Falconer, D. S. *Quantitative genetics*. New York: Ronald Press, 1960.

Fjerdingstad, E. J., Nissen, T., & Røigaard-Petersen, H. H. Effect of RNA extracted from the brain of trained animals on learning in rats. *Scandinavian Journal of Psychology*, 1965, **6**, 1–6.

Flexner, L. B. Loss of memory in mice as related to regional inhibition of cerebral protein synthesis. *Texas Reports of Biology & Medicine*, 1966, **24**, 3–19.

Frank, R., & Kenton, J. Visual cliff behavior of mice as a function of genetic differences in eye characteristics. *Psychonomic Science*, 1966, **4**, 35–36.

Fuller, J. L., & Thompson, W. R. *Behavior genetics*. New York: Wiley, 1960.

Fuller, J. L., & Wimer, R. E. Neural, sensory, and motor functions. In E. L. Green (Ed.), *Biology of the laboratory mouse*. New York: McGraw-Hill, 1966. Pp. 609–628.

Gaito, J. (Ed.) *Macromolecules and behavior*. New York: Appleton, 1966.

Ganong, W. F., Shepherd, M. O., Wall, J. R., Van Brunt, E. E. & Clegg, M. T. Penetration of light into the brain of mammals. *Endocrinology*, 1963, **72**, 962–963.

Green, E. L. (Ed.) *Biology of the laboratory mouse*. New York: McGraw-Hill, 1966.

Grüneberg, H. *The genetics of the mouse*. The Hague: Nijhoff, 1952.

Guide to production, care and use of laboratory animals: An annotated bibliography. *Federation Proceedings, Federation of American Societies for Experimental Biology*, 1960, **19**, 1–196.

Guide to production, care and use of laboratory animals: An annotated bibliography *Federation Proceedings, Federation of American Societies for Experimental Biology*, 1963, **22**, 1–250.

Hall, C. S. The genetics of behavior. In S. S. Stevens (Ed.), *Handbook of experimental psychology*. New York: Wiley, 1951. Pp. 304–329.

Hamilton, T. H. Control by estrogen of genetic transcription and translation. *Science*, 1968, **161**, 649–661.

Harris, V. T. An experimental study of habitat selection by prairie and forest races of deermouse, *Peromyscus maniculatus*. *Contributions* from the *Laboratory of Veterinary Biology*, 1952, **56**, 1–53.

Hirsch, J. Behavior-genetic analysis at the chromosome level. In J. Hirsch (Ed.), *Behavior-genetic analysis*. New York: McGraw-Hill, 1967. Pp. 258–269.

Hydén, H. Biochemical and molecular aspects of learning and memory. *American Philosophical Society*, 1967, **111**, 326–342.

Institute of Laboratory Animal Resources. *Laboratory animals*. Washington: National Academy of Science, 1964.

Jacob, F., & Monod, J. Genetic regulatory mechanisms in the synthesis of proteins. *Journal of Mooecular Biology*, 1961, **3**, 318–356.

John, E. R. *Mechanisms of memory*. New York: Academic Press, 1967.

Kavanau, J. L. Behavior of captive white-footed mice. *Science*, 1967, **155**, 1623–1639.

Keeler, C. E. *The laboratory mouse: Its origin, heredity, and culture*. Cambridge: Harvard Univer. Press, 1931.

King, J. A. Development and behavioral evolution in Peromyscus. Vertebrate Speciation: A University of Texas Symposium, 1961, Pp. 124–147.

King, J. A., Maas, D., & Weisman, R. G. Geographic variation in nest size among species of Peromyscus. *Evolution*, 1964, **18**, 230–234.

King, J. A., Price, E. O., & Weber, P. L. Behavioral comparisons within the genus Peromyscus. *Michigan Academy of Science, Arts and Letters*, 1968, *LIII*, 113–136.

LaBarba, R. C. Emotionality in two strains of mice as a function of maternal handling. *Psychonomic Science*, 1967, **9**, 121–122.

Lane, P. W. (Ed.) *Lists of mutant genes and mutant-bearing stocks of the mouse*. Bar Harbor, Maine: The Jackson Laboratory, 1964.

Lane-Petter, W. (Ed.) *Animals for research.* New York: Academic Press, 1963.

Lehrman, D. S. Gonadal hormones and parental behavior in birds and infrahuman mammals. In W. C. Young (Ed.), *Sex and internal secretions.* Baltimore: Williams & Wilkins, 1961. Pp. 1268–1382.

Levine, R. L. Stability of sucrose drinking curves in gentically heterogeneous mice. *Psychonomic Science.* 1968, **12**, 11–12.

Lindsley, D. L., & Grell, E. H. Genetic variations of Drosophila melanogaster. *Carnegie Institution of Washington Publication,* **627**, 1968.

Lindzey, G., Thiessen, D. D., & Tucker, A. Development and hormonal control of territorial marking in the male Mongolian gerbil (Meriones unguiculatus). *Developmental Psychobiology,* 1968, **1**, 97–99.

Lindzey, G., & Winston, H. Maze learning and effects of pretraining in inbred strains of mice. *Journal of Comparative and Physiological Psychology,* 1962, **55**, 748–752.

Lockard, R. B. The albino rat: A defensible choice or a bad habit? *American Psychologist,* 1968, **23**, 734–742.

Lofts, B., & Murton, R. K. Photoperiodic and psysiological adaptations regulating avian breeding cycles and their ecological significance. *Journal of Zoology,* 1968, **155**, 327–394.

Lund, R. D. Uncrossed visual pathways of hooded and albino rats. *Science,* 1965, **149**, 1506–1507.

Lyon, M. F. (Collator) *Mouse News Letter.* Harwell, Didiot, Berkshire, England: M.R.C. Radiobiological Research Unit.

Machlus, B., & Gaito, J. Drug RNA species developed during a shock avoidance task. *Psychonomic Science,* 1968, **12**, 111–112.

Manning, A. Drosophila and the evolution of behaviour. *Viewpoints in Biology.* 1965, **4**, 125–169.

Manosevitz, M., Lindzey, G., & Thiessen, D. D. (Eds.) *Behavioral genetics: Method and theory.* New York: Appleton, 1969.

Marler, P., & Hamilton, W. J. *Mechanisms of animal behavior.* New York: Wiley, 1966.

Mayr, E. *Animal species and evolution.* Cambridge: Harvard Univer. Press, 1965.

McCarley, W. H. The ecological distribution of the Peromyscus leucopus species group in eastern Texas. *Ecology,* 1954, **35**, 375–379.

McClearn, G. E. The inheritance of behavior. In L. Postman (Ed.), *Psychology in the making.* New York: Knopf, 1962. Pp. 144–252.

McGaugh, J. L., & Petrinovich, L. Effects of drugs on learning and memory. *International Review of Neurobiology,* 1965, **8**, 139–196.

McKusick, V. A. *Mendelian inheritance in man.* Baltimore: Johns Hopkins Press, 1966.

Meissner, W. W. Functional and adaptive aspects of cellular regulatory mechanisms. *Psychological Bulletin,* 1965, **64**, 206–216.

Miller, R. E., & Ogawa, N. The effect of adrenocorticotrophic hormone (ACTH) on avoidance conditioning in the adrenalectomized rat. *Journal of Comparative and Physiological Psychology,* 1962, **55**, 211–213.

Moore, R. E. Ethological isolation between Peromyscus maniculatus and Peromyscus polionotus. *American Midland Naturalist,* 1965, **74**, 341–349.

Morris, D. *The mammals.* New York: Harper, 1965.

Murphy, J. V., & Miller, R. E. The effect of adrenocorticotrophic hormone (ACTH) on avoidance conditioning in the rat. *Journal of Comparative and Psychological Psychology,* 1956, **48**, 47–49.

Newell, T. G. Effect of maternal deprivation on later behavior in two inbred strains of mice. *Psychonomic Science,* 1967, **9**, 119–120.

Ogilvie, D. M., & Stinson, R. H. Temperature selection in Peromyscus and laboratory mice, Mus musculus. *Journal of Mammalogy*, 1966, **47**, 655–660.

Parsons, P. A. *The genetic analysis of behavior*. London: Methuen, 1967.

Ralls, K. Auditory sensitivity in mice: Peromyscus and Mus musculus. *Animal Behaviour*, 1967, **15**, 123–128.

Rensch, B. *Evolution above the species level*. New York: Wiley, 1959.

Rodgers, D. A. Factors underlying differences in alcohol preference among inbred strains of mice. *Psychosomatic Medicine*, 1966, **28**, 498–513.

Rodgers, D. A. Behavior genetics and overparticularization: An historical perspective. In J. N. Spuhler (Ed.), *Genetic diversity and human behavior*. Chicago: Aldine, 1967. Pp. 47–60.

Rosenzweig, M. R. The mechanisms of hunger and thirst. In L. Postman (Ed.), *Psychology in the making*. New York: Knopf, 1962. Pp. 73–143.

Scharrer, E., & Scharrer, B. *Neuroendocrinology*. New York: Columbia Univer. Press, 1963.

Schlesinger, K., & Griek, B. J. The genetics and biochemistry of audiogenic seizures. In G. Lindzey and D. D. Thiessen (Eds.), *Contributions to behavior-genetic analysis: The mouse as a prototype*. New York: Appleton, 1970. Pp. 219–257.

Schwarz, E., & Schwarz, H. K. The wild and commensal stocks of the house, Mus musculus, Linnaeus. *Journal of Mammalogy*, 1943, **24**, 59–72.

Sebeok, T. A. *Animal communication*. Bloomington: Indiana Univer. Press, 1968.

Selander, R. K., & Yang, S. Y. Biochemical genetics and behavior in wild house mouse populations. In G. Lindzey and D. D. Thiessen (Eds.), *Contributions to behavior-genetic analysis: The mouse as a prototype*. New York: Appleton, 1970. Pp. 293–334.

Sheridan, C. L. Interocular transfer of brightness and pattern discriminations in normal and corpus callosum-sectioned rats. *Journal of Comparative and Physiological Psychology*, 1965, **59**, 292–294.

Sidman, R. L., & Green, M. C. Retinal degeneration in the mouse: Location of the *rd* locus in linkage group XVII. *Journal of Heredity*, 1965, **56**, 23–29.

Sidman, R. L., Green, M. C., & Appel, S. H. *Catalog of the neurological mutants of the mouse*. Cambridge: Harvard Univer. Press, 1965.

Simpson, G. G. Principals of classification and a classification of mammals. *Bulletin of the American Museum of Natural History*, 1945, **85**, 1–350.

Smith, M. H. Behavioral discrimination shown by allopatric and sympatric males of Peromyscus eremicus and Peromyscus Californicus between females of the same two species. *Evolution*, 1965, **19**, 430–435.

Spieth, H. T. Mating behavior within the genus Drosophila (Diptera). *Bulletin of the American Museum of Natural History*, 1952, **99**, 401–474.

Staats, J. Behavior studies on inbred mice: A selected bibliography. *Animal Behaviour*, 1958, **6**, 77–84.

Staats, J. Behavior studies on inbred mice: A selected bibliography, II. *Animal Behaviour*, 1963, **11**, 484–490.

Staats, J. (Ed.) Standardized nomenclature for inbred strains of mice: Third listing. *Cancer Research*, 1964, **24**, 147–168.

Staats, J. The laboratory mouse. In E. L. Green (Ed.), *Biology of the laboratory mouse*. New York: McGraw-Hill, 1966. Pp. 1–9.

Sturtevant, A. H. *A history of genetics*. New York: Harper, 1965.

Sumner, F. B. Does 'protective coloration' protect?—results of some experiments with fishes and birds. *Proceedings of the National Academy of Science of the United States of America*, 1934, **20**, 559–564.

Sumner, F. B. Studies of protective color change. III. Experiments with fishes both as predators and prey. *Proceedings of the National Academy of Science of the United States of America*, 1935, **21**, 345–353.

Tata, J. R. Hormones and the synthesis and utilization of ribonucleic acids. *Progress in Nucleic Acid Research*, 1966, **5**, 191–250.

Terry, R. J., Roland, A. L., & Race, J., Jr. Effect of eye enucleation and eyelid closure upon the brain and associated visual structures in the mouse. *Journal of Experimental Zoology*, 1962, **150**, 165–184.

Thiessen, D. D. *Gene organization and behavior*. New York: Random House, 1970, in press.

Thiessen, D. D., Friend, H., & Lindzey, G. Androgen control of territorial marking in the Mongolian gerbil. *Science*, 1968, **160**, 432–434.

Thiessen, D. D., Owen, K., & Whitsett, M. Chromosome mapping of behavioral activities. In G. Lindzey and D. D. Thiessen (Eds.), *Contributions to behavior-genetic analysis: The mouse as a prototype*. New York: Appleton, 1970. Pp. 161–204.

Thiessen, D. D., & Rodgers, D. A. Alcohol injection, grouping, and voluntary alcohol consumption of inbred strains of mice. *Quarterly Journal of Studies on Alcohol*, 1965, **26**, 378–383.

Thiessen, D. D., & Rodgers, D. A. Behavior genetics as the study of mechanism-specific behavior. In J. N. Spuhler (Ed.), *Genetic diversity and human behavior*. Chicago: Aldine, 1967. Pp. 61–72.

Tryon, R. C. Genetic differences in maze-learning ability in rats. *Yearbook of the National Society for the Study of Education*, 1940, 39, Pp. 111–119.

Turner, C. D. *General endocrinology*. (4th ed.) Philadelphia: Saunders, 1966.

Vandenberg, S. G. (Ed.) *Methods and goals in human behavior genetics*. New York: Academic Press, 1965.

Vandenberg, S. G. (Ed.) Contributions of twin research to psychology. *Psychological Bulletin*, 1966, **66**, 327–352.

Vanderberg, S. G. (Ed.) *Progress in human behavior genetics*. Baltimore: Johns Hopkins Press, 1968.

Watson, J. D. *Molecular biology of the gene*. New York: Benjamin, 1965.

Weiss, J. M., McEwen, B. S., Teresa, M., Silva, A., & Kalkut, M. F. Pituitary-adrenal influences on fear responding. *Science*, 1969, **163**, 197–199.

Williams, G. C. *Adaptation and natural selection*. Princeton: Princeton Univer. Press, 1966.

Winston, H. D. Heterosis and learning in the mouse. *Journal of Comparative and Physiological Psychology*, 1964, **57**, 279–283.

Wynne-Edwards, V. C. *Animal dispersion in relation to social behaviour*. New York: Hafner, 1962.

Comparative Psychology

STANLEY C. RATNER

DEPARTMENT OF PSYCHOLOGY
MICHIGAN STATE UNIVERSITY
EAST LANSING, MICHIGAN

Comparative psychology is in a state of change. Three major themes are mingling and, I believe, will eventually converge into a bona fide comparative psychology. The themes involve: animal behavior, general-experimental psychology, and the comparative method. These themes provide a working definition of our topic. *Comparative psychology involves the analysis of the behavior of organisms, including man, by means of the comparative method.*

But before we examine this proposition about comparative psychology, I want to identify myself as a comparative psychologist and trace the origins

115

of my interest, although I suspect that tracing origins is susceptible to major errors and opportunities to uncover these errors are small. If the analyst is a Freudian he seeks psychodynamic explanations; if he is a behaviorist he seeks prior conditioning explanations. I am a comparative psychologist and at the same time I am trying to explain why I work in this area. To do this I will also become doctrinaire and use the language of comparative psychology. My constructs of analysis are: *contacting* and *territoriality*. However, one noncomparative construct will also be invoked, namely *negativism*. But even this construct can be seen as an aspect of territorial behavior, namely, as a response to the condition of crowding.

Contacting is a consummatory activity that has had and continues to have high priority in my repertoire of consummatory activities. When I contact things, for example, I approach them, view them, and sometimes handle them. I do similar things with abstract or imaginative things but with less movement. So, for example, I frequently contact new words, listen to them, repeat them, and may put them with other words. Comparative psychology seemed to provide many opportunities for contacting my environment and then contacting the imaginative materials associated with these prior contacts.

The academic influences that fit, propelled, and formalized these interests came first from interactions with a learning theorist, Professor Charles C. Perkins at Kent State University, who worked in the Hull–Spence theoretical framework. But two characteristics of such research and theory were less than positive to me. Such theory disregarded or failed to use many of the observations made about the diverse behaviors of laboratory animals in the learning apparatus, and the area of study was already very crowded. I then met Professor J. Robert Kantor at Indiana University, whose dedication to the behavior (interbehavior) of organisms was a natural extension of stimulus-response (S–R) learning theories. The relevance of Professor Kantor's views was reinforced by my study with Professor W. K. Estes who frequently asked the question, "What does the animal do in the apparatus?" Thus, my doctoral and predoctoral research emphasized observation, measurement, and theoretical analysis of several components of an animal's behavior during acquisition and extinction of learned responses (Ratner, 1956). Professor I. J. Saltzman, my thesis chairman, encouraged my work by allowing me to do it with minimal restraint.

Formal opportunity to work in comparative psychology came when I joined the faculty of Michigan State University and became responsible for the uncrowded area of comparative psychology. Almost unlimited facilities existed for contacting behaviors of organisms and the provocative interest of students encouraged these contacts. A year of research and study with zoologists at Cambridge University and other Continental centers made me understand something of the style of zoology and the meaning that zoologists attached to comparative study. Thus, I began to understand that the study of behavior by zoologists had a different theoretical perspective from the study of behavior by comparative psychologists. My first attempt to organize this understanding for review by colleagues and students appeared in the book *Comparative Psychology* (Ratner & Denny, 1964). Professor Denny and I spent several years reviewing the experiments and the ideas of animal behaviorists and comparative psychologists. Our ideas represented an example of coordination between strict S–R analysis of learning and broad contacts with behaviors of organisms. Since the time when Denny and I began to work together to identify, describe, and use a comparative psychology, I have found a territory in comparative psychology. While it is uncrowded, it is not isolated. That is, it is congruent with comparative analysis in a number of areas of study including zoology, but it is not merely a restatement of the theory of evolution as it relates to behavior of organisms. The remaining sections of this chapter will amplify and illustrate these ideas, and I believe move us to a bona fide comparative psychology.

You may wonder at the idea that a bona fide comparative psychology does not yet exist since the label comparative psychology has been applied to books and psychological journals for many decades. The *Journal of Comparative and Physiological Psychology* is publishing its 66th volume and it was entitled the *Journal of Comparative Psychology* for many years. In 1914 John B. Watson (the father of behaviorism) published a text entitled *Behavior: An Introduction to Comparative Psychology* (1967) and Watson's treatise was not the earliest. Margaret F. Washburn published the first of several editions of her book on comparative psychology in 1908. These texts were followed by others, each of which dominated the view of comparative psychologists for some time. Examples are: *Principles of Animal Psychology* by Maier and Schnierla (1935), and the three-volume treatise entitled *Comparative Psychology* written by Warden, Jenkins, and Warner (1935, 1936, 1941).

It is my premise that the previously mentioned journals and books reflect the long term interest in comparative psychology, but they represent incomplete approaches to it. In general, these approaches are deficient in the use of comparative method and overemphasize either animal behavior or general-experimental psychology. While both animal behavior and general-experimental psychology are essential for a true comparative psychology, they are not sufficient for it. They lack the organization that comes from the use of the comparative method. *Comparative Psychology* by Ratner and Denny (1964) represents one of the first attempts to put all of these components into a single analysis and this analysis was further elaborated by Ratner (1967).

I. Animal Behavior

Because comparative psychology deals with the analysis of behavior of organisms, the study of animal behavior constitutes the first ingredient of comparative psychology. Such study is one of the oldest areas of biological study. This area traditionally excludes man, so that information about the behavior of man must come from other investigators. This exclusion is an unfortunate one because man is then put into a unique category with special and often mystical theories used to characterize him. With the exception of the area of human behavior, investigators of animal behavior have made many contributions that are important for comparative psychology, and recently zoologists who specialize in animal behavior are extending their analyses to humans (Lorenz, 1965).

A. Reasons for the Study of Animal Behavior

This section could be entitled "Why Are People Interested in Animals?" Put this way, the diverse reasons for interest in animals would probably be found to range across theological, scholarly, economic, and even neurotic human behaviors. Ratner and Denny (1964, p. 1) identify four main reasons for such study. They are: (a) interest in the animal itself; (b) interest in the animal as an economic element; (c) interest in one species as a model for others; and (d) relevance of animal behavior for the theory of evolution.

Interest in the Animal Itself. As suggested above, people are interested in the behavior of animals for a variety of reasons, but the fact of their interest is clear. Consider the extensive use of animal pictures in advertising, attendance at zoos, and the pet industry. Such interest makes the behavior of any species appropriate material for professional or amateur study. Reports in *National Geographic* illustrate both professional and amateur interests. Bird watching and photographic safaris illustrate another expression of interests in animals and animal behavior. The contribution of amateurs to the total understanding of animal behavior is significant and will be discussed in Section III which describes the "stages approach" to comparative analysis.

Animals As Economic Elements. The behaviors of many species of animals are of great economic consequence. In some cases the behaviors are a positive consequence, but in many they are negative. The training and use of Seeing-Eye dogs, watchdogs, and horses suggest a few of the positive uses of animal behavior. Joy Adamson illustrates the negative consequences of animal behavior in an early section of her story of Elsa, the lion cub that was "born free." "A Boran tribesman had been killed by a man-eating lion. It was reported to George (senior game warden in Kenya) that this animal, accompanied by two lionesses, was living in some nearby hills, and so it became his duty to track them down." (Adamson, 1960, p. 17.)

Aspects of behaviors of starlings, crows, pigeons, mosquitoes, rabbits, etc., have negative economic consequences for many people. Intensive study and understanding of the behavior of each of these species is therefore important in order to reduce these negative consequences. The effect of the stimulus of the figure of an owl on starlings, pigeons, and crows has been studied and investigators thought that they could control the behavior of these species of birds with the owl's figure. The effects are strong but temporary, and some of you may have seen pigeons perched on the heads of owls. Clearly, more study is necessary.

Behavior of One Species As a Model for Others. The most familiar study of animal behavior by psychologists involves using the behavior of one species as a model of other behaving organisms or behavioral systems. So, for example, thousands of psychologists and students measure the behaviors of laboratory rats, pigeons, school children, worms, monkeys, and so forth, where the primary focus is on the animal as a model of a behaving organism. Chapanis (1961) has discussed some of the logic and the confusion associated with the use of models by psychologists. Using his definitions the laboratory rat, for example, can be considered as a model since it is: ". . . a representation or likeness of certain aspects of complex events . . . [p. 115]." Specifically, Chapanis would consider the animal as a *replica model.*

One unfortunate factor that is associated with the use of an animal as a model behavioral process is that the investigator frequently knows very little about the particular species, the model, that he is using. So, for example, information about biology and the living habits of model animals, such as rats, is often unknown to investigators. Kenk (1967), a biologist who specializes in the study of the flat worm, planaria, describes some of the difficulties that investigators of planaria learning have encountered when using supply house information about the worms. Among the problems are those associated with identification of species, relating the living conditions and experimental situations to the requirements of particular species, and recognizing the limits of the generality of experimental findings. But similar problems can arise if the model involves rats or even school children, if the investigator knows little more about his model than its name and the fact that he wants it to be a model of a generalized species.

While failure to know the model is one problem associated with this type of study of individual species, positive features of such studies are evident. Psychologists have learned a great deal about learning from intensive study of the behavior of rats. The data in Skinner's treatise *Behavior of Organisms*

(1938) is based on the study of no more than 10 laboratory rats. Subsequent appreciation of the large and subtle effects of schedules of reward also arose from studies of rat learning.

The use within the past 10 years of planaria, the flat worm, as a model of learning and chemical change during learning has permitted psychologists, biologists, and chemists to perform hundreds of experiments investigating such problems (Corning & Ratner, 1967). Another model animal used for experimental study of learning and chemistry of learning is the laboratory rat (John, 1967).

Relevance for the Theory of Evolution. Of the various reasons for the study of animal behavior, the study of it for its relevance to the theory of evolution is the most unfamiliar to students of general psychology. The theory of evolution with its concepts of *natural selection, selection pressure,* and *adaptation* is essential in the training and thinking of zoologists, but is frequently omitted from the training of psychologists. However, zoologists have not used behavior of organisms in relation to the theory of evolution as extensively as they have used structural and physiological factors. One reason for this is almost self-evident. The theory of evolution is largely supported by fossil evidence and behavior leaves no direct fossils. The other reason for the de-emphasis on behavioral data arises, I believe, from the fact that psychologists and zoologists have an inadequate vocabulary to describe behavior. An eminent student of evolution, Simpson (1958), also comments on this problem: "There is an imperative need for taxonomy of behavior, including necessarily definitions of distinguishable categories of behavior [p. 155]."

In spite of the problems associated with analysis of behavior, zoologists, including Charles Darwin, have worked extensively on the two-way relations between behavior and evolution. As Hinde and Tinbergen (1958) point out: "Species-specific behavior is in part the product of evolutionary process. Likewise, the behavior of a species must influence the course of its evolution [p. 251]." The study of animal behavior in relation to evolution is the particular concern of *ethologists* such as Lorenz (1965), Tinbergen (1951), Thorpe (1956), and Hinde (1966).

B. *Concepts and Methods for the Study of Animal Behavior*

Concepts and theoretical analyses specifically related to behaviors of infrahumans are relatively well developed. These concepts are applied particularly when the worker is interested in animal behavior, per se, and not behavior of one species as a model for explaining the behavior of other species. A concept used particularly with animals is *instinct*. Analyses of behavior published at the turn of this century often referred to "instinct."

The concept at that time meant an inherited pattern of behavior or motivation more complex than a reflex. However, uncritical use of the concept led to its downfall.

Recent Instinct Theory. Recent redefinition and reconsideration of the concept of instinct has led many contemporary workers, particularly the ethologists, back to it. As used by Tinbergen (1951), for example, the concept refers to complex patterns of behavior that: (*a*) are unlearned; (*b*) are specific to particular species; (*c*) are triggered by particular stimuli; and (*d*) are more difficult to elicit after repeated elicitations. The fighting behavior of male stickleback fish is considered an instinct in the newer sense. The behavior occurs within this species with a characteristic pattern of movements, and it occurs, or, in Tinbergen's terms is "released," when the male sees the red belly of another stickleback during the mating and nesting seasons. Tinbergen found that the fighting pattern may be released by any red-bellied object shaped like a fish which is close to the nesting site.

The principles used in tying and casting flies for fishing constitute an informal use of the notion that certain stimuli or releasers may be used to elicit the feeding response in fish. That is, when a fisherman is tying flies, he does not duplicate the insect in detail; he only imitates those aspects of the insect that he suspects are the releasers for the feeding response of the fish.

The concept of instinctive behavior suggested above is even more complex than is suggested by the listed criteria. Moreover, the concept of instinctive behavior involves a set of interlocking concepts which are still undergoing development by investigators such as Tinbergen (1951), Thorpe (1956), and Lorenz (1957). One novel aspect of the present formulation of instinct involves the concept of "fixed-action patterns," stereotyped responses that animals make. These responses are presumed to provide the chief source of animals' motivation and not vice versa, as is typically assumed in psychological terms. Thus, a releaser (a stimulus which naturally elicits some response) leads to one element in the response sequence and this pattern leads to the next element in the sequence, and so forth. The occurrence of the sequence leads to the subsequent components and increasing strength of the response.

Nest building, courting rituals, fighting patterns, and other such complex behaviors have been analyzed in terms of releasers and fixed-action patterns. An ethological analysis describes these behavior patterns, called consummatory acts, such as nest building and copulating, without assuming that the animal is working for the goals of having a nest or producing young. Rather, it is assumed that when an appropriate releaser is present a response is elicited. This releaser-response sequence leads to the next sequence, and so forth through a chain. In these instances, the chain of S–R units is not learned as it is in the case of development of a chain in the Skinner box; rather, the chain is instinctual.

Classes of Animal Behavior. Another set of concepts proposed primarily as a description of animal behavior has been presented by Scott (1958). His descriptive system is oriented around an assumption that has been guiding the thinking of zoologists since the time of Charles Darwin. The assumption is that the behavior of organisms is "adaptive." Precisely what is meant by the concept adaptive is not clear. As with the psychologists' concept of reward, each worker makes use of the assumption as it fits his other assumptions. Scott identifies the following types of adaptive behavior: ingestive behavior, shelter seeking, agonistic behavior (fighting), sexual behavior, care-giving behavior (particularly to the young), eliminative behavior, allelomimetic behavior (responding in the same way as other animals that are in close proximity), and investigative behavior. I use some of these concepts in a Section IIIB where I propose a classification of behavior for use in comparative psychology.

This set of concepts or similar sets suggests classes of behavior for experimental study and provides a structure into which descriptions of animal behaviors may be fitted. In investigating animal behavior using these concepts, the psychologist may study the stimulus conditions associated with each type of behavior, the form of the behavior, and the conditions leading to changes in the behavior. The behavior patterns suggested by Scott may be, and in some cases have been, further analyzed in terms of instinct theory and/or in terms of learning theory.

Concepts Applied to Behavior of Invertebrates. A detailed descriptive system to analyze some aspects of behavior of invertebrates has been proposed by Fraenkel and Gunn (1961). Their system is devised to "deal with the orientation of animals, the directions in which they walk or swim and the reasons why particular directions are selected [p. 5]." An assumption underlying the descriptive system is that orienting reactions of animals are unlearned. This assumption is similar to that underlying the description of instinctive behavior. The reactions of moths to flame or other sources of light is one such example of an unlearned orienting response. Fraenkel and Gunn attempted to make a systematic analysis of such reactions that was applicable to species of invertebrates from amoeba through insects. The forms of the movements of these various species differ. Thus, the descriptive system is relatively complex, but very useful for analyzing behavior of many species. It may even be applied to the behavior of vertebrates, although little research along these lines has been undertaken.

Three classes of orienting reactions are identified. They are: *kineses, taxes*, and *compass* reactions. Each class is further subdivided in terms of details of the animal's movements, but these subdivisions will not be discussed.

A *kinetic reaction* is one in which the animal moves in an *undirected manner* in response to some stimulus. When stimulation is terminated or when the movements have led the animal to another stimulus condition that does not elicit kinetic reactions, then the undirected movements stop. An example of kineses is the reaction of a paramecium to an increase in thermal (temperature) stimulation. If the water in which a paramecium is swimming is heated, the animal becomes more active and eventually stops when it has moved into a cooler area. Such a reaction is called a thermokineses. In general, organisms with generalized sensitivities or undifferentiated receptors show kinetic reactions.

In a *tactic reaction* an animal moves in a *directed manner* toward or away from some stimulus. Thus, taxes are classified as positive (movements toward) or negative (movements away). In the cases of a positive tactic response the animal moves along the gradient of stimulation toward the source. Obviously then, the tactic reactions require rather highly developed receptors that are sensitive to the intensity of stimulation. For example, earthworms show negative tactic responses to photic stimulation. That is, they move away from the source of photic radiations. If the stimulus is presented only briefly, then withdrawal is momentary. As in the case of kinetic reactions, the name of the source of stimulation is often included in the description of the tactic reaction. So for example, this behavior of the earthworm is called a negative phototactic reaction. Other sources of stimulation that are associated with *directed movements*, either toward or away, are: chemical gradients (chemotaxes), water pressure gradients (rheotaxes), body contact gradients (thigmotaxes), and gradients of gravitational pull (geotaxes). A further complication in the analysis of orienting reactions comes from the fact that the reactions intereact so that reaction to one gradient may be affected by reaction to another (Ratner and VanDeventer, 1965).

Compass reactions, also called *transverse orientations*, are directed reactions in which the animal moves or adjusts itself to be at some fixed angle in relation to the direction of the gradient of stimulation. The most familiar examples of compass reactions involve the orientation of insects, such as ants and bees, to photic radiation. These animals often move about by temporarily navigating a path that is at some fixed angle from the direction of sunlight. Thus, for example, a bee may repeatedly orient from a source of food to the hive using a heading in relation to the angle of the sunlight. Such reactions require a receptor made up of a number of sensitive elements that are pointed in different directions—the eye of the insect. Transverse orientations are also made in response to gravitational fields. In this case an animal maintains some fixed orientation to the earth's gravitational field. Unlike other compass reactions, gravitational reactions are not movements toward some source, but are rather ways of maintaining the body in space or in water.

Modification of Innate Behavior: Learning. There is an interesting and important question that follows from considering some aspect of animal behavior as innate behavior. To what extent may such behavior be modified in the lifetime of an animal? Can innate orienting and instinctive behaviors be changed? One view of learning is that it involves changing innate behaviors. Skinner (1938), for example, conceived of two kinds of learning procedures. One, a modification of reflexes and smooth-muscle responses, was called *respondent learning*. The other type, a modification of movements and skeletal-muscle response, was called *operant learning*. These procedures may be viewed as modifications of two innate behavior processes. However, Skinner was not particularly concerned with the characteristics of the innate behavior processes. Denny and Ratner (1970) also make the assumption that learning involves the modification of innate behavior.

Field Studies. Some of the important studies of animal behavior have been conducted as field studies, which involve *observing the animals in their natural settings.* The field study differs from the laboratory experiment particularly in terms of the degree to which the experimenter controls the conditions of the experiment, including the independent variable. The field study is characterized by a low degree of such control and on the surface seems to be a weak substitute for the laboratory experiment. However, conditions exist under which field studies are distinctly advantageous, particularly when used in conjunction with laboratory studies. Advantages arise when the species cannot be readily established in the laboratory, which is true for many nondomesticated species, and when variables which affect their behavior cannot be reproduced. Another circumstance in which field studies are advantageous is *when hypotheses are being formulated* about psychological processes of animals. That is, observing the species in a wire cage in the laboratory provides few ideas about what and how the animal learns, what it sees, and so forth.

Field studies are somewhat rare in psychological investigations of animal behavior, although the method is frequently used in social psychology and is a familiar tool of the biologist. Some of the prerequisites of the field method are: (*a*) information about the natural history of the species and the particular group of organisms under study, and (*b*) a technique for rapid identification of the individuals under study. Identification may be arranged by marking the individuals or becoming familiar enough with each to recognize it from bodily and postural characteristics.

C. Animal Behavior: Summary

Information, concepts, and methods that relate to the study of animal behavior provide the first of three ingredients that we will combine into a bona fide comparative psychology. The information, concepts, and methods regarding animal behavior arise from study of the animal: (a) as a natural animal, (b) as an economic element, (c) as a model of other processes, and (d) for its relevance to evolution.

Observation and study of animal behavior has gone on for thousands of years, so that a great deal is known. At the present time, ethologists, who specialize in animal behavior, offer a systematic vocabulary for the description of innate behavior. They postulate two classes of innate behavior. One class involves *orienting movements* of animals, especially invertebrates; and one class involves *instinctive behaviors*. The *field method* is one important method for collecting data and testing hypotheses.

II. GENERAL-EXPERIMENTAL PSYCHOLOGY

The second component of a true comparative psychology involves contributions from general-experimental psychology. The contributions come from both general psychology and experimental psychology. Since comparative psychology involves psychological study, it must emphasize psychological as opposed to zoological processes and theories. This distinction has been missed by ethologists such as Konrad Lorenz (1950), who states: "An American journal masquerades under the title of *Comparative Psychology* although . . . no really comparative paper has ever really been published in it [p. 240]." Lorenz seems to mean that no research has been published that flows directly from the theory of evolution which is the central theory in comparative biology. While the comparative psychologists must be aware of the comparative study of animal behavior by zoologists, I assume that the comparative psychologist has another focus. This focus is to relate animal behavior and general experimental psychology with the comparative method in order to produce a true comparative psychology.

A. Characteristics of General-Experimental Psychology

General-experimental techniques have both strong positive characteristics and some perplexing limitations as they are used in comparative psychology. The limitations come primarily from aspects of the attitude and style of experimental psychologists. I consider characteristics to be negative when they move the emphasis of the research from the animal and its behavior to the apparatus and the investigator's concepts. Clearly, all research is bound to some extent by the concepts and apparatus of the investigator, but failure to know and acknowledge the animal and its behavior makes an experimental study of little use for the purposes of comparative analysis. This is true because comparative psychology is *naturalistic and comprehensive.* Thus, experimental studies that are contrived (apparatus-or concept-bound) and very narrow in scope are limited in value. Examples are studies that deal specifically with highly selected samples of humans or animals, and studies that are designed to test the relevance of specific concepts from miniature theories.

B. Contributions from General-Experimental Psychology

The characteristics of general-experimental psychology that coordinate positively with comparative psychology are many and varied. Two of the general contributions involve the methodology of experimental psychology, and analysis in terms of stimulus and response. Specific contributions involve content from studies of learning and content from studies in areas such as sensory and physiological psychology.

Methodology. We have already reviewed the contributions to comparative psychology of the field method of the naturalist and ethologist. The experimental method and particularly the laboratory-based experimental method for the study of behavior, is one general contribution from experimental psychology. The salient features of the experimental method for analysis of behavior are familiar, but will be noted. The first feature involves *control of variables* and the second involves *manipulation of variables.* Because one stage of comparative analysis (discussed in Section III) involves identification of variables that affect behavior, the importance of techniques for such identification is clear. That is, control and manipulation of variables are essential in order to identify these variables and analyze the extent to which the variables are interacting with each other and influencing responses of organisms. Zoologists who study animal behavior have only recently begun to use experimental procedures. This has come about as the kinship between zoological and psychological approaches to behavior has grown.

Statistical procedures, some of which are common in general-experimental psychology, also contribute to comparative analysis. Several types of statistical procedures are important. They are the procedures of inference and control, description, and measurement. The procedures of inference and control, such as randomization and tests of significance, are tied to the interpretation of results of experiments and the methodology of comparative psychology. Descriptive statistics, that involve indexes such as means, medians, and standard deviations, are clearly important.

The statistics of measurement are a less familiar part of general-experimental psychology, yet they are especially important in comparative analysis. Guilford (1954) discusses the details of many of the statistical procedures that, I believe, can be used in comparative study. The psychophysical methods for establishing sensory and perceptual thresholds, and methods relating to the reliability of measurement are among those that comparative psychologists have used. Investigators use the psychophysical methods to establish basic sensory information regarding animals and man, and they use methods associated with psychological testing to evaluate characteristics of the behavior measures (Ratner, 1968).

Stimulus–Response Analysis. The basic language of behaviorists is not a necessary part of general-experimental psychology, but it is closely associated with the experimental study of behavior from the time of John B. Watson and Ivan Pavlov. As Ratner and Denny (1964) point out, it is particularly useful for comparative psychology. This is true because the vocabulary and concepts used by ethologists to describe orienting and other innate behaviors is also a language that directly uses or implies the concepts of stimulus and response. So, for example, psychologists who study learning speak of unconditioned stimuli and unconditioned responses; ethologists speak of releasing stimuli and fixed action patterns. The comparative psychologist can readily coordinate these two vocabularies as he brings together the ideas of animal behavior and general psychology with the comparative method.

Relevant Content from General-Experimental Psychology. Virtually every topic that general-experimental psychologists have studied has some relevance for comparative psychology. This includes experimental study of social process, behavior development, physiological mechanisms, behavior genetics, learning, and sensory process. Typical books in comparative psychology have chapters that deal with these topics, and a typical issue of the *Journal of Comparative and Physiological Psychology* reports experiments on each of them. The overlap between the general study of animal behavior and general-experimental is so great that a typical issue of the journal entitled *Animal Behavior* also reports experiments on each of these topics. For example, an issue of Volume 16 of *Animal Behavior* published in 1968 has research reports with the following titles: "Social Inertia and Stability in Chickens," "Effects of Age on Taste Discrimination in the Bobwhite Quail," "Discrimination Learning in the Pigeon Following Unreinforced Training on the Negative Stimulus," and "Effects of Testosterone Propionate and Luteinizing Hormone on Agonistic and Nest Building Behavior of *Quelea quelea*" (*Quelea quelea* is a weaver bird). You can see that the species that are investigated in these reports from *Animal Behavior* are

TABLE 1

SOME AREAS OF PSYCHOLOGICAL STUDY AND REFERENCES THAT PROVIDE NATURALISTIC
AND COMPREHENSIVE INFORMATION[a]

Area and selected topics	Reference
General	
History	Kantor (1963, 1968)
Theory	Denny & Ratner (1970)
Methodology	
Experimentation	Webb, Campbell, Schwartz, & Seechrest (1966)
Apparatus	Tinbergen (1958)
	Stokes (1968)
Experimental	
Perception	Schiller (1957)
Learning	Breland & Breland (1966)
Physiological	
Sensory	Marler & Hamilton (1966)
Genetics	Hirsh (1967)
Animal	
Early experience	Sluckin (1965)
Motivation	Bolles (1967)
Developmental	
Infancy	Kuo (1967)
Parent–young relations	Rheingold (1963)
Social	
Sexual behavior	Beach (1965)
Language	Lenneberg (1967)

[a] The areas of psychological study are the first seven of eleven section
headings with sample topics from each from the *Psychological Abstracts* of the
American Psychological Association.

slightly unfamiliar, but the variables and processes under investigation are
common to general-experimental psychology.

Among the important classes of variables that experimental psychologists have investigated are those that deal with behavior development,
internal factors, genetic factors, sensory processes, and behavior modification.
Table 1 shows various areas of psychological study and coordinated readings
from the area of animal behavior. I will illustrate some of the relations
between animal behavior and general-experimental psychology with examples from learning, although I assume that such relations exist for other
areas of experimental study.

Amateur and professional investigators of animal behavior make several
points about animal behavior and learning (behavior modification) that
provide an important perspective for the psychologist who studies learning.

Reports by amateurs (including historians and anthropologists) clearly reveal that animal training is a very old art and probably has extended to more species than experimental psychologists have used in the laboratory. Elephant training in India, for example, is at least several thousand years old. If you were to read about this training you would find it full of mystery, but you would also find that these amateur students of learning were aware of the operation of many variables that influence learning by this particular species. Describing elephant training, for example, Hallet (1968), an amateur observer, reports:

... calves were then roped or netted, brought to the station, tethered to trees, and accustomed to the sight, sound, smell, and manner of men over a 10-month training period: Their *cornacs* talked to them, sang traditional Hindu songs, and plied them with sugar cane ... The songs were all-important. Emotional as they are, elephants show extreme sensitivity to music. Circus elephants sway in time to marches, trumpet excitedly when trumpets blow, and fall asleep during symphonies [p. 84].

Two ideas from this short selection are of particular interest. The first concerns the elaborate *pretraining procedures* that the trainers, *cornacs*, used. The sentences that describe this ancient procedure resemble sentences from the method section of an experimental report in a psychology journal. The second idea concerns the use of music with elephants. Assuming the point is valid, it represents the use of information about characteristics of the particular species that can be used in the training of the species. To generalize the point even further, we can say that every species has species-specific behaviors that involve fixed responses to specific stimulus configurations, releasing stimuli. An investigator can use species-specific behaviors to enhance learning as the *cornacs* do. But such behaviors also place limits on learning. Breland and Breland (1966), two experimental psychologists, have made this point repeatedly and clearly as a result of 18 years of work with animals. During this time they trained more than 8000 animals of more than 60 species at their farm in Hot Springs, Arkansas. As an example of the use that the Brelands made of their appreciation of animal behavior, they discussed the observation of alternation by the rat in a T-maze as follows:

Why should the rat turn left when it has found food by turning right? First, consider the nature and magnitude of the reinforcement. Rats in their wild state often feast upon great hoards of food ... they may dig into a grainery and drag home a whole ear of corn ... or may gnaw a hole in a sack of wheat. To run a labyrinth and encounter only a tiny bit of food at the end might be a pretty good indication to the rat to try the other path next time. Secondly, the rat makes his living by exploring dark corridors ... it may be to his advantage in the long run to try a new way ... [p. 65].

I do not mean to de-emphasize the importance of learning as investigated in systematic ways by experimental psychologists. However, I want to emphasize several things: (*a*) neither Pavlov, Thorndike, nor Skinner invented the procedures for modifying behavior; (*b*) we are in a strong position to understand behavior modification if we understand and appreciate the behavioral repertoire of the species we are studying. Denny and Ratner (1970) discuss these points in detail in their analyses of motivation, classical conditioning, and operant learning.

C. General-Experimental Psychology: Summary

The second ingredient in comparative psychology comes from general-experimental psychology. While some aspects of the general-experimental approach are eschewed, the contributions from the laboratory and statistical methods are noted. In addition, data from the experimental analysis of most of the topics in general psychology, such as developmental, perception, and learning, can be related to comparative psychology.

Aspects of the study of animal behavior are combined with the experimental study of learning to show how these two themes relate to produce a *naturalistic* and *comprehensive* comparative psychology.

III. COMPARATIVE METHOD

The third component of a true comparative psychology consists of applying the comparative method to the data of behavior of organisms. Thus, in this section, we will integrate material from animal behavior, general-experimental psychology, and the comparative method. But before we do this, it is necessary to distinguish among the various approaches to comparative psychology and to present the background ideas that show that comparative analysis involves a formal method.

A. The Accidental Tie between Evolution and Comparative Psychology

The typical view of comparative psychology that appears in a number of introductory chapters of comparative psychology books and in descriptions of courses in comparative psychology emphasizes evolution and comparisons. Stone (1951), for example, in the third edition of his book on comparative psychology says: "Comparative psychology, as a term, is applied to the study of diverse animals—chiefly studies that are intended to bring out differences and similarities [p. 1]." Stone then points out the relations between comparative psychology and various comparative biologies, such as anatomy and physiology. This view of comparative psychology that made it akin to comparative biology began to shift by 1960 when

Waters (1960), a respected and mature comparative psychologist, identified two major tasks of the comparative psychology: "(1) The analysis of an animal's behavior repertoire. This task involves discovering and cataloging the kinds or forms of behavior the animal exhibits . . . (2) The problem of comparing the different types of animals with respect to the likenesses and differences of the behavior observed [p. 6]." Notice that the first task that Waters identifies involves the first stages of comparative psychology as we will describe it in this section, although the second task and the major portion of the book (Waters, Rethlingshafer, & Caldwell, 1960) are related to comparative biology in the traditional way. In 1964 Ratner and Denny (1964) described comparative psychology, for the first time, as an enterprise that differed from comparative biology, and recently Ratner (1967) identified the stages of the comparative method and used them for a formal analysis of behavior of organisms.

Why Psychology Accepted the Evolutionary Approach. The question remains about how comparative psychology became tied to comparative biology and why this represents a weak comparative psychology. The relations between comparative psychology and comparative biology grew through the gradual dissemination of the theory of evolution after it was proposed by Darwin and widely dispersed through all other areas of study, especially the poorly developed ones such as psychology.

Psychologists, sociologists, political scientists, economists, and others used the idea of evolution in a global way to explain and describe the phenomena with which they dealt. For example, psychologists postulated the evolution of behavior or consciousness simply by tying words about behavior to evolution of animal form; economists postulated the evolution of economic systems, typically by putting their system as the highest evolutionary form and imagining the order of "lesser forms." Thus, evolution was used uncritically and without recourse to the aspects of Darwin's theory that proposed mechanisms of evolutionary change. You might get some feeling for the widespread acceptance and imitation of this aspect of comparative biology by thinking about the current widespread acceptance and imitation of quantitative procedures, especially those involving the computer. In summary, then, comparative study, especially in psychology, was tied rather directly to comparative biology as psychologists saw biology being investigated and used after Darwin's contributions. This meant that aspects of the theory of evolution and aspects of biological research that involved comparing species or structures were adopted as the style and spirit of comparative psychology.

The Failure of the Evolutionary Approach in Psychology. The inappropriateness of the evolutionary approach to comparative psychology can be characterized as "putting the cart before the horse." Psychologists took the end product of millennia of observations and systematic study by naturalists and professional biologists, namely, the theory of evolution, and started at that point with psychology. The consequences of this activity led to a very weak version of ethology and research that is best described as *capricious comparison.*

Capricious comparison, for example, involves taking two or more species of animals, jamming them individually into a piece of apparatus, such as a T-maze, and discovering the number of trials each species requires to reach criterion for negotiating the maze. At the conclusion of this experiment the investigator reports that the species differ or, in some cases, do not differ. While the experiment has a conclusion, the research has no theoretical or comparative conclusion beyond the naked facts and some global statements about higher and lower evolutionary forms. Such research is called capricious insofar as the investigator's selection of the animals he tests and the testing situation come about from the accident of having these animals and the apparatus available. Such experiments are sometimes fun to perform, but the results have little meaning if the apparatus and the details of the procedure, such as the size of the apparatus and the amount of reward, are not individually adjusted to the species. Even if these adjustments are made, the investigator has little to conclude.

Many studies were conducted by comparative psychologists where the comparison was implicit. Human problems were roughly scaled to animal proportions and animals were tested. If the animals failed, the investigator spent years adjusting procedures to lead to successful solutions by the infrahuman species to which the particular investigator was partial. Delayed response, multiple-maze alternation, and detour problems were some of the favorite ones. The early volumes of psychological journals that reported animal research contain many reports of such studies. However, many people continued to believe that comparisons of this capricious sort constitute the content of comparative psychology.

I do not mean to suggest that comparisons among behaviors of different species are inappropriate in all cases. It is appropriate if the behavioral measures are representative of some important or valid process, and if the relations among the species are based on information about evolution. Ethologists routinely conduct and interpret such studies (see for example recent issues of the journals *Animal Behaviour* or *Behaviour*), but such investigators are functioning as comparative behaviorists. Testing behaviors of different species is also appropriate if the investigator is asking questions about the *generality* of a behavior process, such as imprinting, orientation to temperature, etc. We will consider the value of such research in Section III.B and distinguish it from capricious comparison.

B. *The Stages Approach to Comparative Psychology*

My dissatisfaction with a comparative psychology that involved capricious comparison or a weak version of comparative biology led me to review the question of what is meant by comparative psychology.

My answer to this question soon led to the idea that comparative psychology involves a method that I call the *stages approach*. Furthermore, I concluded that biology and chemistry are two areas of study in which the method has been used with ultimate success. Thus, I will use the remaining portions of this chapter to describe the stages approach and to illustrate its use in psychology. The assertion that biologists and chemists used such a method requires substantiation, and is itself a topic for extensive study, but we can use items from the history of both biology and chemistry as guides without fully accepting or rejecting this assertion.

Ratner and Denny (1964) made the first approximation to the stages approach by identifying five aims of comparative psychology. I then re-evaluated these aims (Ratner, 1967) and set them into a formal system of analysis that involves six sequential stages that constitute the comparative method. The stages and descriptive statements about each are shown in Table 2. My premise regarding these stages is that they are sequential, but development within one stage allows reanalysis both in preceding and in subsequent stages. You can think of comparative psychology as developing by "successive approximations." We know that at the final stage we want a general theory of behavior of organisms. We start building the first stage (background information), this leads to the first systematic attempts at classification, the stage involving systematic classification permits both more adequate collection of background information and the first systematic attempts to develop powerful research preparations for the study of the behavior classes that were proposed in stage II, classification stage. The procedure continues through the development of a general theory.

In biology, for example, it appears that the comparative method, although unrecognized, slowly moved investigators from observing in the field to classification, and so forth, toward a general theory, the theory of evolution. As the stages approach is presently conceived, stages I–IV are *preparatory stages* that precede specific comparisons. Stages V and VI are the stages that involve comparison and general theory.

Stage I: Background Information. One of the most conspicuous characteristics of the queen of comparative studies, biology, is the breadth and depth of the background information that Darwin and other biologists had available. Naturalists, gentlemen, professional biologists, explorers, and many others had walked through the woods or in other ways viewed the

TABLE 2

THE STAGES APPROACH TO COMPARATIVE ANALYSIS[a]

Order	Stage	Major activity
I	Background information	Search for informal and formal information sources
II	Taxonomy	Develop functional classification system
III	Research preparations	Specify valid and reliable examples of each class
IV	Variables	Identify variables that affect classes
V	Origins and comparisons	Trace origins of classes and compare classes
VI	General theory	Identify general mechanisms that relate all classes

[a] Adapted from Denny and Ratner (1970).

biological scene and written about it. The life histories of hundreds of species of birds, mammals, and other creatures have been carefully reported. In the spirit of these activities, the collection and reporting of similar information regarding the behavior of organisms constitutes the first stage of comparative analysis in psychology. In this case, background information is required both about behaviors and organisms. It seems on the surface that the comparative psychologist should have little trouble because he himself is a behaving organism. Unfortunately, although this advantage seems to provide the useful starting point, it otherwise constitutes a very limited sample.

Background information gives the investigator a broad feeeling for the events that interest him and provides ideas about the gross characteristics of these events. In addition, the investigator gets perspective about the events and whatever existing theories are available.

The idea of background information is not unique to comparative analysis. Every research study involves a search of the literature at some point in the inquiry. But the search for background information of a comparative analysis must: (a) come early in the inquiry, and (b) use both *formal* and *informal* sources of information. The reasons that the background search comes early have been noted above. The reasons that both formal and informal sources are important are tied to the ideas of *breadth* and *perspective*. Remember that the final goal of comparative analysis is a general theory. Breadth and perspective in the early stage of analysis fit into this ultimate goal. In addition, a thorough search of background information increases the chance that the inquiry is valid. Professor M. E. Bitterman, for example, reports (in conversation) that he spent more than two years preparing to do behavioral research with sea crabs.

Charles Darwin's reflections (*Autobiography*) on the course of developing the theory of evolution illustrate the use of background information. Darwin reports:

> After my return to England it appeared to me that . . . by collecting all facts which bear in any way on the variation of animals and plants under domestication and nature, some light might perhaps be thrown on the whole subject. My first notebook was opened in July, 1837. I worked on true Baconian principles, and without any theory collected facts on a wholesale scale, more especially with respect to domesticated productions, by printed inquiries, by conversation with skillful breeders and gardeners, and by extensive reading. When I see the list of books of all kinds which I read and abstracted, including whole series of Journals and Transactions, I am surprised at my industry.

For the comparative psychologist one of the primary sources of background information about behaviors in animals (other than humans) comes from the area of *animal behavior*. You may remember that animal behavior constitutes the first component of comparative psychology, and stage I is one of the points at which animal behavior enters comparative analysis. The field of animal behavior has formal sources, such as journals and professional books; and informal sources that include naturalists, animal breeders, hunters, and animal management personnel. *Biological Abstracts*, that are available in most libraries, are well indexed both for behavior classes and species.

While psychologists are typically conscientious about searching formal sources for background material about human behavior, they seem to make little use of informal sources. Alcoholics Anonymous and Christian Science, for example, deal with thousands of adult humans in ways that bear some relation to clinical and social psychologies. The great southern preachers seem to be experts at persuasion. If a psychologist wanted to get some breadth and perspective on human behavior he might profit from contact with these informal sources.

Stage II: Behavior Classification. After an investigator has some feeling for the breadth and general characteristics of behavior of organisms, he is ready to sort behavior into classes. This is an extremely difficult and elusive task, but biologists and chemists, for example, had a similar task and eventually achieved success. Classification, taxonomy of behavior, yields the most tentative results, because the classification system undergoes change as background information and later stages of analysis are improved. The chapter titles of many psychology texts reflect the present state of classification of behavior. From these titles we see that psychologists propose categories such as personality, motivation, emotion, thinking, etc. It is my contention that these classes have emerged primarily from folklore and historical accident.

The focus of stage II in the comparative analysis is to do a self-conscious job of identifying major classes of behavior that represent our best judgments from the most adequate collection of background information.

The importance of classification of behavior can be seen in a number of ways. First, consider the state of chemistry if chemists did not know what elements they had in their test tubes. Consider also the difficulty of doing zoological work with sea animals if zoologists only had the classes of sea animal, land animal, and air animal. The zoologist might indiscriminately and unknowingly mix fish with lobsters and shrimp. The "error term" in such research work would be very large. Also, consider the importance that psychologists have attached to narrow spectrum classifications, such as the one Hilgard and Marquis (1940) provided when they reviewed learning and proposed two types of learning: classical conditioning and instrumental learning. This classification system is still in use.

It is difficult to imagine biology without an adequate taxonomy of animal forms and chemistry without a periodic table. But such conditions did exist for a long time while these sciences were working through the preparatory stages of comparative analysis. While chemists and biologists have been successful, comparative psychologists have not yet provided an adequate classification of behavior. Denny and Ratner (1970) present a tentative classification that draws heavily on concepts from animal behavior. They propose that behavior of organisms can be described in terms of three major types of behavior that we consider to be innate, using the terms descriptively: appetitive (orienting) behaviors, consummatory behaviors, and postconsummatory behaviors. *Appetitive behaviors* involve actions that precede and move an organism toward consummatory behaviors. Examples are courting, searching for food, and freezing when an unfamiliar noise occurs. *Consummatory behaviors* involve the vital activities of organisms such as copulating, feeding, reacting to predators, and caring for the body surface. Consummatory activities are rigidly stereotyped in form in many species. However, this stereotypy is decreased to some extent in a number of domesticated species, including humans. *Postconsummatory behaviors* are only relatively stereotyped and follow immediately after consummatory behaviors. Their function is to move the organism to the next appetitive–consummatory–postconsummatory sequence.

Table 3 presents the list of classes of consummatory behaviors and examples of each. In reviewing the list and examples you will see that not all animals show in an obvious way all of these behaviors. Nesting and caring for the young are minimal in some species, fighting is minimal in others, and so forth. However, among the classes of physiological processes we

TABLE 3

Taxonomy of Consummatory Behaviors and Related Biological Processes Arranged
in Order of Behavioral Development in Higher Vertebrates[a]

Behavior class	Biological system	Example
Resting	Recuperative	Sleeping
Contacting	Arousal	Visual following
Eliminating	Eliminative	Urinating
Drinking	Ingestive	Sucking
Feeding	Ingestive	Pecking
Care of body surface	Skin sensitivity	Grooming
Predator defenses	Defensive	Freezing
Fighting	Defensive	Biting
Sexual behavior	Reproductive	Ejaculating
Nesting	Reproductive	Fur pulling
Care of the young	Reproductive	Retrieving

[a] Adapted from Denny and Ratner (1970).

also find that some processes, such as fluid ingestion, are minimal in one species and prominent in others. That is, different classes of activities have different degrees of conspicuousness when applied across species. I believe that this is a characteristic of the organization of animals and their behavior and is not a negative recommendation for the classification system. In addition, the list in Table 3 is heavily loaded with behaviors that characterize the activities of infrahumans and may omit a number of behaviors that characterize humans. For example, how should we classify the activities that are involved in writing a chapter such as this one? Can we subsume such human behavior within the present system of classification or should other categories be added? By stretching the categories in Table 3 and by examining closely the behaviors of writers we might be able to subsume writing, theater, music, etc. For example, writing about a topic and displaying this writing might be a highly evolved form of establishing and marking a territory that leads to avoidance from some competitors and deference from competitors and other people. The concepts of territory and territorial marking are used by analogy in this case, but careful analysis of both human and infrahuman territorial behavior may show that the concepts are appropriate once the later stages of comparative study are advanced. On the other hand, we may have to add new categories that reflect unique human behaviors, even if these occur for only a small part of the population, as done by Maslow (1954).

One of the ideas behind the classification of behavior such as the one shown in Table 3 is that it permits a psychologist to describe behavior of the individual organism in these terms. We can say that a rat is showing the appetitive and consummatory components of feeding, or resting. We can also apply this to human behavior. When young men are in the presence of females, much of the behavior of these young men can be described as courting, the appetitive component associated with attracting females for copulation. The men may strut, flex arms, and engage in man-to-man sparring, much as the young males of other species do.

Certain circumstances and procedures modify components of these behavior classes. So Denny & Ratner (1970) see the process of learning as the modification of some features of innate behavior. One common procedure of modification used with rats involves changing the appetitive component of feeding and reacting to predators (threatening situations). In a T-maze, for example, the rat gradually runs faster and more unerringly to food. In this case, we build a chain of appetitive responses associated with feeding and reduce by *habituation* some of the rat's responses to threat. Hormonal changes, for example, modify the structures and sensitivities of the animals that are involved in appetitive or consummatory behaviors (Denny & Ratner, 1970, Ch. 6), and so modify these behaviors.

Procedures for classifying events are relatively complex and generally unfamiliar to psychologists. In addition, the procedures that are available are not directly applicable to psychology. Jensen, a comparative psychologist, has made an attempt to describe a method for classification. Jensen (1967) applies the system of polythetic classification to types of learning of invertebrates. The basic premise of this system, called *polythetic taxonomy*, is that things are grouped together as Jensen states "by overall similarity, i.e., by the presence of a sizeable number of the many characteristics typical of the group [p. 45]." This classification procedure, based on work by Sokal and Sneath (1963) is contrasted to the older procedure of classification by *monothetic similarity*. In monothetic classification events are grouped together if they share one important characteristic. Jensen believes that the use of monothetic classification has led to the controversy about whether lower organisms learn.

A second important consideration in classification involves the use of *functional classification* as opposed to *structural classification*. This means identifying classes and putting events together based on "what is happening" or "what they do" rather than putting them together on the basis of "sharing some static or structural feature." An example of functional classification comes from Skinner (1938) who classified neutral stimuli as S^Ds, S^Δs, or S^rs based on how an animal responded to the stimuli, rather than the physical properties of the stimuli.

The classification that is suggested in Table 3 attempts to use polythetic functional principles. Other characteristics and requirements of classification are illustrated by Bitterman's discussion of classification of types of learning (1960).

Stage III: Research Preparations. I mentioned in our discussion of stage II that not all classes of behavior are shown with clarity by all animals under all conditions. In other words, the study of a class or process of behavior requires a situation (preparation) in which the process shows itself clearly. The third stage of comparative analysis deals with the discovery and characterization of *research preparations* that have sufficient clarity to permit study of the class or process noted in stage II. Research preparations can be thought of as "good examples" or "archtypes," but these labels do not express the full sense of powerful research preparations.

Before we consider the full meaning of this stage of comparative analysis, the question of why comparative analysis includes this stage are legitimate. The answer lies partly in tradition and partly in the characteristics of comparative analysis. The tradition of comparative study as seen in biology and chemistry includes the search for clear examples of classes and processes. Zoologists, for example, continue to seek preparations for research that have properties that are clearly characteristic of a particular phylum or the classes within a phylum. The phylum Annelida (segmented worms) and the class Oligochaete has many members, some of which show the features of this class more clearly than others. The familiar research preparation for this class is the earthworm, *Lumbricus terrestris.* Other species within this class are not as suitable as research preparations. Similarly, physiologists use the giant axon (nerve) of the squid as the structure involved in the preparation to study some aspects of nerve physiology. The axon is long, large in diameter, relatively accessible, readily procured, and most important, is true neural tissue. So the tradition of comparative analysis suggests that comparative psychology has as one of its stages the search for powerful research preparations. Although this is a weak reason by itself, I believe the tradition has come about for two important reasons. First, the comparative investigator has proposed the system of classification and he properly follows this by identifying examples of each class. Second, the comparative investigator is steeped in background information, so his range of choice of preparation should be larger than that of the investigator of a single process.

We can consider an anthropologist to be a comparative sociologist, and when we do, the reasons that anthropologists go to "strange places" make more sense. On the one hand, they may be collecting background information, but a lot of this has already been done. On the other hand, the anthropologist may be identifying or using a research preparation that has the characteristics of the particular social process that is of interest to him, such as a particular type of kinship system.

Self-conscious attention to research preparations is not yet a part of psychological research, partly, I believe, because a bona fide comparative psychology is just developing. But psychologists already have some research preparations that are coordinated with the narrow spectrum classification that they use. The classification of types of learning into instrumental learning and classical conditioning has research preparations for each member of his class. The maze and lever-pressing apparatus with food for hungry laboratory rats constitute preparations for the study of instrumental learning; the salivary eliciting procedure and eyelid-closing procedures used with dogs and humans constitute research preparations for classical conditioning.

Powerful research preparations have a number of characteristics that are implied in the description of the use of the giant axon of the squid as one preparation for the study of neural activity. The characteristics are: (*a*) the preparations represent the class or process in a *valid* way; (*b*) the preparation yields *reliable* information about the class; (*c*) the process under study is *clear* in the preparation; and (*d*) the preparation is *convenient*.

In the case of classes of psychological processes the evaluation of the validity and reliability of the research preparation is technically feasible but otherwise very difficult. These evaluations are difficult even with psychological tests, such as intelligence tests where techniques for such procedures are well developed. However, I believe that if psychologists are concerned with the question of preparation they are then better able to reach later stages of analysis.

Webb, *et al* (1966) illustrate some of the details for establishing validity and reliability of preparations. In general, these procedures consist of detailed evaluations of the preparation using methods for standardizing the procedures, and methods developed by students of measurement to assess reliability. For example, Ratner (1968) has studied the reliability of the preparation involving learning by planaria. The results of this study were disappointing, since the reliability of performance of the planaria in a learning situation was very low. Wilson and Collins (1967) studied the reliability of observers who scored planarian learning and found that observers agreed with one another in scoring behavior on a single trial, but if we relate this finding to that of Ratner's (1968) we see that the animals are very erratic from trial to trial. There is the further question of whether the behavior changes that the planaria show can be considered as valid examples of learning (Jensen, 1967).

To say that a powerful research preparation shows the process clearly means that it is maximally conspicious and unconfounded by other processes. The laboratory rat, and especially the albino rat, makes a weak preparation for the study of visual factors in learning. Learning for this animal has visual components, but they are confounded with olfactory, auditory, and kinesthetic components. The fact of this confounding means that many control experiments and procedures are necessary to tease out visual factors for this animal. In a powerful research preparation, visual factors should predominate as they would in a preparation that used birds as the test animal. So, we see that within the past few years investigators who are interested in stimulus control of learning involving visual factors use pigeons. Investigators who are interested in maze learning or shock-avoidance learning use rats.

Preparations for comparative psychology involve more than the test animal itself, although we frequently talk about the preparation in terms of the test animal. A preparation includes: *the animal, the test situation, the procedures for measurement,* and *the antecedent conditions.* Weakness at any of these parts of the preparation, such as unreliable measurement or unspecified antecedent conditions, reduces the value of the preparation.

In summary, then, the third stage of comparative analysis involves the identification of powerful research preparations that are coordinated with the classification system established in stage II. You can see that the background information and the content from the study of animal behavior enter into establishing powerful research preparations. The examples of each behavior class that are noted in Table 3 suggest preparations that are useful for the study of each behavior class, although the test situation, etc., are not specified.

Stage IV: Variables. Stage IV of the comparative analysis involves the identification of variables or factors that affect the behavior classes that are identified in stage II. For identification of variables the investigator uses the preparation he developed or found at the previous stage of analysis. If we were using the narrow spectrum classification of types of learning suggested by Hilgard and Marquis (1940), we would begin to search for variables that affect each class using the most powerful preparations of instrumental and classical learning that are available. (Much of the work on identification of variables has already been done for these classes.)

When we are concerned with broad spectrum classification for comparative psychology, a number of variables immediately suggest themselves. These variables are: (*a*) age of the animal; (*b*) sex of the animal; (*c*) species; and (*d*) the many temporal conditions, such as intertrial interval, stimulus duration, trial duration, and trial frequency. If we find that any of these variables affect the behavior, we can then begin to study the interactions among these variables.

Notice that at this stage of comparative analysis, the contributions of general-experimental psychology enter comparative analysis. Notice also the necessity for powerful research preparations where the class of behavior exposes itself in a clear and unconfounded way. If powerful preparations are not available, the investigator will not be able to detect the effects of variables. If very little is known about the behavior process, the investigator may need to use *field* studies to get some hints about the types of variables that affect the behavior. This is frequently done by ethologists and their methods are particularly useful at such a time (Hinde & Tinbergen, 1958; Klopfer & Hailman, 1967). I have used the field method in my research at several points in the study of predator defenses called animal hypnosis (Ratner, 1967).

Stage V: Comparisons and Relations.   One of the most fully developed examples of comparison in psychology comes from the narrow spectrum classification of type of learning developed by Hilgard and Marquis (1940). Following their comparison, Professor Kimble (1961) made another comparison of instrumental and classical learning in a book entitled *Hilgard and Marquis' Conditioning and Learning.* His analysis assumed that the classification of types of behavior modification was valid and that powerful research preparations had been used to identify variables and their effects. Based on these assumptions (some of which are questionable, at least to me), and a detailed examination of the procedures and effects of variables in relation to instrumental and classical learning, Kimble notes that many kinds of experiments remain to be done in order to draw firm conclusions about the relations between instrumental and classifical learning. He goes on to note: "... classical conditioning and instrumental learning possess many features in common. They seem to respond similarly to manipulations of many variables. The only important exception is intermittent reinforcement which is more detrimental to classical than to instrumental conditioning [p. 107]." Kimble then speculates about the general rules or logic for concluding that processes are similar or concluding that they are different. He had gotten to stage V of a narrow-spectrum comparative analysis.

Professor Kimble did not propose that his carefully assembled volume be considered an exercise in comparative analysis, but it is a good example of stage V of the comparative method. This is true for several reasons: (*a*) it compares *behavior processes,* and the comparison of behavior constitutes a domain of psychology; (*b*) the comparison comes after careful development of the earlier stages of analysis; (*c*) the results of the comparison suggest specific problems that require further experimental study.

I had the opportunity to do an exercise in comparative analysis that moved from the preparatory stages, I–IV, to stage V (Ratner, 1967). In this case, I was concerned with a large and unorganized mass of naturalistic and experimental material that had been called "animal hypnosis." Previous attempts to deal with this material had started immediately at stage V, although this was not recognized by the investigators. Pavlov, the father of classical conditioning, related animal hypnosis to inhibitory neural processes (1955); Gilman and Marcuse (1949) related it to fear; and Volgyesi (1966) related it to human hypnosis in a lengthy treatise on hypnosis.

The approach I took for this narrow-spectrum comparative problem included all five stages of comparative analysis. I started by reviewing both formal and informal sources of background information that related to the problem of animals that became immobile. Material from animal behavior and general-experimental psychology were brought together by the comparative method. At stage V, I concluded that the behaviors that were called animal hypnosis were related to the class of behaviors we called *predator defenses*. In keeping with the taxonomy of behavior noted in Table 3 on page 137, these reactions are best described as *immobility display*. I concluded that the responses called animal hypnosis represent one of the kinds of displays animals make when predators attack them. Freezing, secreting offensive chemicals, and piercing vocalizing are other displays in this class of reactions. Now that this tentative comparison is made, we are ready to sharpen our preparation and return to the laboratory and field for more sophisticated study of immobility display. With additional information and thought, I may modify the classification of behavior, find new preparations, or increase my understanding of the effects of variables on this behavior

Stage VI: General Theory. The final stage of comparative analysis involves postulation of the general mechanism or mechanisms that relate all of the behaviors of organisms. In chemistry this took the form of the theory of atomic structure and function, in biology it took the form of the theory of evolution. Earlier attempts at general theory had occurred in both biology and chemistry and these theories were approximations to the later and more adequate ones. In addition, subsequent work in particular stages has led to modification of the statements of general mechanisms. These points illustrate again the continuous interplay among the stages of analysis.

Psychology certainly has no shortage of proposals for general theory; but the theories have shortages at every stage of analysis. Examples of these theories are psychoanalytic theory, generalized forms of learning theory, and generalized forms of neural or chemical theories. The general mechanisms that are proposed by these theories, such as pleasure–pain principles, S–R reinforcement principles, or DNA–RNA principles, have precursors in earlier general theories that were based on even slimmer support. I made a review of mechanisms that have been proposed for the analysis of learning and memory and found every current mechanism in very old writing (Ratner, 1967). So, for example, Aristotle proposed a classification of memory involving short term memory and long term memory and he proposed a general theory to relate these processes. The classification is useful but his theory is inadequate.

It is my premise that general theory and its associated mechanisms will develop from conscientious attention to the three components that appear to be converging into a bona fide comparative psychology. Specifically, this involves the application of the six stages of comparative analysis to the content and ideas of animal behavior and general-experimental psychology.

IV. CONCLUSIONS

Comparative analysis is required when the events under investigation have *diversity*. So, psychology, like a number of other areas such as biology, economics, political science, and even chemistry, require comparative analysis. While the label, comparative psychology, has been used for many decades, it has meant several different things including the uncritical application of comparative biology and capricious comparison. But comparative psychology is in a state of change at this time and three themes are coming together to produce a true comparative psychology. The three themes arise from: animal behavior, general-experimental psychology, and the comparative method, called the stages approach to comparative analysis.

I believe that the stages approach that involves six mutually dependent stages of theory and research will lead to a general theory of behavior. This theory will relate the diversity of behavior of organisms much as the theory of evolution has related the diversity of animal forms.

REFERENCES

Adamson, J. *Born Free*. New York: Pantheon, 1960.
Beach, F. A. *Sex and Behavior*. New York: Wiley, 1965.
Bitterman, M. E. Toward a comparative psychology of learning. *American Psychologist*, 1960, **15**, 704–712.
Bolles, R. C. *Theory of motivation*. New York: Harper, 1967.
Breland, K., & Breland, M. *Animal behavior*. New York: Macmillan, 1966.
Chapanis, A. Men, machines, and models. *American Psychologist*, 1961, **16**, 110–121.
Corning, W. C., & Ratner, S. C. *Chemistry of learning*. New York: Plenum, 1967.
Denny, M. R., & Ratner, S. C. *Comparative psychology*. (Revised ed.) Homewood, Ill.: Dorsey, 1970.
Fraenkel, G. S., & Gunn, D. D. *The orientation of animals*. New York: Dover, 1961.
Gilman, T. T., & Marcuse, F. L. Animal hypnosis. *Psychological Bulletin*, 1949, 141–165.
Guilford, J. P. *Psychometric methods*. New York: McGraw-Hill, 1954.
Hallet, J. P. *Animal Kitabu*. New York: Random House, 1968.
Hilgard, E. R., & Marquis, D. G. *Conditioning and learning*. New York: Appleton, 1940.
Hinde, R. A. *Animal behavior*. New York: McGraw-Hill, 1966.

Hinde, R. A., & Tinbergen, N. The comparative study of species-specific behavior. In A. Roe & G. G. Simpson (Eds.), *Evolution and behavior*. New Haven: Yale Univer. Press, 1958. pp. 251–268.

Hirsh, J. (Ed.) *Behavior-genetic analysis*. New York: McGraw-Hill, 1967.

Jensen, D. D. Polythetic operationism and the phylogeny of learning. In W. C. Corning & S. C. Ratner (Eds.), *Chemistry of learning*. New York: Plenum, 1967. Pp. 43–55.

John, E. R. *Mechanisms of memory*. New York: Academic Press, 1967.

Kantor, J. R. *The scientific evolution of psychology*. Vol. I. Granville, Ohio: Principia Press, 1963.

Kantor, J. R. *The scientific evolution of psychology*. Vol. II. Granville, Ohio: Principia Press, 1968.

Kenk, R. Species differentiation and ecological relations of planarians. In W. C. Corning & S. C. Ratner (Eds.), *Chemistry of learning*. New York: Plenum, 1967. Pp. 67–73.

Kimble, G. A. *Hilgard and Marquis' conditioning and learning*. New York: Appleton, 1961.

Klopfer, P. H., & Hailman, J. P. *Introduction to animal behavior*. Englewood-Cliffs, N. J.: Prentice-Hall, 1967.

Kuo, Z.-Y. *The dynamics of behavior development*. New York: Random House, 1967.

Lenneberg, E. H. *Biological foundations of language*. New York: Wiley, 1967.

Lorenz, K. The comparative method in studying innate behavior patterns. In Symposium of the Society for Experimental Biology. Vol. IV. *Physiological Mechanisms in Animal Behavior*. London and New York: Cambridge Univer. Press, 1950.

Lorenz, K. The nature of instinct. In C. E. Schiller (Ed.), *Instinctive behavior*. New York: International Universities Press, 1957.

Lorenz, K. *Evolution and modification of behavior*. Chicago: Univer. of Chicago, 1965.

Maier, N. R. F., & Schnierla, T. C. *Principles of animal psychology*. New York: McGraw-Hill, 1935.

Marler, P. R., & Hamilton, W. J. *Mechanisms of animal behavior*. New York: Wiley, 1966.

Maslow, A. H. *Motivation and personality*. New York: Harper, 1954.

Pavlov, I. P. *Selected works*. Moscow: Foreign Language Publishing House, 1955.

Ratner, S. C. Effect of extinction of dipper approaching on subsequent extinction of bar pressing and dipper approaching. *Journal of Comparative and Physiological Psychology*. 1956, **49**, 576–581.

Ratner, S. C. Comparative aspects of hypnosis. In J. E. Gordon (Ed.), *Handbook of clinical and experimental hypnosis*. New York: Macmillan, 1967. Pp. 550–588.

Ratner, S. C. Reliability of indexes of worm learning. *Psychological Report*, 1968, **22**, 130.

Ratner, S. C., & Denny, M. R. *Comparative psychology*. Homewood, Ill.: Dorsey, 1964.

Ratner, S. C., & VanDeventer, J. M. Effects of water current on responses of planaria to light. *Journal of comparative and physiological Psychology*, 1965, **60**, 138–140.

Rheingold, H. L. (Ed.) *Maternal behavior of mammals*. New York: Wiley, 1963.

Schiller, C. H. (Ed.) *Instinctive behavior*. New York: International Universities Press, 1957.

Scott, J. P. *Animal behavior*. Chicago: Univer. of Chicago Press, 1958.

Simpson, G. G. Behavior and evolution. In A. Roe & G. G. Simpson (Eds.), *Evolution and behavior*. New Haven: Yale Univer. Press, 1958. Pp. 507–536.

Skinner, B. F. *The behavior of organisms*. New York: Appleton, 1938.

Sluckin, W. *Imprinting and early learning*. Chicago: Aldine, 1965.

Sokal, R. R., & Sneath, P. H. A. *Principles of numerical taxonomy*. San Francisco: Freeman, 1963.

Stokes, A. W. (Ed.), *Animal behavior in laboratory and field*. San Francisco: Freeman, 1968.

Stone, C. P. Introduction. In C. P. Stone (Ed.), *Comparative psychology* (3rd ed.). Englewood Cliffs, N. J.: Prentice-Hall, 1951. Pp. 1–8.

Thorpe, W. H. *Learning and instinct in animals.* London: Methuen, 1956.

Tinbergen, N. *The study of instinct.* London and New York: Oxford Univ. Press (Clarendon) 1951.

Tinbergen, N. *Curious naturalists.* London: Country Life, 1958.

Volgyesi, F. A. *Hypnosis of man and animals.* (2nd ed.) Baltimore: Williams & Wilkins, 1966.

Warden, C. J., Jenkins, T. N., & Warner, L. H. *Comparative psychology.* Vol. I. New York: Ronald Press, 1935.

Warden, C. J., Jenkins, T. N., & Warner, L. H. *Comparative psychology.* Vol. II. New York: Ronald Press, 1936.

Warden, C. J., Jenkins, T. N., & Warner, L. H. *Comparative psychology.* Vol. III. New York: Ronald Press, 1941.

Waters, R. H., Rethlingshafer, D. A., & Caldwell, W. E. *Principles of comparative psychology.* New York: McGraw-Hill, 1960.

Waters, R. H. The nature of comparative psychology. In R. H. Waters, D. A. Rethlingshafer, & W. E. Caldwell (Eds.), *Principles of comparative psychology.* New York: McGraw-Hill, 1960. Pp. 1–17.

Watson, J. B. *Behavior, an introduction to comparative psychology.* New York: Holt, 1967.

Webb, E. J., Campbell, D. T., Schwartz, R. D., & Seechrest, L. *Unobtrusive measures: Nonreactive research in the social sciences.* Chicago: Rand McNally, 1966.

Wilson, R. A., & Collins, G. D. Establishment of a classically conditioned response and transfer of training via cannibalism in planaria. *Perceptual and Motor Skills,* 1967, **24,** 727–730.

Developmental Psychology[1]

LEWIS P. LIPSITT

DEPARTMENT OF PSYCHOLOGY
BROWN UNIVERSITY
PROVIDENCE, RHODE ISLAND

As I understand the charge given me, it should be my purpose here to indicate what I perceive to be important recent trends in the field of developmental psychology, particularly as these have affected my own research pursuits and theoretical inclinations. It will be my aim to provide some historical background to the kind of research which I do, to express some of the biases which characterize the approach of my laboratory to the exploration of the origins of human behavior, and to indicate some areas in which significant advances should be made in the near future.

I shall dwell on the early learning processes of humans, because that is where my research life is, and I will try to reflect on the importance of such processes for a fuller understanding of various applications of knowledge about child development and learning, particularly with respect to educational and psychotherapeutic processes. It is my belief, and I may as well state it

[1] This research was supported by USPHS Grant No. HD 03911.

147

at the outset, that child development or, more specifically and emphatically, the study of learning processes in children is crucial for the advancement of educational and therapeutic programs in a society which so clearly has heavy demand for these.

The science of learning processes in the maturing human deals, after all, with the experiential circumstances which facilitate or retard the educational process, and it relates at the same time to the influence of various classes of events (such as familial circumstances and relationships) which produce psychogenic distresses later in life. Broadly speaking, the science of learning processes *is* the study of the effects of earlier experience on later behavior. Moreover, the study of learning in children inevitably yields findings regarding the effects of individual differences in the determination of behavior, and these are importantly related to the origins and assessment of abilities and achievements, or intelligence. The science of learning processes is thus critical for the full understanding of personality functioning. In order to achieve a high level of understanding within the fields of education and psychotherapy, which are two areas germane to the applied psychology of learning, it will be necessary to make considerably more progress than has yet been possible concerning basic learning processes of humans, particularly in the first few years of life.

I. DEVELOPMENT OF PROFESSIONAL INTERESTS

In contemplating the origins of my own interest in learning processes of infants and children, I cannot help but be struck by the extent to which the potentiality of practical applications dictated my choice of career and the focus of my specific research pursuits within that career. I am also frequently surprised at the response of others when I inform them that I was at one time in a training program to become a clinical psychologist and that, in fact, I worked during my military years entirely in the field of clinical psychology. Apparently a person doing my type of research and carrying the label of experimental child psychologist is not easily perceived as having much concern for the affairs of the world and the well-being of babies. But I can see very clearly that my social welfare motivations, which were obvious before but are apparently subtler now, have shaped the natural history of my scientific concerns and have provided motivational supports when progress in the laboratory was slow.

While working as a clinical psychologist, following master's-level practicum experience, I became appreciative of the propositions, put forth most profoundly by Freud, that (*a*) early experiences constitute important determinants of later behavior, (*b*) all behavior has causes which, in principle, can be discovered given the appropriate scientific investigatory tools, and (*c*) only an empirical approach could possibly result ultimately in a complete understanding of the origins of human behavior and the development of techniques for behavioral remediation when psychological distresses emerge. In my interactions with distressed and disturbed persons, the conclusion gradually emerged that the facts about human development, and most particularly learning processes in the maturing human, are not as yet very well documented, and consequently the practitioner (whether therapist or educator) has very little substantive knowledge on the basis of which to proceed in the formulation of proper educational and reeducational programs for those in need of such services. It was perhaps at about the same time that I became finally and fully convinced that the understanding of learning processes per se would eventually provide the key to the mysteries of personality functioning. My acquaintanceship with the writings of Dolland and Miller (1950), as well as others who were concerned with the accomplishment of a rapprochement between psychoanalytic and learning theories, helped to turn my career attentions in the direction of learning processes of children.

These, then, were some of the personal determinants, along with a few fortuitous circumstances (which should not be belittled), which converged to enable my choice in 1954 of the Iowa Child Welfare Research Station (now the Institute of Child Behavior and Development) at the University of Iowa to conclude my graduate training. The tradition at Iowa turned out to have an exceedingly important influence upon me through its reinforcement (or perhaps better, fortification) of my developing views about the importance of the scientific study of learning processes, for it was at that institution that some well-known studies were conducted on the extreme effects which environmental factors can have on later behavior (e.g., Skeels, 1966; Skeels & Harms, 1948; Skeels, Updegraff, Wellman, & Williams, 1938; Skodak & Skeels, 1949; Wellman, 1940, 1945). It was also at Iowa that Kurt Lewin and Robert Sears had such remarkable impacts on the history of child development research in the United States, Lewin through his insistence upon an empirical and (sometimes) an experimental approach to the study of behavior's causes, and Sears through his adoption of the learning-process approach to the understanding of personality and human development. Actually, Sears introduced during his time at Iowa an approach which has endured perhaps even longer than he would have wished; it was Sears who gave the study of child development and behavior a great thrust ahead in his support of learning theory *propositions* and of the hypothetico-deductive method which he had learned, like Dolland and Miller, at Yale. While some studies of learning processes had been conducted with children prior to the ascendancy of Sears in the field, few of these studies were theoretically based. The Sears orientation, which, it will be remembered, enabled the deduction of displacement behavior from approach and avoidance gradients of the learning theorist (Hollenberg & Sperry, 1951; Sears, Whiting, Nowlis, & Sears, 1953) was such as to give heart to the child psychologist who was then despairing of ever being able to integrate meaningfully the enormous number and variety of functional relationships pertaining to child behavior which by then had become available.

At Iowa, it was not long before the empirical stamp of the institution was thoroughly impressed upon me, through the teachings of such staff members as Boyd R. McCandless, Charles C. Spiker, Alfred Castaneda, Orvis C. Irwin, Howard V. Meredith, and Irene E. Harms. Besides these and other staff members in the child institute, there was the entire Department of Psychology that influenced importantly the experimental child psychology training program through which we graduate students progressed. Needless to say, there was a heavy dosage of the Hull–Spence orientation to the study of learning processes, but I (and I believe most others) had few regrets about this, for the effect of the training was to enhance one's theoretical, method-ological, and philosophy-of-science skills rather than to win students to a monolithic theoretical orientation. The teachings in particular of Spiker, Kenneth W. Spence, I. E. Farber, Judson S. Brown, Don Lewis, Harold Bechtoldt, and Gustav Bergmann enabled the student to examine the credibility of various empirical propositions irrespective of the theoretical source or research bias of the experimenter.

When I say that the move of child psychology toward the assimilation of the learning-theory approach might have been more than Sears expected or wished, I am referring to the fact that Iowa graduates are generally appreciated these days as having overworked the Hull–Spence theory on behalf of the understanding of child behavior. These critics generally suppose that there is more, much more, to the individual child, and more skill involved in the understanding of the whole child, than can possibly be accomplished through the meticulous laboratory techniques and machinations of the learning theorist. Just how these critics have been able to know in advance what are the potentialities and limitations of the learning-theory approach has always been beyond my understanding, so I have simply tried to pursue the facts without any misgivings over the theoretically obsessed or their objectors. It has always seemed to me that the Iowa "philosophy" is frequently misunderstood by others; the fact of the matter is that no one was required to take an oath of subscription to any particular theoretical orientation; rather the investment of "the Iowan" is in the empirical verifica-tion of factual propositions regardless of their theoretical origins.

This is perhaps a rather overpersonalized background of the work which I wish now to describe in some detail. I hope that I have conveyed through this recitation enough background that you will appreciate the sense of elation which I had in 1957 when it became possible, following my work at Iowa, to accept a position at Brown University. A most attractive aspect of the position was that, first, this old and highly respected Department of Psychology was contemplating expansion of its research and teaching resources into the experimental child psychology area, and second, a situation had arisen at Brown whereby there would be available a population of infants (part of a national collaborative project) who would be followed by various scientific and professional personnel through the age of seven years and it would therefore enable the child psychologist to have access to infants. I remember well the communications which I had at that time with the late Professor Harold Schlosberg, then Chairman of the department, whom I asked if it might be possible for me to carry on some much-needed conditioning work with newborns and older infants through the mechanism of the collaborative project. His reply was that it not only would be possible, but that he and his department would be most enthused about that sort of innovation. Harold Schlosberg remained from then until his death a very important facilitator of this work, defending it on occasion when some could not grasp its possible scientific importance or its practical implications, and providing excellent advice on numerous occasions (and insisting that he not be credited). I mention here the influence of Harold Schlosberg on this research program especially to make the point that often our stereotypes of experimentalists and clinicians preclude the possibility of our imagining such people as having multiple interests, complex motivations, and varied loyalties. There are some who cannot imagine Schlosberg being interested in children. But then, there are many who cannot believe that Walter S. Hunter once wrote a chapter on paranoia.

II. A New Direction for Child Psychology

I have already alluded above, perhaps somewhat chauvinistically, to the rather important role I believe the University of Iowa played in the history of the child development movement and the science of child psychology. It must be remembered that the child development field was intent for many years on the development of "maturity-measuring" techniques, i.e., developmental tests, a preoccupation which grew out of the attachment which child developmentalists had for morphological models borrowed from structural biology (Gesell & Ilg, 1949; Harris, 1963). While the morphological models were quite appropriate for studies of physical growth, and although excellent data have been collected by some anthropometrists interested in plotting physical growth attributes as a function of chronological age, the assessment of behavioral properties of the child and the search after causes or explanatory principles underlying these have not yielded an exciting body of facts. Age as an explanatory variable is simply not very illuminating, for although behavior may be correlated well with age (and some behaviors obviously are), it is often the case that the role of age in the relationship does not go beyond the correlational level (Spiker & McCandless, 1954). Perhaps this point is made most clearly by recalling that available data (e.g., that of Smith, 1926) indicate clearly that children's word output or vocabulary increases in an orderly manner with age, just as does the length of sentences spoken by the maturing child. Few persons, however, would be inclined to argue from such data that age has been a direct *cause* of such behavioral output; rather one would suppose that interacting sets of factors have been responsible, such as changes in the neural biochemistry of the child and exposure to certain stimulating or learning conditions, both of these factors themselves functions of age.

The adoption of the morphological model by child developmentalists was in some ways unfortunate, for there emerged a tendency, however unwarranted, toward the simultaneous adoption of a genetic bias with respect to intellectual endowment. This view, reviewed well by Hunt (1961), held that intelligence is essentially determined at birth and that experiential precursors have rather minimal intellectual consequences. Although there were certainly those who obviously did not adopt the extreme hereditary position, the prevailing view probably did inhibit the search for and discovery of the special capacities of infants for assimilation of sensory stimuli and infant response to learning conditions in the environment.

Unfortunately, a middle-of-the-road position with respect to the relative contributions of constitutional and experiential determinants of child behavior is more difficult to enunciate (like many moderate political views) than an extreme position of either sort. It seems that if a person favors or is fascinated by experiential or learning factors in his own research pursuits he is regarded as an environmentalist; on the other hand, if he concentrates upon genetic attributes of the organism, he is regarded as an extreme hereditarian.

I hope the point has now been adequately made that we child developmentalists should avoid the tendency to assess the relative contributions to behavior and development of either constitutional or environmental factors. Anastasi (1958) is correct when she says that such an approach cannot possibly lead us to definitive answers regarding the causes of behavior change; rather than asking *how much* of behavior is attributable to one or another antecedent or determinant, we should be asking *how* each of the pertinent variables does its work.

III. RESEARCH ON NEONATES AND OLDER INFANTS

Twelve years ago, we began a sensory assessment and conditioning laboratory at the Providence Lying-In Hospital, an institution especially affiliated with Brown University for purposes of cooperating in the National Collaborative Project sponsored by the National Institute of Neurological Diseases and Blindness. This collaborative project involved 14 different institutions which collected and processed extensive obstetrical, pediatric, psychological, and speech–hearing data on some 50,000 children throughout the country. As a collaborating institution, Brown University collected newborn data and is still in the process of collecting follow-up data on almost 4000 children, who are administered various standard testing procedures at prescribed ages up to the eighth birthday. The newborn laboratory at the Providence Lying-In Hospital was founded under the auspices of the collaborative project but now continues independently, with the phasing out of the obstetrical portion of the National Collaborative Study. Although much of the research carried out in this newborn laboratory pertains to the study of basic perceptual and learning processes of neonates, we are of the opinion that such research is, or at least will ultimately be, relevant to the socially important search for a better understanding of the origins and possible remediation of such early childhood afflictions as cerebral palsy, mental retardation, and other sensory and learning defects. We have tried in this work to find out what the newborn child can appreciate sensorily, what he may learn, how his psychophysiological and other behavioral characteristics are altered through life experience, and the extent to which very early learning circumstances may have an enduring effect upon later behavior. Needless to say, we are far short of some of the intended goals of this research program presently, partly because we were starting with relatively little information, partly because studies with newborns are sometimes painfully tedious, and partly because successive stages in the buildup of knowledge in this area depend upon the prior achievement of more basic information. For example, in order to study longitudinally the persisting effects of early experience, it is necessary to devise appropriately reliable early learning circumstances, for it is a statistical reality that the long-term predictive power of a given attribute can be no greater than its initial reliability. Our results thus far therefore pertain principally to which behaviors infants may manifest at given ages and the stimulating conditions required to produce them. While we are interested ultimately in the processes underlying change in behavior over extended periods of time, most of the processes with which I shall be concerned here relate to relatively small time durations.

The newborn laboratory in which this work is carried on is equipped with a stabilimeter bed, a polygraph for the permanent recording of various behavioral and autonomic responses, various timing units and stimulating devices for the automatic presentation of stimuli and polygraphic monitoring of such presentations, sterilization equipment, and so on (Lipsitt & DeLucia, 1960). Numerous sensing devices, including electrodes for heart-rate recording, a pneumobelt and associated pressure transducer for recording of breathing, an automatic nipple device (DeLucia, 1967) with associated transducer to allow analog recording of the infant's sucking activity and controlled feeding, a cardiotachometer providing immediate quantitative transformation of the electrocardiograph record, and an integrator associated with the stabilimeter enabling the cumulative recording of body-activity, all provide for a degree of automation that leaves the experimenter relatively free to make close visual observations of the infant. Figures 1 and 2 provide views of the overall laboratory and of a newborn in the experimental situation respectively.

In this laboratory it has been demonstrated that the human newborn (by this will be meant throughout this paper the first four days of life) is quite exceptionally sensitive to differences in intraoral stimulation from moment to moment and that reinforcement contingent upon sucking behavior may either enhance or diminish that activity. In one study, Lipsitt and Kaye (1965) compared the sucking behavior of infants who were provided either with a nipple, a length of surgical tubing, or a nipple–tube alternation on successive trials. This study demonstrated that the baby's sucking rate is greater to an ordinary commercial nipple than it is to a less flexible and less rounded piece of tubing. Furthermore, the group which was administered the nipple and tube on an alternating basis could be seen to have its nipple-sucking behavior diminished temporarily by the previous presentation of the tube, while tube-sucking was enhanced by previous nipple-sucking experience. Perseverative effects of prior experience such as this help to lead us to the conclusion that the newborn human is a creature capable of learning, but it is necessary to provide clear-cut examples of the enhancement of associative processes in order to make the learning argument more forcefully. A subsequent study therefore utilized the tubing as a conditioning stimulus.

Lipsitt, Kaye, and Bosack (1966) administered a dextrose solution through that tube on specified trials to one group of infants in such a manner that these infants received the dextrose in association with tube-sucking. A control group, on the other hand, was given the same amount of dextrose and was administered identical experience with the tube, but in this group tube-sucking and dextrose were not allowed to occur simultaneously. For the control group the dextrose was administered during the intertrial interval and through an oral syringe rather than through the tube. Under these conditions, the experimental group showed a significant increase in tube-sucking behavior, and showed response decrement during extinction trials; the control

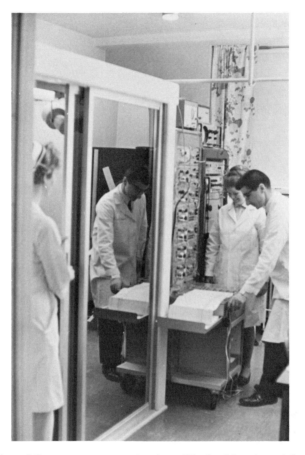

FIG. 1. A view of the sensory assessment and conditioning laboratory at the Providence Lying-In Hospital.

group, on the other hand, showed no such increase in sucking to the tube across trials.

It may be noted that this set of procedures bears certain similarities to classical or respondent conditioning, in that the tube in the mouth may be regarded as a conditioning stimulus while the administration of dextrose solution is analogous to the delivery of the unconditioned stimulus. However, the experimental paradigm bears some similarities as well to operant conditioning procedures. Conceptualized in the latter way, the tube in the infant's mouth assures or at least facilitates the execution of a low-incidence operant behavior which becomes enhanced, relative to the "baseline" level, in the group which is administered dextrose "contingent upon" the occurrence of

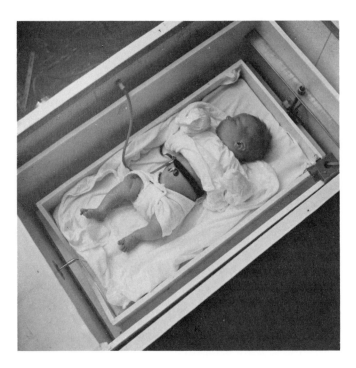

Fig. 2.   A view of a newborn infant in the conditioning laboratory.

that sucking behavior. Consequently, the behavior is increased on test trials following conditioning experience and is diminished during extinction trials.

In the experiment cited above, the control group which did not receive the dextrose reinforcement contiguous with the tube-sucking experience actually showed a relatively large diminution of response to the tube over the entire conditioning session. This tendency for response to wane over trials with successive presentations of a constant stimulus has been quite well documented in the newborn child by numerous researchers. The phenomenon, called habituation, is a particularly useful process for the assessment of sensory capabilities in the very young or otherwise inarticulate organism, for it is possible to determine whether the subject can discriminate among multiple stimuli by utilizing a habituation series followed by a dishabituation procedure.

Engen, Lipsitt, and Kaye (1963) presented two groups of newborns with two odorants (anise oil and asafoetida), each of these groups getting the olfactory stimuli in opposite order. One group received 10 trials of anise followed by 10 trials of asafoetida, and the other group received the two odorants in reverse order. Each of the groups received the first odorant once

again after the second odorant had been administered. The results of the
study clearly indicated that olfactory habituation occurs in the newborn in
that, over the 10-trial runs, stabilimeter activity and respiratory disruption
diminished greatly, and also showed that habituation to one odorant transfers
to a second such that response to the second series is less than if this odorant
were given first. Moreover, dishabituation occurs, as represented by the fact
that recovery of response to the first odorant occurs following administration
of the second odorant (which is a time-out period with respect to the first
stimulus).

Engen and Lipsitt (1965) followed this olfactory study with another in
which neonates were administered an odorant mixture consisting of amyl
acetate and heptanal along with a nonodorous diluent in 20 trials. Following
such trials and without a change in the intertrial interval, tests were given
with one or the other component in solution with the nonodorous diluent.
Figure 3 shows the response over those 10 trials for ten subjects exposed to
the mixture. Following these presentations and the documentation of a
response-decrement phenomenon, the amyl acetate odorant when presented
alone produced recovery of response. The level of response on these recovery
trials was the same as that of a comparable control group (represented by

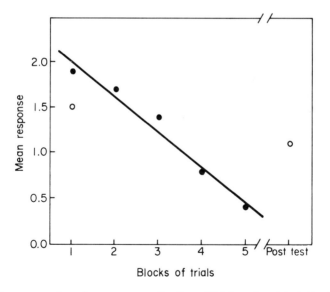

FIG. 3. Average number of responses as a function of trials and post-test stimulus (amyl
acetate). ●: mixture of 50% diethyl phthalate, 33.3% amyl acetate, 16.7% heptanal.
○: 33.3% amyl acetate. Circle at the left indicates basal response to amyl acetate by
independent group of subjects. $R = -0.39\ T + 2.41$. (Reproduced with permission of
authors and publisher, Engen and Lipsitt, 1965).

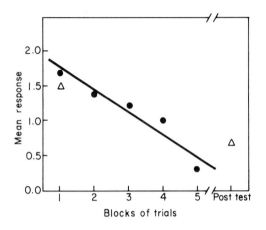

FIG. 4. Average number of responses as a function of trials and post-test stimulus (heptanal). Triangle at left shows basal response ●: mixture of 50% diethyl phthalate, 33.3% amyl acetate, 16.7% heptanal. △: 16.7% heptanal. $R = 0.32\ T + 2.028$. (Reproduced with permission of authors and publisher, Engen and Lipsitt, 1965).

the left open circle, over trial-block 1 in Fig. 3) that had had no trials with the mixture. A comparable group of newborn subjects, whose data are represented in Fig. 4, was administered the heptanal solution following habituation to the mixture. This group also yielded the expected recovery although not to the level produced by amyl acetate.

It was of considerable fascination to us that the ordering of odorant similarity (the order being *mixture* to *heptanal* to *amyl acetate*) was the same as that produced by articulate adults who were requested to make similarity judgments of the same stimuli in a psychophysical experiment. It can thus be concluded that the human newborn is apparently capable of discriminating components of odorant compounds and that higher nervous system function must be somehow implicated in the process. Our reasoning is that the character of the method, involving as it does the later administration of components of a previously presented olfactory compound, is such as to preclude the possibility that the habituation effect which was obtained through the repetitive presentation of a constant stimulus could be attributed to a peripheral or sensory loss of stimulus reception. Rather it appears that the newborn has processed information relating to the "identity" of the compound and that the single constituents of that compound are each clearly identified as discriminably different from the previously experienced odorant mixture.

The most recent work of our newborn laboratory has tried to capitalize as much as possible upon the natural or congenital response repertoire of the infant organism, on the assumption that those responses which are best executed at birth and which are most clearly associated with specific stimulating conditions are the ones which are most likely to be amenable to experiential manipulation. Thus we suppose that response systems which are present early in the fetal life of the child, and which perhaps have the longest evolutionary history and the clearest functional (ethological) significance, will yield most easily to the pressures of environmental necessity, especially if the environmental necessity is one which simply demands that the topography of the response be altered in order to effect greater incidence of reinforcement. In short, the rooting reflex, or the head-turning response to tactile stimulation near the mouth, should be an exceptionally good candidate for conditioned alteration, if the conditioning circumstances imposed upon the child simply demand a more facile or more frequent execution of the response to enable the receipt of greater amounts of food.

With these suppositions in mind, Siqueland and Lipsitt (1966) elaborated upon conditioned head-turning techniques reported earlier by Papousek (1959, 1960, 1961), and utilized tactual stimulation applied to the face along with dextrose reinforcement. The general procedure involved, on each trial, touching the infant at the corner of the mouth, a procedure that characteristically elicited ipsilateral head-turning on approximately 30% of the trials prior to conditioning training. Such rooting behavior is ordinarily considered as a respondent inasmuch as it requires eliciting stimulation. In the present experiments, however, a procedure was used whereby this "respondent" was reinforced as if it were an operant or instrumental behavior on any trial in which the ipsilateral response was executed within a prescribed time limit. Thus on conditioning trials when the infant turned his head appropriately to the tactile stimulus, a bottle was quickly offered into the baby's mouth availing him of the opportunity to suck and be nutritively reinforced. In all three of these experiments conducted by Siqueland and Lipsitt utilizing these techniques, auditory stimuli preceded and continued simultaneously with the tactile stimulus, to determine whether classically conditioned anticipatory head-turning would increase in frequency over conditioning trials, and to provide the possibility of studying discriminative behavior.

In the first study, the procedure consisted of sounding a buzzer for five seconds, during the latter half of which the left cheek of the infant was stimulated. If an ipsilateral response occurred, dextrose was administered for two seconds. Eighteen infants in the second and third days of life received 30 conditioning trials, with 30-second intertrial intervals, while a matched control group received the same stimulations, but were provided the dextrose eight to ten seconds following termination of the tactile stimulus. The matched control group received the dextrose noncontingently with respect to their own behavior; that is, reinforcement in this group was delivered on a schedule dictated by the behavior of matched subjects in the experimental group. For the experimental subjects, response to the tactile stimulus increased over a one-half hour training period from approximately 30 to 80%, while the control group merely declined in frequency of ipsilateral head-turning, presumably due to habituation of the nonreinforced rooting reflex. The results of this experiment are presented in Fig. 5.

A further elaboration of this conditioned head-turning technique involved the utilization of two groups of newborns, two to four days of age, who were provided with differential reinforcement for two responses, left and right head-turning. In this study two different auditory stimuli were utilized, a tone and buzzer, with trials being alternated between left and right cheeks, and with buzzer associated with stimulation on one side and tone with stimulation on the other. Tone and buzzer were each positive stimuli for half of the infants, and a basal "test" enabled the experimenters to apply positive

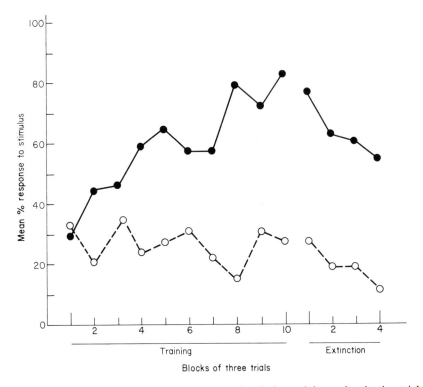

FIG. 5.   Mean percent responses to eliciting stimulus during training and extinction trials for experimental and control groups. ●—●: experimental group ($N = 18$). ○ - - - ○: control group ($N = 18$). (Reproduced with permission of authors and publisher, Siqueland & Lipsitt, 1966.)

(reinforced) training to the less-preferred head-turning side. For the subjects in the experimental group, dextrose was delivered, following ipsilateral turns to the positive stimulus (for example, tone plus touch to the left), but not following turns to the negative stimulus (for example, buzzer plus touch to the right). As in the first study, control infants received the same number of reinforcements, but dextrose was delivered on a delayed basis following the tactile stimulation and *not* contingent upon head-turning. Learning was reflected through relative shifts in percentages of responding to the positive and negative stimuli over trials. The experimental group rose in responding to the positive stimulus from approximately 20 to 75%, while the control group merely declined from 20%. It was thus concluded that learned differentiation of head-turning behavior in the newborn child can be accomplished within a relatively short experimental session.

In still a third variation on this conditioned head-turning method, Siqueland and Lipsitt next utilized the two auditory stimuli as positive and negative cues for reinforcement on only one side of the face to determine whether a still more difficult discrimination might be learned by newborn infants. In this study, 16 infants between 48 and 116 hours of age were divided into two groups. For the first group, the tone was positive and the buzzer negative, while for the second group, buzzer was positive and tone negative. The method was such that head-turns in response to stimulation of the right cheek in the presence of one auditory stimulus were reinforced, but such right head-turns in the presence of the other auditory stimulus resulted in no such reinforcement. After such training, the positive stimulus became the negative, and the negative stimulus became positive for both groups, thus enabling the study of reversal learning in a second facet of the study. As in the previous studies, a 30-second intertrial interval was used, and the tactile stimulation coincided with the last half of the auditory stimuli. The results of this study may be seen in Fig. 6. Responding increased markedly to the positive stimulus from a level of about 20% to approximately 70%, while response to the negative stimulus changed little during the first phase of the study. When the stimulating conditions were reversed, behavior shifted appropriately such that by the end of this phase the previously negative but now positive stimulus produced more right head-turning responses than the now negative stimulus.

With these experiments it became especially clear that the newborn child adapts remarkably to the learning circumstances that the environment may provide, particularly when these learning conditions are crucially relevant to a well-elaborated response system such as that involving head movement, sucking, and food ingestion. It should be added that in none of the three experiments did the infant subjects tend to demonstrate increases in classical anticipatory responding during the sound-stimulus presentations which preceded the onset of the tactile stimulus. The effect of the training condition

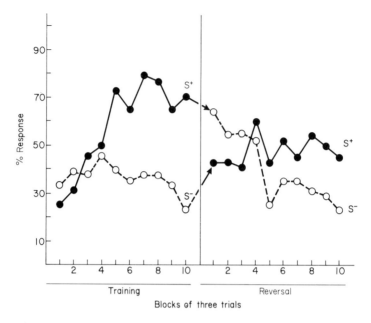

FIG. 6. Comparison of percentage responses to positive and negative stimuli during original training and reversal trials. (Reproduced with permission of authors and publisher, Siqueland & Lipsitt, 1966.)

seems to have been in *potentiating* an operant response system of the infant. A low-frequency respondent was operantly conditioned through the presentation of reinforcement contingent upon the appearance of the response. It is apparent from the differential behavior demonstrated in the third experiment of the series, however, that the auditory stimuli did have discriminative or signal functions for the infant; acquisition of the differential behavior to the positive and negative stimuli could not possibly have occurred had the infants not "used" the auditory stimuli discriminatively.

In another study of conditioned head-turning, Siqueland (1968) further capitalized upon the ethological or functional importance of this response system by treating it as a free operant. Continuous polygraphic monitoring of the infant's head-turning activity, along with the utilization of a protractor arrangement for making rapid assessments of magnitude of head-turn, enabled Siqueland to reinforce immediately, during conditioning periods, all head-turns of 10° or greater in either direction. An interesting aspect of the present study is that the reinforcer used involved only the insertion of a blank nipple or "pacifier" into the infant's mouth for a prescribed time; no nutrient was provided.

Three groups of eight infants, all in their third and fourth days of life, were administered five-second presentations of the nonnutritive nipple for reinforcement. The experimental procedure was such as to allow comparison of three reinforcement schedules. The sequence of events was as follows: (*a*) three-minute baseline period, (*b*) 25 reinforcements delivered under one of three schedules, (*c*) five-minute extinction period. (*d*) 15 additional reinforcements, and (*e*) a three-minute reextinction period. Training in a continuous reinforcement (CRF) group was such that each successive 10° turn was reinforced until 25 such reinforcements had been obtained. The second group received a ratio schedule such that reinforcements occurred early in learning in a 2 : 1 ratio and later in a 3 : 1 ratio. The third group was actually reinforced for *not* engaging in head-turning activity. This "pause group" received the nipple after each 20-second period in which no 10° movement occurred. The three groups, then, were equivalent with respect to numbers of reinforcements received prior to each extinction phase, although reinforcement patterns varied.

Figure 7 shows that large differences in behavior occurred in the three groups during the extinction phases. In line with most data comparing ratio reinforcement schedules with continuous reinforcement, the ratio group produced reliably more responses, and the pause group emitted the smallest number of responses. While the Siqueland and Lipsitt (1966) study provided some of the clearest evidence of "controlled-operant" conditioning (Spiker, 1960, p. 390), the Siqueland (1968) study demonstrated the most striking free-operant conditioning yet documented in human newborns. Moreover, the Siqueland study clearly revealed that the opportunity to suck nonnutritively may serve as a very powerful reinforcing event for the newborn child.

As might be expected, many of the response assessment procedures developed over the past decade in work with young infants are likely to have significant implications for the more refined cataloging of the discriminative capacities of the inarticulate infant. Because it is impossible to ask the infant to report to us when he detects a difference between stimuli, or when he notes the similarity, it is necessary to devise autonomic and behavior measures which have some likelihood of reflecting the differential response of the infant to distinctive stimuli. We have already seen, in some of the olfactory research reported earlier (Engen, Lipsitt & Kaye, 1963; Engen & Lipsitt, 1965), that the habituation procedure followed by the introduction of dishabituation trials constitutes one method of documenting the discriminative ability of the newborn. Another procedure that could possibly be used would be one like that in the third head-turning conditioning experiment of Siqueland and Lipsitt (1966). In that study, the newborns showed clearly through their discriminative head-turning behavior that they detected the difference between the tone and the buzzer which served as positive and negative stimuli. The

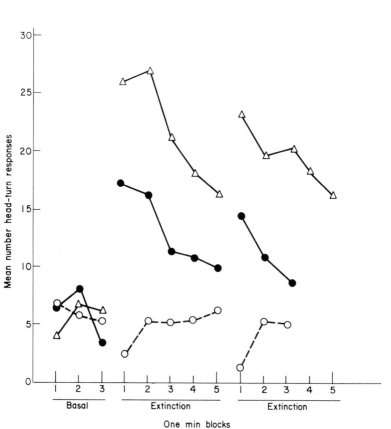

Fɪɢ. 7. Mean number of head-turns for three groups of newborns under three different conditions of reinforcement. The data plotted are for the basal and two extinction phases only. The ratio group ($\triangle$—$\triangle$, $N = 8$) received a partial reinforcement schedule, the CRF group ($\bullet$—$\bullet$, $N = 8$) received continuous reinforcement, and the Pause group ($\bigcirc$ - - -$\bigcirc$, $N = 8$) was reinforced during conditioning periods for refraining from head-turning. (Reproduced with permission of author and publisher, Siqueland, 1968.)

foregoing techniques, however, are rather tedious and time consuming for deployment on behalf of stimulus-differentiation objectives, so we are presently betting more on a recently devised technique that may have psycho-physical utility.

The Soviet investigator Bronshtein (1958) reported, with his colleagues, the fascinating finding that suppression of ongoing behavior in infants may be induced through the presentation of exteroceptive stimulation. The "Bronshtein effect" is represented as follows. If an infant is sucking on a nipple, the sudden introduction of a sound, odorant, or other stimulus tends to disrupt the sucking pattern and sometimes cause the sucking behavior to cease entirely for a period of time. Although Bronshtein reported that habituation of this disruption tends to occur with repetitive exposure to the stimulus, the sucking interruption method may be used for documentation of sensory reception irrespective of whether such habituation occurs.

Semb and Lipsitt (1968) recently conducted a study in which the suppression of sucking effect was demonstrated in newborns. In this study a tone was sounded on occasions when the infant was sucking but was also sounded on other occasions when the infant was not sucking. This enabled the separate documentation of both sucking suppression (like that of Bronshtein) and sucking instigation. When the infant was not sucking, activation of sucking was readily induced through presentation of the auditory stimulus. The sucking activation phenomenon, in fact, tended to occur considerably more frequently than did the sucking suppression phenomenon.

The specifics of this study were as follows. Thirty newborns received a series of 91 db acoustic stimuli, each of one second duration. The infants' respiration activity and body movement were monitored polygraphically, and an event marker simultaneously recorded presentations of the tone. The sucking behavior of the infants was continuously monitored on the polygraph, and the automatic nipple (DeLucia, 1967) remained in the infant's mouth throughout the experimental session. Control or "mock" trials were given throughout the session to provide an indication of basal sucking changes in the absence of any acoustic stimuli, and these control trials were recorded polygraphically like the auditory trials.

A suck was defined in terms of the magnitude of deflection of the polygraph pen connected with the sucking apparatus. At any given time the subject could be sucking or not. Under the sucking condition he might either stop or not stop sucking when the auditory stimulus was sounded. Similarly, under the nonsucking condition, the infant might either start sucking or not. A minimal intertrial interval of approximately 15 seconds was employed, but the tone or the "mock" stimulus were administered only if, after the intertrial interval, the baby had been in either a sucking or not-sucking state for at least two seconds. Whether a given trial was a suppression or an activation test depended solely, then, upon the sucking behavior of the infant at the appointed time of stimulation. The data, shown in Fig. 8, were treated in terms of probability of change in sucking condition as a function of stimulus (or "mock" stimulus) presentation. Comparison of control trials with stimulus presentation trials indicated that response of either type, sucking suppression or sucking instigation, was reliably greater when tones were used than when "mock" stimuli were used. Thus the data clearly indicate that the particular auditory stimulus utilized in this study was unquestionably heard by the subjects. Moreover, the phenomenon of

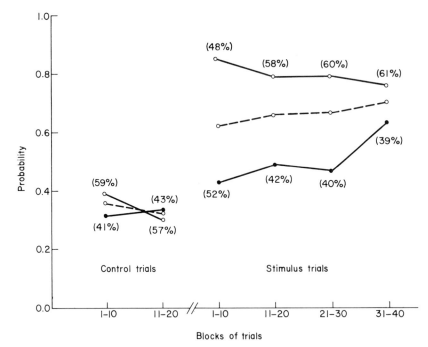

FIG. 8. Probabilities of response initiation, P(AS/NS), ○—○; response cessation P(NS/AS), ●—●; and change in state of either type P(CS) ○ - - ○. Probabilities are plotted as a function of blocks of 10 successive control and stimulus trials, respectively. Percentages, in parentheses, refer to proportion of trials subject was in each conditional state prior to trial initiation. (Reproduced with permission of authors and publisher, Semb & Lipsitt, 1968.)

sucking instigation or activation occurred with reliably greater frequency than did the phenomenon of sucking suppression. For at least the particular auditory stimulus utilized in this study, habituation of neither sucking suppression nor sucking instigation occurred over trials. Success in converting the suppression and instigation data to likelihood ratios led the authors to comment on the psychological usefulness of the technique as follows (Semb & Lipsitt, 1968):

The method described here and response measures, as documented, appear likely candidates for the study of sensory processes in the infant. The method is flexible in that it can be used regardless of the child's sucking rate, as long as the rate meets some minimal arbitrary criterion. Response cessation and response initiation are inversely related; thus in an infant sucking at a high rate, response cessation will indicate sensitivity to environmental changes, but in an infant sucking at a low rate, response initiation or enhancement will indicate his perception of sensory events. In the analysis of the data one can consider the conditional probabilities of both measures, either as separate entities compared with control trials, or in terms of likelihood ratios [p. 596].

Thus the technique enables, at least in principle, the computation of likelihood ratios for a series of stimuli, utilizing both sucking suppression and instigation such that the presence and magnitude of discriminability of the series of stimuli could be determined for each individual subject.

It has become apparent, from some of the studies which we have recently conducted involving the simultaneous recording of heart rate and sucking behavior, that these two response systems are quite related. We have seen, for example, what we have termed a "heart-rate mounding" effect, which involves temporary enhancement of heart rate during sucking bursts. Normal newborn sucking activity tends to occur in volleys, separated by interburst intervals, as seen in Fig. 9. As may also be observed, there is a tendency for the cardiotachographic record to reflect the waxing and waning of heart rate coincident with the onset and offset of sucking bursts. Further research relating to this interesting phenomenon is in progress to determine whether the extent to which this heart-rate mounding constitutes an individual difference variable which may be predictive of later behavioral measures, and to determine as well whether the superimposition of exteroceptive stimulation in the presence of the heart-rate mounding tends to further accentuate the mound. If this turns out to be the case, as we suspect it is from preliminary

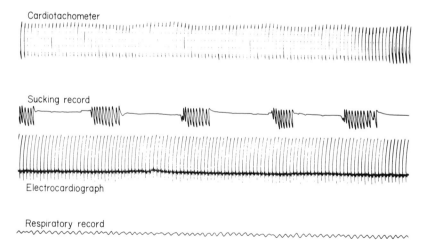

FIG. 9. Polygraph record from newborn showing relation of "heart-rate mounding" to sucking behavior. Bottom pen represents respiration, next pen up is basic electrocardiograph recording, next pen is sucking activity, and top pen is electrocardiographic transformation of heart-rate. It may be noted that when a sucking burst commences heart rate quickens (represented by increased density of beats on electrocardiograph pen and shortened cardiotachograph pen-swings.)

data, it is possible that some composite of the sucking response measure and heart rate may constitute an interesting dependent variable relevant to the "excitability" of the very young human.

Numerous response systems in the human newborn seem to be interrelated in quite interesting ways. The coincidence of the sucking and cardiac response systems just mentioned is one example of this sort. Some of these inter-relationships seem to have an obviously functional symbiotic significance. For example, a touch to the baby's cheek near the mouth not only elicits a head-turning response ("rooting reflex") but tends also to potentiate sucking activity as well. Very frequently as the baby engages in the head-turning activity the tongue and lips can be seen to engage in anticipatory sucking activity (Babkin, 1953).

Perhaps an even more interesting example of the synergistic action of seemingly independent response systems, also documented by Babkin, is the tendency for the newborn child to respond to pressure on the palms with a turn of the head toward midline and a simultaneous opening of the mouth ("the Babkin reflex"). Bruner (1968) has recently described the intricate interplay between visual fixation and hand manipulation behaviors in the course of development within the first year of life. Such response systems seem particularly suited for modification through learning experiences, partly because of their ontogenetic precocity which facilitates their unconditioned occurrence, and partly because of the apparent functional utility of these responses in enabling the infant to survive and thrive.

As has been pointed out, the head-turning response is remarkably sus-ceptible to learned alteration within the newborn period (Papousek, 1967; Siqueland & Lipsitt, 1966). Kaye (1965) has shown that it is also possible to condition the Babkin reflex during the newborn period, utilizing arm movement or kinesthetic stimulation as the conditioning stimulus. Bruner's observations of infants as they age suggest strongly that increased opportunity to practice eye–hand coordinations increases the infant's facility in engaging in this type of activity, until the infant's independent eye and hand response systems seem eventually to anticipate one another.

At the risk of seeming overly anthropomorphic (or is it "adultomorphic?") it would not miss the mark by far to suggest that those response systems of the young infant which are performed with the greatest ease, grace, or facility tend to be the ones which are probably most subject to alteration through the superimposition of environmental stimulation. The conditioning circum-stance will quite possibly "take" best if the stimulus features of the environ-ment facilitate the organism's accomplishment of a complete behavior chain, such as might occur through the introduction of dextrose reinforcement contingent upon an infant's head-turning activity when stimulated on the cheek. Thus it is well for investigators of early conditioning phenomena in children to avail themselves of whatever ecological and ethological information is available concerning the intricate and multifaceted response systems of the age organism under study. Because so little descriptive information of this sort is available, especially with the newborn child, it usually becomes necessary for each investigator to become his own ethologist.

I should now like to turn my attention to the technique of "conjugate reinforcement," a procedure for inducing learned changes in behavior which capitalizes greatly on the ability of the young child to utilize one response system in the service of another. In studies of learning processes in infants a major objective is to seek environmental events or stimulating conditions which tend to promote and sustain some observed behavior. Much of the behavior of infants and young children, and perhaps even that of adults as well, seems to have a self-reinforcing and thus self-perpetuating character. Systematic attempts to include such behaviors within a theoretical framework have only recently begun. For example, White (1959) has introduced the term "competency striving" for those instances of behavior which draw upon internal stimulation and satisfaction for their motivational energization, rather than the obvious reduction of some somatic drive condition. The suggestion, like that of Butler (1953), who used the term "curiosity motivation," is that the sheer exposure to sensory stimulation and the opportunity to engage in behavior which yields further novel stimulation or provides opportunity for mastery of a task can serve just as well as the so-called primary motivators (e.g., food and water for hungry and thirsty organisms). Harlow, Harlow, and Meyer (1950) have used the term "manipulation drive" to refer to behavior which occurs in the absence of the traditional primary drives. Pfaffmann (1960) has spoken aptly of these captivating experiences and quests as involving "the pleasures of sensation." J. McV. Hunt (1965) speaks of infants as having needs for sensory inputs and he suggests that the particular kind of sensory input sought by the infant may be quite different at successive ages. While the older child tends to be a novelty-seeking organism, more frequently the young infant seeks what Hunt calls "recognitive familiarity," which is to say that he tends toward conservatism with respect to stimulus heterogeneity.

A rather interesting technique involving the administration of reinforcement to infants was originated by Lindsley and his colleagues (Lindsley, Hobika, & Etsten, 1961; Lindsley, 1962, 1963), who utilized a type of reinforcement that promises to have considerable applicability in the study of infant behavior. *Conjugate reinforcement* utilizing sensory stimulation, the prototype of which is the hand-generator flashlight in which illumination intensity is directly controlled by the rate and pressure of response on a trigger or other handle, is implemented by presenting a continuously available event contingent upon some prescribed behavior. The event's intensity varies directly and immediately with response strength, manifested in such aspects as rate or intensity. Unlike episodic reinforcement schedules of the usual type, such as the delivery of food pellets or grains (or candies for children), conjugate reinforcement is characterized by continuous availability in amounts commensurate with some response characteristic.

Conjugate reinforcement strikes many observers as more like "real life" for infants than episodic intrusions of reinforcement events. When the infant sucks on a nipple, for example, the amount of liquid obtained is a function of the frequency and pressure characteristics of the response. As the infant sucks more rapidly or with greater vigor he has the opportunity to optimize his own reinforcement intake. Under the conjugate reinforcement procedure, the child acts to produce his own stimulus intake, and he has the opportunity to set his response level to accord with his need for the stimulation available. This is essentially what an infant does when he lies supine in the crib or on the floor turning his head back and forth, moving his eyes, and adjusting other portions of his body to optimize visual stimulation.

Our first utilization of the conjugate reinforcement technique was with 12-month-old children who were placed on a seat in front of an apparatus containing a clear plastic panel (Lipsitt, Pederson, & DeLucia, 1966). The infant's response to this panel activated a power supply which was capable of varying the degree of illumination behind the panel and in the apparatus. Opportunity to see inside this otherwise darkened box was proportional to the infant's rate of response, which produced higher brightnesses with higher rates and lesser illumination with lower rates. Cessation of responding caused the inner box to go dark. Within the viewing box was an attractively colored clown figure attached to a motor shaft which caused the clown to rotate continuously. Cumulative responses were recorded by reading electrical counters every 15 seconds. A basal period involving no reinforcement was followed by a conditioning phase during which the visual reinforcement was available in increasing amounts with increasing rate of response. Extinction, reconditioning, and reextinction sessions followed. Infants of 12 months of age showed reliable increases in responding under these conditions in as short a session as 15 minutes, and diminution of such behavior was apparent upon withdrawal of the conjugate reinforcement contingency.

Recently Rovee and Rovee (1969) have reported on a study utilizing their own two-month-old son and other children of the same age in a study which utilized dancing mobiles hanging above the infants' cribs as the rein-forcer for limb activity. Uzgiris and Hunt (1965) had previously observed, in a study of their own involving the use of mobiles, that infants of about this age seem to sense the effect their own body movements have upon mobiles hanging above them; some seem fascinated not only with the moving visual stimulus but with the opportunity to effect the movement themselves.

To the extent that this is so, such a state of affairs would be an example of Butler's (1953) "curiosity motivation," or the "manipulation drive" of Harlow *et al.* (1950). In the Rovee study, the infants were first exposed to the mobile for several weeks prior to the experimental day. For the experimental session, the infants' leg movements became the response of interest and observations of leg responses were made from one end of the crib outside of the child's view. First a three-minute baseline period was administered during which each child's basal level of right-foot kicks was counted. Following this, a 15-minute acquisition period was instituted, in which the mobile was connected to the child's right leg with a light string such that increases in leg movement would result in commensurate increases in mobile activity. This conjugate reinforcement phase was followed by a five-minute extinction session with the string disconnected. It was possible to continue the session with two subjects for a 46-minute period involving a ten-minute reacquisition session followed by five minutes of reextinction. For four of the children, the experimental session was terminated after the first extinction condition. The data for the six experimental subjects are shown in Fig. 10, in comparison with two control groups receiving identical but noncontingent visual stimulation.

The control groups establish that the enhancement of leg-kicking activity

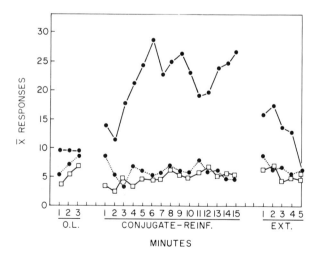

FIG. 10. Mean response rate as a function of reinforcement condition over 46 minutes. ●—●, conjugate reinforcement group; ● - - - ●, noncontingent visual group (no cord); □ — □, noncontingent visual and touch group (cord attached). (Repro - duced with permission of authors and publisher, Rovee & Rovee, 1969.)

in the experimental subjects was attributable to an acquisition or associative process and not due merely to an increase in excitement with increased visual stimulation. The data quite clearly indicate that reinforcement provided by the visual feedback enhanced operant leg-flexion responses. In addition to documenting that limb movement increased, relative to operant level, when the mobile was "hot" and that detachment of the string resulted in diminution of leg activity, the Rovees also observed that the infant responses changed over the course of conditioning from gross body activity to refined and smooth limb-thrusts after experience with the cord attached to the leg. Moreover, bursts of kicking were often followed by long pauses, during which the infant's eyes remained fixed on the now-swaying mobile figures.

Smith and Lipsitt (in preparation) have also documented such conditioning through the use of conjugate mobile reinforcement and have noted that in the course of conditioning the infants often stop to "test" the effect they are apparently having on their own visual environment. Rather than engaging in continuous leg-kicking activity during "hot" periods, the leg thrusts occur in bursts and pauses, with the infant seeming to pause for assimilation of the differential consequences of his activity and inactivity. Testing her own son, Mrs. Smith conducted a study in which she repeatedly tested the child between two and five months of age with numerous mobile objects varying in color, form, and auditory stimulation. An automatic counter was attached to the infant's limb simultaneously with attachment of the cord leading to the mobile. In this study, the two-month-older learned quickly to move his limb appropriately to activate the visual reinforcer, and limb movement coincided, in successive conditioning and extinction periods, with the availability of reinforcement. The data from this child indicated that infants of this age will apparently respond in a mobile-activation setting for long durations without great fatigue or boredom. In addition, it appears, as may be seen in Fig. 11, that the mobile technique may be useful in determining discriminative abilities and stimulus preferences of infants as young as two months old.

An interesting observation made in this study was that after repetitive conditioning and testing with the mobiles being controlled by the infant, the introduction of an extinction period sometimes results in the occurrence of crying and other fussy behavior. Such behavior indicates the presence of a frustration state occasioned by the absence of expected mobile movement when the infant's limb is moved, and such occurrences indicate further the apparently powerful effect which conjugate reinforcement may have upon the very young child. However, because such agitated behavior is in opposition to the usual indicant of extinction behavior, namely diminution of leg-kicking responses, the occurrence of this type of response usually interferes with the recording of the response. It has been found that the crying

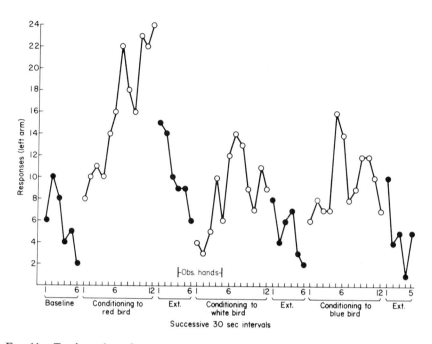

FIG. 11. Total number of responses from one 76-day-old subject in mobile conjugate reinforcement learning situation, over successive phases of testing. Number of responses increases during conditioning phases relative to baseline and extinction phases. More responses are shown to the red stimulus than either the white or blue stimulus. (Reproduced with permission of authors, Smith & Lipsitt, in preparation.)

behavior can often be eliminated merely by resuming the conditioning circumstance, i.e., reconnecting the mobile and the child.

Siqueland has evolved an ingenious technique, in the Brown University infant laboratories, for the extensive study of babies' visual exploratory behavior made possible through the execution of sucking behavior by the infant. Siqueland's conjugate reinforcement situation is instrumented in such a way that when the infant engages in high-intensity sucks on an automatic nipple device, the illumination of slides projected on a screen in the infant's line of vision is commensurately enhanced. The situation is a good example of synergy between two seemingly independent response systems, for infants even as young as one month of age seem quite quickly (in one session) to optimize their visual stimulation by adjusting their sucking behavior appropriately, either producing high-intensity sucks to maximize the screen's illumination or even refraining from engaging in such sucking behavior if *this* condition now maximizes visual intake.

One of Siqueland's (1969) studies divided 30 infants into three groups, a reinforcement group (Group R), a stimulus withdrawal group (Group W), and a baseline control (Group C). The latter ten subjects yielded a baseline reference for 10 minutes of nonreinforced sucking, while the other two groups were administered a 13-minute session of conditioning, extinction, reconditioning, and reextinction. Reinforcement occurred for Group R contingent upon sucking in the conditioning period, while in Group W sucking produced withdrawal of the visual stimulus, each high-amplitude suck in the latter group occasioning a five-second delay in onset of the picture on the screen. In both of the conditioning groups, chromatic slides showed cartoon figures,

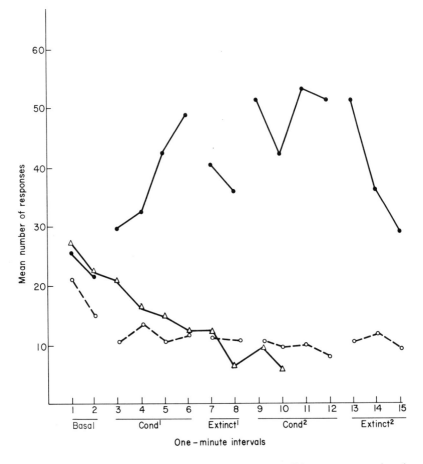

FIG. 12. Mean number of responses for three different conditions over successive phases of testing. ●—●: sucking reinforcement group. ○ - - ○: stimulus withdrawal group. △—△: baseline group. (Reproduced with permission of author, Siqueland, 1969.)

pictured faces, and other forms for 30 seconds each in four-minute conditioning blocks. As can be seen in Fig. 12, Group R produced rapid acquisition of high-amplitude sucking, while Group C did not change. Group W decreased slightly in amount of high-amplitude sucking with the overall effect of the experiment clearly showing that visual stimulation does indeed function as a reinforcer to maintain sucking activity in infants.

In another study, Siqueland has demonstrated that sucking behavior in 12-month-olders, which is by this age at a relatively low level compared with earlier sucking behavior of infants, may be established again quite quickly through the use of visual feedback. One group of ten infants received three replications of a set of four stimuli over two four-minute sessions while a second group received a single replication of an eight-simulus set. Striking sucking-rate increases for both groups occurred as compared with baseline controls of the same age, and response decrement followed reinforcement termination. An additional effect obtained in this study was that of satiation resulting from repetitive stimulus presentation in the four-stimulus group as compared with the high and stable response rates for the eight-stimulus group, the latter having been administered the less repetitive series of stimuli.

IV. Promising Recent Research Developments

I should like to draw this presentation to a conclusion by mentioning two recent developments in our infant laboratories, and to say a word about applications and prospects for the future understanding of infant behavior (and hence human development). The first of these developments, recently achieved by Siqueland (1969), relates to important effects obtained with premature infants through the administration of compensatory handling and learning experiences. Work with the premature infant is particularly exciting for a number of reasons. First, examining the capabilities of the premature infant prior to the normal date of birth gives some insight into the perceptual and learning prowess of the as yet unborn infant. This is not strictly true, of course, for the infant once born, however prematurely, can never be quite the same physiologically or psychologically as the fetus of the same age. In all likelihood, neural structures are affected by extrauterine experience just as lung tissue is altered by the changed respiratory condition of the child after birth. Nevertheless, documentation of learning capacity in the premature infant prior to normal date of birth may give some clues as to the extent to which normal neonatal learning might be facilitated if appropriate techniques could be developed.

Another reason that premature children are of considerable intrinsic interest is that this class of children as a group is well known to be in developmental jeopardy for years after birth, presumably as a result of the handicap of not having benefit of the full fetal period or as a result of some prenatal aberration which itself precipitated or caused the premature birth. Premature infants are more subject than full-term babies to perinatal death, they contribute heavily to populations of the cerebral palsied, the mentally retarded, school failures, and so on. In short, this is a group of infants for whom significant advances might be made physiologically and psychologically with the advent of new techniques of care.

It has been suggested by a previous participant in this National Science Foundation Institute in Psychology, Barbara Rothschild (1967), among others, that the considerable social and stimulus isolation to which the premature infant is subjected under routine care procedures for premature babies may be a contributing factor to the eventually high incidence of emotional disturbance in this group of people. In a study conducted by Siqueland, premature infants participating in a stimulus-enrichment program received daily handling both between and during feedings by nurses especially trained in the care of the premature. Some simple conditioning procedures were also instituted in which the babies were trained to keep their eyes open in order to receive nonnutritive sucking reinforcement and auditory (vocal) feedback. When the eyes-open behavior of those trained infants was compared with comparable behavior in a control group receiving only noncontingent stimulation of this kind, evidence was obtained of a reliable conditioning effect over the course of a ten-day training period. Premature infants aged 5–15 days, then, displayed operant conditioning behavior.

Of further interest in the Siqueland compensatory-handling study is the fact that when handled and nonhandled premature babies were compared at four months of age on the Siqueland visual reinforcement task, the sucking behavior of the two groups was very different. Figure 13 shows the conditioned sucking behavior for five sets of twins, one member of each pair having been handled and the other member a nonhandled subject while under care in the premature nursery. At four months of age the five experimental and five control infants were given 18 minutes of conditioning with visual patterns. Four of the five handled twins sucked at higher rates for visual reinforcement than their control pairs. All five of the handled subjects produced evidence of conditioning, while only two of the five matched controls showed evidence of such conditioning.

In addition, Siqueland has compared the conditioning performance of independent (nonsibling) groups of 16 handled and 16 nonhandled prematures in the same task with the result that the differences are essentially the same as those found for the differentially treated twins. It appears at this stage that the compensatory handling and stimulation procedure with prematures results in better learning performance at four months of chronological age. We believe that part of the developmental deficit which premature

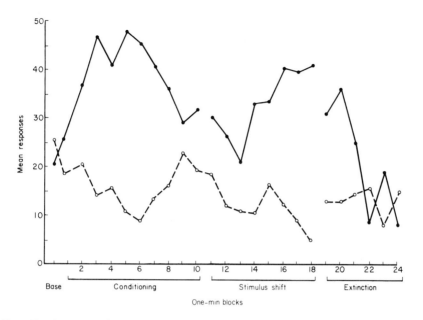

FIG. 13. Mean number of responses made by experimental and control twins over successive phases of testing. ●—●: experimental. ○ - -○: control. (Reproduced with permission of author, Siqueland, 1969.)

infants characteristically show is due to the general stimulus deficits to which the premature is routinely subjected simply in the course of routine care. It should be emphasized that the nonhandled prematures in the studies just described were not administered a deficit or deprivation condition but were simply provided with the usual care accorded the premature infant in a modern lying-in hospital.

Finally, I have been fascinated and challenged recently by the study of infant cardiac reactivity to exteroceptive stimulation. Numerous studies, reviewed by Graham and Clifton (1966) and Graham and Jackson (in press), have indicated that the phenomenon of cardiac deceleration is quite rare in the human newborn, although this characteristic of heart-rate responding is frequent, if not typical, in the older infant. Graham and her colleagues, largely on the basis of studies utilizing auditory stimulation which seems to yield mostly cardiac accelerative responses in the newborn, have suggested that acceleration is part of a defensive response system, while deceleration is relevant to more mature orienting behavior (Sokolov, 1963). Recently, I and a student, Carol N. Jacklin (also a former participant in these National Science Foundation Institutes) discovered quite serendipitously that cardiac deceleration seems to occur in the newborn when an olfactory stimulus of moderate intensity is used as the stimulus. We were conducting an experiment in which we had hoped to document perseveration or transfer over a two-day period of an habituation effect in the newborn child (an objective which, incidentally, failed). When we looked at the heart-rate records, it was apparent that immediately following the onset of the olfactory stimulus, a preponderance of decelerative responses first occurred which only after a few seconds was supplanted by the more characteristic and longer lasting accelerative component. Figure 14 shows the comparison of heart-rate activity, with respect to both accelerations and decelerations, in an experimental group which received the odorant, and a control group which received only mock or blank trials (i.e., no odorant). The assessment of accelerative and decelerative heart-rate occurrences was determined on the basis of comparison of each of the 20 heart-beats following stimulation with the heart-rates represented during a basal period for the 10 beats just prior to the onset of the stimulus.

Statistical comparison of the experimental and control groups, each of 10 subjects, indicated that the stimulated group produced more decelerative responses immediately following onset of stimulation than did the control group (Lipsitt & Jacklin, 1969). Moreover, a correlation of 0.64 was obtained over the two-day testing period, indicating that the tendency toward cardiac deceleration in response to exteroceptive stimulation is a reliable individual difference variable. Especially since cardiac deceleration is thought to be a "mature" response, these results are particularly encouraging. They suggest, first, that some sensory systems may be more amenable to the production of orienting behavior than others, and these sensory systems might possibly be the better candidates for more profound conditioning effects. Secondly, if cardiac deceleration is truly an indicant of physiological maturity, in some neurophysiological sense, then those infants with the greatest tendencies toward deceleration may be most susceptible to behavioral alteration through conditioning circumstances. That cardiac deceleration has shown reliable day-to-day consistency offers special encouragement for the further utilization of this measure as an index of maturity.

V. CONCLUDING REMARKS

To close, finally, I should like to say that it has been my hope to share here some of the excitement of our progress in the Brown University infant laboratories in the exploration of conditioning processes of children, and hopefully in the field of child development as a whole. While I do not think that I have been fully responsive to the charge that I reflect broadly

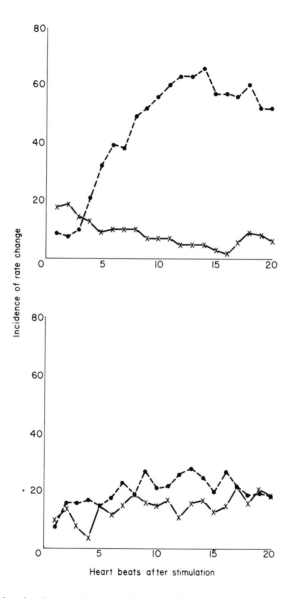

FIG. 14. Accelerative (● - - ●) and decelerative (X–X) changes in response following stimulation for top: an experimental group ($N = 10$), and bottom: control group ($N = 10$) of newborns. The experimental subjects were administered an asafoetida odorant on 10 successive trials. (Reproduced with permission of authors, Lipsitt & Jacklin, 1969.)

on the entire field of child development, I have hoped that through presentation of recent advances in my own laboratories and the work of my colleagues and students, I could convey the message that the serious adoption of experimental manipulative techniques for the study of infant and child behavior over the past two decades has yielded some advances.

As I conclude this paper, the world is anticipating an imminent landing by astronauts on the moon, a feat which two decades ago would have been considered virtually impossible to accomplish in such a short span of time. That such an astronomical goal (literally and figuratively) has been achieved with such speed and precision is due principally to the extensive investment of human resources in a project considered of great social and scientific value. Advances that might be made in other scientific areas if humans will consider them worthy of dedicated exploration are staggering to imagine. I have a sustaining faith that a well-developed experimental psychology of infant behavior would illuminate psychological processes having important diagnostic, educational, and remediational implications. In addition, such a pursuit would probably provide even greater intellectual challenges than now exist. Anyway, the chase is fun.

REFERENCES

Anastasi, A. Heredity, environment, and the question "How?" *Psychological Review,* 1958, **65**, 197–208.

Babkin, P. S. Head-turning reflexes in infants (Russian). *Zhurnal Nevropatologii Psikhiatrii, S. S. Korsakova,* 1953, **53**, 692–696.

Bronshtein, A. I., Antonova, T. G., Kamenstkaya, A. G., Luppova, N. N., & Sytova, V. A. On the development of the functions of analyzers in infants and some animals at the early stage of ontogenesis. In *Problemy evolyutaii fisiolgicheskikh funktsii.* Moscow–Leningrad Academiya Nauk USSR, 1958. (Translation obtained from U.S. Department of Commerce, Office of Technical Services.)

Bruner, J. S. *Processes of Cognitive Growth: Infancy.* (Vol. III. Heinz Werner Lecture Series). Clark Univer. Press with Barre Publishers, 1968.

Butler, R. A. Discrimination learning by rhesus monkeys to visual exploration motivation. *Journal of Comparative Psychology,* 1953, **46**, 95–98.

DeLucia, C. A. A system for response measurement and reinforcement delivery for infant sucking-behavior research. *Journal of Experimental Child Psychology,* 1967, **5**, 518–521.

Dollard, J. & Miller, N. E. *Personality and Psychotherapy,* New York: McGraw-Hill, 1950.

Engen, T. & Lipsitt, L. P. Decrement and recovery of responses to olfactory stimuli in the human neonate. *Journal of Comparative and Physiological Psychology,* 1965, **59**, 312–316.

Engen, T., Lipsitt, L. P., & Kaye, H. Olfactory responses and adaptation in the human neonate. *Journal of Comparative and Physiological Psychology,* 1963, **56**, 73–77.

Gesell, A., & Ilg, F. L. *Child Development: An Introduction to the Study of Human Growth.* New York: Harper, 1949.

Graham, F. K., & Clifton, R. K. Heart-rate change as a component of the orienting response. *Psychological Bulletin*, 1966, **65**, 305–320.

Graham, F. K., & Jackson, J. C. Arousal systems and infant heart rate responses. In H. W. Reese and L. P. Lipsitt (Eds.), *Advances in Child Development and Behavior*, 1970, Vol. V, in press.

Harlow, H. F., Harlow, M. K., & Meyer, D. R. Learning motivated by a manipulation drive. *Journal of Experimental Psychology*, 1950, **40**, 228–234.

Harris, D. H. Child psychology and the concept of development. In D. S. Palermo and L. P. Lipsitt (Eds.), *Research Readings in Child Psychology*. New York: Holt, 1963. Pp. 21–31.

Hollenberg, E. & Sperry, M. Some antecedents of aggression and effects of frustration in doll play. *Personality*, 1951, **1**, 32–43.

Hunt, J. McV. *Intelligence and experience*. New York: Ronald Press, 1961.

Hunt, J. McV. Traditional personality theory in the light of recent evidence. *American Scientist*, 1965, **53**, 80–96.

Kaye, H. The conditioned Babkin reflex in human newborns. *Psychonomic Science*, 1965, **2**, 287–288.

Lindsley, O. R. A behavioral measure of television viewing. *Journal of Advertising Research*, 1962, **2**, 2–12.

Lindsley, O. R. Experimental analysis of social reinforcement: Terms and methods. *American Journal of Orthopsychiatry*, 1963, **33**, 624–633.

Lindsley, O. R., Hobika, J. H., & Etsten, B. E. Operant behavior during anesthesia recovery: A continuous and objective method. *Anesthesiology*, 1961, **22**, 937–946.

Lipsitt, L. P., & DeLucia, C. An apparatus for the measurement of specific response and general activity of the human neonate. *American Journal of Psychology*, 1960, **73**, 630–632.

Lipsitt, L. P. & Jacklin, C. N. A report of cardiac deceleration and its stability in human newborns. Paper presented at meetings of The Psychonomic Society, St. Louis, Mo. November, 1969.

Lipsitt, L. P., & Kaye, H. Change in neonatal response to optimizing and non-optimizing sucking stimulation. *Psychonomic Science*, 1965, **3**, 221–222.

Lipsitt, L. P., Kaye, H., & Bosack, T. N. Enhancement of neonatal sucking through reinforcement, *Journal of Experimental Child Psychology*, 1966, **4**, 163–168.

Lipsitt, L. P., Pederson, L. J., & DeLucia, C. A. Conjugate reinforcement of operant responding in infants. *Psychonomic Science*, 1966, **4**, 67–68.

Papousek, H. A method of studying conditioned food reflexes in young children up to the age of six months (Russian). *Zhurnal Vysshei Nervnoi Deyatel'nosti imeni I. P. Pavlova*, 1959, **9**, 136–140.

Papousek, H. Conditioned motor alimentary reflexes in infants. I. Experimental conditioned sucking reflexes (Czechoslovakian). *Ceskoslovenska Pediatrie*, 1960, **15**, 861–872.

Papousek, H. Conditioned head rotation reflexes in infants in the first months of life. *Acta Paediatrica (Stockholm)*, 1961, **50**, 565–576.

Papousek, H. Experimental studies of appetitional behavior in human newborns and infants. In H. W. Stevenson, H. L. Rheingold, and E. Hess (Eds.). *Early behavior: comparative and developmental approaches*. New York: Wiley, 1967. Pp. 249–277.

Pfaffmann, C. The pleasures of sensation. *Psychological Review*, 1960, **67**, 253–268.

Rothschild, B. F. Incubator isolation as a possible contributing factor to the high incidence of emotional disturbance among prematurely born persons. *Journal of Genetic Psychology*, 1967, **110**, 287–304.

Rovee, C. K., & Rovee, D. Conjugate reinforcement of infant exploratory behavior. *Journal of Experimental Child Psychology.* 1969, **8**, 33–39.

Sears, R. R., Whiting, J., Nowlis, V., & Sears, P. S. Some child-rearing antecedents of aggression and dependency in young children. *Genetic Psychology Monographs*, 1953, **47**, 135–234.

Semb, G., & Lipsitt, L. P. The effects of acoustic stimulation on cessation and initiation of non-nutritive sucking in neonates. *Journal of Experimental Child Psychology*, 1968, **6**, 585–597.

Siqueland, E. R. Reinforcement patterns and extinction in human newborns. *Journal of Experimental Child Psychology*, 1968, **6**, 431–442.

Siqueland, E. R. The development of instrumental exploratory behavior during the first year of human life. Paper presented at meetings of Society for Research in Child Development, Santa Monica, California, March 1969.

Siqueland, E. R. & Lipsitt, L. P. Conditioned head-turning in human newborns. *Journal of Experimental Child Psychology*, 1966, **3**, 356–376.

Skeels, H. M. Adult status of children with contrasting early life experiences. *Monographs of the Society for Research in Child Development*, 1966, **31**, 65.

Skeels, H. M. & Harms, I. E. Children with inferior social histories: Their mental development in adoptive homes. *Journal of Genetic Psychology*, 1948, **72**, 283–294.

Skeels, H. M., Updegraff, R., Wellman, B. L., & Williams, H. M. A study of environmental stimulation: An orphanage preschool project. *University of Iowa Studies in Child Welfare*, 1938, **15**, No. 4.

Skodak, M., & Skeels, H. M. A final follow-up study of one hundred adopted children. *Journal of Genetic Psychology*, 1949, **75**, 85–125.

Smith, M. E. An investigation of the development of the sentence and the extent of the vocabulary in young children. *University of Iowa Studies in Child Welfare*, 1926, **3**, No. 5.

Smith, L. & Lipsitt, L. P. Investigations of conjugate reinforcement using mobiles in young infants. In preparation.

Sokolov, E. N. Higher nervous functions: The orienting reflex. *Annual Review of Physiology*, 1963, **25**, 545–580.

Spiker, C. C. Research methods in children's learning. In P. H. Mussen (Ed.), *Handbook of Research Methods in Child Development*. New York: Wiley, 1960. Pp. 374–420.

Spiker, C. C. & McCandless, B. R. The concept of intelligence and the philosophy of science. *Psychological Review*, 1954, **61**, 225–266.

Uzgiris, I. & Hunt, J. McV. A longitudinal study of recognition learning. Paper read at meetings of the Society for Research in Child Development, Minneapolis, Minnesota, 1965.

Wellman, B. L. Iowa studies on the effects of schooling. *Yearbook of the National Society for the Study of Education*; 1940, **39**, Part II. Pp. 377–399.

Wellman, B. L. IQ changes of preschool and non-preschool groups during the preschool years: A summary of the literature. *Journal of Psychology*, 1945, **20**, 347–368.

White, R. W. Motivation reconsidered: The concept of competence. *Psychology Review*, 1959, **66**, 297–333.

A Learning–Behavior Theory: A Basis for Unity in Behavioral–Social Science[1]

ARTHUR W. STAATS

DEPARTMENT OF PSYCHOLOGY
UNIVERSITY OF HAWAII
HONOLULU, HAWAII

I. PERSONAL INFLUENCES AND DEVELOPMENT

Although I had an environmentalistic, deterministic, approach to human behavior as a family inheritance, it was not until I was a graduate student that the formal field of learning became central in my thinking. Actually, not until I began reading on my own in the philosophy of science and of psychology did the general products of psychology begin to fit together in a meaningful integration in the context of laboratory-derived principles of

[1] This paper was written in part under the support of the Office of Naval Research Contract N000 14-67-C-0387-0007 with the University of Hawaii, 1969.

183

learning. Readings in the scientific empiricism of Hull, Spence, and Stevens (see Hull, 1943a,b; Spence, 1944, 1948; Stevens, 1939) began to provide a general basis for considering the then contemporary concepts and observations in psychology in the learning framework and also began my concern with the philosophy of the science. My thinking and research have continued to be related to a basic philosophy, which constitutes a unifying guide, although the philosophy has itself developed under the press of my further experimental, theoretical, naturalistic, and clinical work.

At any rate, I began at this time to become familiar with Hull's learning theory and to realize the importance of a formal learning theory in my own interests in psychology. From the beginning I had a "functional" philosophy in the sense that if learning principles were valid one should be able to demonstrate the principles clearly in various situations, with functional behaviors, including those of real life. Experimentally, for example, I began to test the principles of learning in the context of animal learning, with my only available subject, a pet cat. Thus, using classical conditioning procedures I tested the possibility that the cat would come to respond to the word "no" by stopping what she was doing, if the word was first paired with an aversive stimulus. The training was very effective. I also tested the possibility that an instrumental response, that of approaching me, could be brought under the control of the verbal stimulus of the cat's name by reinforcing better and better approximations to the final skill I desired (see Staats, 1968a). I also trained the animal to respond to other verbal stimuli, and this work constituted my first extension of learning principles to language—experimental-naturalistic work which was the prototype of formal experiments I later conducted.

In addition, I began to analyze human behavior in terms of the learning principles. This included a critical analysis of traditional personality theories and the clinical actions of psychologists and psychiatrists that stemmed from the psychodynamic theories they held. Although taking my degree in general experimental psychology, I completed training in and took a Veterans Administration internship in clinical psychology. In this position I had an opportunity of seeing that a learning theory of human behavior would lead to different treatment of abnormal behavior than did the prevailing psycho-analytic conception. Thus, I began to make extensions of learning principles to the analyses of human behavior which had been conducted using other theories. Analysis of clinical problems in learning terms has continued to be one of my major interests (see Staats, 1957, 1963, 1964, 1968a, 1970, a, b). Dollard and Miller's early book (1950) was important at the beginning, but I felt that their use of psychoanalytic theory as the basic model of personality was in error.

Another problem which concerned me at that time involved Maier's

(1949) frustration-fixation concept. I felt that the experimental results of him and his associates could be, and should be, dealt with in learning terms. I spent many hours attempting to do so within the confines of Hull's learning theory (1943b). It was in this work that I began to realize that the important parts of Hull's theory for the analysis of behavior resided in the learning principles and analyses of the behavior into stimulus response (S–R) elements, and that his formal theoretical concepts did not add much to such efforts. (See Staats, 1959b, for the paper I finally published on this problem.)

Among the most influential courses I took as a graduate student at UCLA was one by Maltzman in which he presented his not yet published Hullian model for problem solving (see Maltzman, 1955). In the progress of this course I read a number of papers on problem solving from a gestalt orientation. Again, I felt that it was important to extend the learning principles (in this case Maltzman's extension of Hull's habit family hierarchies) to specific behaviors and to derive experimental (or treatment) hypotheses from the abstract theoretical analysis. I thus analyzed Maier's two-string problem in terms of habit families and set up an experimental situation to test the hypothesis that the individual's process of problem solving depends in part upon the nature of the hierarchy of responses he has previously learned to problem objects. My experimental results (see Staats, 1955) were suggestive but not definitive. However, Maltzman later employed the experimental situation in several additional studies and more firmly substantiated the learning analysis (Maltzman, 1960; Maltzman, Brooks, Bogartz, & Summers, 1958).

In any event, although this work was important to me, and although I had outlined a series of experimental studies of problem solving, by the time I had completed my dissertation I was convinced that there were areas of human behavior more basic and more central than the experimental anologues of problem solving. For one thing, I decided then that an analysis of problem solving as a unitary type of activity was erroneous. Rather a variety of learned skills appeared to be basic to problem solving, centrally among which for humans was language. For this and other reasons I will mention shortly, my concerns focused more on the study of language.

I may say here that my interests were from the beginning broad. I was interested in basic learning theory as the foundation of my conceptual scheme. But I also considered all aspects of complex human behavior to be learned, and in my view the development of a learning theory involved extensions into all areas of human behavior. To have interests ranging from basic learning theory to the various areas of human behavior in clinical, child, educational, and social psychology may seem like an imposing undertaking. However, when defined in the way that I did at that time, the task was not as impossible as it might seem. My area of speciality became basic learning theory, and any extension of the principles of learning to a type of human behavior. Articles of interest to me were likely to appear in a variety of sources, it is true. However, they did not constitute a large percentage of those in those sources.

Another strategem that made the task more manageable has been my plan to move progressively into more and more complex behaviors. Thus, although interested in clinical, social, child, and educational psychology from the beginning, I have not concentrated my efforts in these areas until an adequate foundation for broad considerations of these topics could be made from my more basic work. As it turns out I have been making this progressive advancement to more complex areas of human behavior, but the things I learn in doing so send me back to more basic considerations. So the work does turn back upon itself, although a general movement is still involved, and the progression to the more complex is still my plan.

Always in this task, however, consideration of language has remained a focal interest. In my view it is the development of language that especially marks man off from his subhuman progenitors. Language is involved in all human activities. There is no study of human behavior that does not have to include language as a central consideration. Language appeared to me to be the key to comprehensive treatments of problems in experimental psychology, in clinical psychology, in educational psychology, in child psychology, and in social psychology, as well as in the other social and behavioral sciences. Language is the most complex type of human behavior and regardless of the area being dealt with, clinical, child, or what have you, if one deals with language successfully the other problems of behavior will follow relatively easily. Thus, although I have published research in a number of areas of psychology, I almost invariably deal with the topics as they relate to language behavior in that area. In my dissertation I had considered language to be very central to problem solving. At this time I also became familiar with Cofer and Foley's original and important article (1942) on semantic generalization which had elaborated Hull's concept of the pure stimulus act (1930), as well as Osgood's later, related, analysis of mediating responses and word meaning (1953). While by no means covering the complexity of language, the conception of implicit meaning responses to words, developed through conditioning, was important.

Other reading that was central to my early learning theory development came from several sources. The philosophy of science already mentioned constituted one basic ingredient. Another influence arose from the writings of Hull (1943a) and Spence (1944), Dollard and Miller (1950), Osgood (1953), and Mowrer (1954). It was only later, in the second half of the 1950's that I became familiar with Skinner (1953, 1957). Skinner's books, however, fitted very well into my views, which were by then pretty well crystallized, and corroborated my earlier explorations with the instrumental conditioning of language behaviors. In some cases, as will be discussed further on, Skinner's learning terminology was an improvement over Hull, although each theory required innovation to become a comprehensive basic learning theory and to serve as a foundation for a behavior theory. At any rate, these were the seedings for my work. It was in the work itself, however, that my formulation grew, changed, and was extended. It was in the conduct of the work (conducting experiments, and reading about them, teaching, and in theorizing myself) that I could see the uses, and inadequacies, of the already existent learning theories. These evaluations convinced me that a "third-generation" learning theory was needed, unlike the common conclusion that the age of general theory building was past.

To continue, however, in 1955 I took my first academic position in the Department of Psychology at Arizona State University. It then became possible to pursue in formal experimentation the principles I had already tested in experimental-naturalistic studies. My first goal was to test the principles of classical conditioning in language learning. That is, I had already tested with the cat the hypothesis that pairing a word stimulus with an aversive unconditioned stimulus which elicited a negative emotional response would condition the emotional response to the word. My first experimental venture in this area was to text this analysis with humans, although it was not until 1958 that I and my associates completed a formal study of this type, the first order conditioning of word meaning (Staats, Staats, & Crawford, 1962). Before that I had already completed what was supposed to be the second type of experiment, the demonstration that higher-order conditioning of responses to words also occurred. That is, according to my analysis, since some words are conditioned stimuli that elicit responses (and thus are meaningful), it should be possible to pair such words with a new word and thereby condition the responses to the new word. Thus, my hypothesis was that if a nonsense syllable verbal stimulus was paired with different words that elicited a positive emotional response attitude the response should be conditioned to the nonsense syllable. My first experiment confirmed this expectation. My wife Carolyn then conducted two replication studies with different types of meaning responses (that is, Osgood's potency and activity meanings) as part of her doctoral dissertation, which gave further support to my analysis and experimental procedures. These findings were later elaborated with a series of my studies (Staats & Staats, 1958, 1962; Staats, Staats, & Heard, 1960) as well as by experiments conducted by others[2] (for example, Abell, 1969;

[2] There is presently a controversy concerning whether this type of conditioning can occur without awareness (see Page, 1969; Staats, 1969). Several recent studies are particularly relevant in indicating that awareness is not necessary (Ertel, Oldenberg, Sirz, and Vormfelde, 1969; Miller, 1966; Zanna, Kiesler, and Pilkonis, 1970).

DiVesta & Stover, 1962; Early, 1968; Ertel, Oldenberg, Siry & Vormfelde, 1969; Miller, 1966; Paivio, 1964; Pollio, 1963). In addition to the experimental support that connotative word meaning responses such as emotional or evaluative responses were learned according to classical conditioning principles, it occurred to me that what we call sensations are actually responses. There was very suggestive experimentation to that effect (see Leuba, 1940; Ellson, 1941; Phillips, 1958). And naturalistic experience suggests the same. I introduced the concept of the conditioned sensory response to an analysis of language first in 1959 (Staats, 1959a). My suggestion was that some words are meaningful because they are systematically paired with sensory objects and events, and thus come to elicit conditioned sensory (or image) responses (which themselves have stimulus properties). This analysis was also confirmed experimentally (Staats, Staats, & Heard, 1960) and the concept of the conditioned sensory response was employed later in analyses by Mowrer (1960), Sheffield (1961), Adams (1968), and Paivio (1965, 1969).

My interest in instrumental conditioning principles had not abated, however, as well as my interest in extending learning principles to the consideration of complex, functional, repertoires of human behavior. Bijou and his associates (see Orlando and Bijon, 1960), had tested the principles of reinforcement with children employing operant conditioning apparatus. These were studies to test the relevance of the basic principles from the animal laboratory, and the behaviors were simple motor responses, and the reinforcers were simple also, edibles like M & M candies. However, my work with animals and humans in naturalistic situations indicated to me that the principles applied as well to complex, functional, human behaviors.

Studying such complex behaviors was an integral part of my program. Thus, by 1959, I had developed a more sophisticated reinforcement system for the study of such behaviors which are only acquired over a long period of time involving many, many, training trials. The reinforcement system was based upon tokens which were accumulated and exchanged for some material reinforcer the subject had chosen to work for. With this token-reinforcer system varying kinds of behavioral repertoires, with varying kinds of subjects, could be studied *and treated*. In my laboratory I continued to extend the instrumental principles and the token-reinforcer system to aspects of children's language learning (see Staats, 1963, 1966, 1968a,b; Staats & Butterfield, 1965; Staats, Finley, Minke & Wolf, 1964; Staats, Minke, Finley, Wolf, & Brooks, 1964; Staats, Minke, Goodwin, & Landeen, 1967; Staats, Staats, Schutz, and Wolf, 1962). Dissemination of the general value of the token-reinforcement system led to its service as the foundation of a number of projects and studies (Ayllon & Azrin, 1969; Wolf, Giles, & Hall, 1968; Bushell, Wrobel, & Michaelis, 1968; Birnbrauer, Wolf, Kidder, & Tague, 1965).

The foregoing mentions some of my experimental work, each unit of which derived from the learning theory which I had synthesized. In addition to the specific extensions in the experimental work my interests were moving forward on a broad front in dealing with other complex behaviors. By 1960, I had extended my learning analysis to a sufficient number of areas to feel that it was possible to stipulate a set of integrated learning principles which had broad extensions to complex human behavior. Some experimental literature was also available which could be organized in this effort. I thus planned my *Complex Human Behavior* (Staats, 1963) and *Human Learning* (Staats, 1964) books on the basis of my learning theory of that vintage. As I wrote the first (which included collaborative contributions from my wife Carolyn) I saw even more clearly the need for a new learning theory as the foundation for a general conception of human behavior. The possibilities for integration at the basic level as well as at the human behavior level appeared to be confirmed, if not complete or in final form. Although this was a theoretical effort, studies since that time have provided considerable support for this view.

One example of areas that could be unified by an integrated learning analysis involved the British behavior therapy studies, which predominantly utilized Hullian theory and classical conditioning procedures, as well as the American studies employing instrumental conditioning principles which came to be called behavior modification. Actually, the theoretical terminologies were antagonistic, but when I considered the findings in terms of a unified set of learning principles the complementary relationship could be seen. My interest in the integration of these areas prompted in 1961 a sabbatical visit to Maudsley Hospital, Eysenck's center of early behavior therapy development. It was possible in discussions with H. Eysenck and S. Rachman to bring into conjunction our American operant clinical studies and the British Hullian behavior therapy studies.

My efforts presently continue in extending the experimental work, including that of providing an integration of learning principles, in demonstrating the importance of learning principles and procedures in dealing with human behavior and behavior problems (see the already mentioned studies as well as Staats, 1968b, 1970), and in theoretical extensions of the basic learning theory. Some of this is in more recent books, *Learning, Language, and Cognition* (Staats, 1968a), *Child Learning, Intelligence, and Personality* (Staats, in press (a)), and articles. It is clear, however, that the task is only begun. The learning theory, and attendant procedurse, have great potential for understanding, predicting, and controlling human behavior. It is possible to see how such a learning theory will become a foundation to the various areas of psychology ranging from basic learning areas through traditional human learning areas in experimental psychology to clinical, social, child, and educational psychology and on to such social and behavioral sciences as sociology, anthropology, economics, education, and history. Most psychologists study in a particular area and thus are not aware of what occurs in other areas, or of the common principles that might be employed to unify the various areas. This will change when a common theoretical orientation is adopted throughout psychology, as well as the other social and behavioral sciences. This development is possible now. One of the needs in this development is a learning theory which is integrational on the basic level, and which also has been constructed with the goal in mind—that of serving as the basis for a general conception of man. It will not be possible to treat in detail the learning theory that is proposed, or its empirical basis. However, it will be possible to characterize the theory. Before doing this, however, a brief section will in very general terms characterize the field of learning in a critical manner which is relevant to the present approach.

II. CRITICAL OVERVIEW OF THE FIELD OF LEARNING

The philosophical background of the field of learning had its immediate forebears in British empiricism which suggested that man's mind is formed by his experiences. Learning began to emerge as a scientific field with the laboratory stipulation of the principles by which environmental occurrences (stimuli) can affect the behavior of an organism. Thus, the first stage in the development of the field was in the laboratory specification of the basic principles of learning, or conditioning.

Pavlov began the discovery of the principles of classical conditioning and Thorndike began the discovery of the principles of instrumental conditioning. In each case there was an interest not only in the basic principles themselves but also in the relevance of the principles for consideration of human behavior.

However, the empirical principles were not yet well specified, the systematic organization of the findings in the field was incomplete, the learning terminology was not yet well developed and derived heavily from the pre-experimenal past, and the statement of the basic set of principles (theory) was simplistic. Thus, the accounts of human behavior in terms of the learning principles, such as Thorndike's and also Watson's, were not comprehensive. Neither did the learning theories provide an adequate basis for studying or dealing comprehensively with important human behaviors. While these accounts influenced heavily later applications of learning to human behavior (such as Hull's and Skinner's), the formulations of Thorndike and Watson proved to be much better as stimulants to the development of the *basic* aspects of the field of learning.

In the next stage of development, the primary feature of the field of learning was that of theory building and competition among the theories. This stage included (*a*) continuing advancements in experimental methodology for systematic research on the basic principles, (*b*) systematic consideration of logical methods and terminological rules, (*c*) construction of general theoretical frameworks to incorporate basic experimental findings, (*d*) concentration upon animal studies, and (*e*) theory-oriented research to advance one theory and to challenge competitors.

The theories of Guthrie, Tolman, Hull, and Skinner were major at this second level of development. Each systematist drew upon the earlier formulations of Pavlov, Thorndike, and Watson, but developed individual characteristics of his own. Hull dominated this stage. The accepted (if some times implicit) goal of this area of theorizing was to establish a higher-order (more abstract) set of principles to explain the lower-order empirical principles of conditioning. Questions concerning what underlies learning (S–R habit versus an expectancy or cognitive map), and what underlies reinforcement, and so on, are illustrative of the characteristic approach. Hullians were also interested in such "higher-order" theoretical terms as *drive reduction* and *habit strength*, and so on. Skinner evidenced his acceptance of this methodological approach to theory with his higher-order "explanatory" term *reflex reserve* which was postulated to explain some of the empirical principles of instrumental conditioning. In this effort, Hull also attempted to employ mathematical formulations. The end "specialization" of this general theoretical methodology (in an evolutionary sense), and in the use of mathematics, can be seen in the emergence of the mathematical models approach to learning.

This nature of the field of learning, it may be suggested, was not a stable one in terms of producing a paradigm which offered a long-term path for the advancement of the science. None of the theories has been complete in this sense. Much research was generated to test the theories, but the differences were not resolved, and much of the work did not fall into the mainstream of developing the field of learning. Thus, Skinner was correct in this context in criticizing the emphasis upon theory in the field, although the message was unclear in the article (1950), and has remained so. He did not stipulate what theory is or should be in learning or the behavioral sciences, or indicate the role or advantages of theory. The message was accepted as a restriction to experimentation, preferably or exclusively using operant conditioning and single-organism research methods. Skinner's statement of the philosophy of the experimental analysis of behavior contained the injunction to find out about behavior by taking it into the laboratory where operant conditioning variables could be manipulated and the important variables found. This antitheory philosophy has drawn those who have followed the operant approach into a focus upon experimentation unguided by a larger framework or context—and without a philosophy to seek such generality.

To continue, however, the emphasis at this stage of the development of learning was the competition of the major learning theories. Some of the issues were of basic orientation, for example, between strict behaviorists, like Hull, and those who still retained some mentalistic flavor, like Tolman. Much of the research which aimed to advance one of these approaches at the expense of the other did not achieve this purpose. It is edifying to note in retrospect that the S–R behaviorism of Hull won out because of the products it produced, not because of success in "crucial" experiments. That is, Hull's approach convinced more experimentalists of its value, and the theory led to more experimentation and a larger number of extensions. Attempts to devise crucial comparisons of the learning theories, as in the latent learning controversy, came to naught. (The author makes the same prediction for such contemporary issues as "awareness versus conditioning" studies, the "psycholinguistic versus learning" approaches to language, and so on.)

The differences between Hull and Skinner, however, in the general senses to be discussed were not large. Little done under one systematization could not have been derived from the other. There were differences of emphasis and differences in terminology and experimental apparatus that divided followers into two camps. Oddly enough, even though Skinner's was a two-factor (instrumental and classical conditioning) approach and Hull's a one-factor approach (which did not differentiate instrumental and classical conditioning), Hullian researchers have worked with both instrumental and classical conditioning procedures, while Skinnerians have restricted themselves to instrumental principles by employing only operant apparatus. In addition, Hull elaborated his theoretical terms greatly and employed mathematics, as mentioned. These characteristics did have a great impact upon psychology which would not have been inspired by Skinner's systematization. In terms of the learning principles themselves, however, there is little that could not be done from either framework. Skinner's own work with schedules of reinforcement involved the elaboration of the principle of reinforcement, and operant conditioning apparatus is more appropriate for this than are mazes. Hull's approach was more general, however, in terms of utilizing various types of experimental apparatus. Both researchers, following their predecessors Watson and Thorndike, exhibited an interest in extensions to the human level, with Hull showing the earlier interest. Perhaps, in summary the major differences have been (1) in the use of stimulus–response analyses of the behaviors being dealt with; Hull diagramming behaviors liberally and Skinner not employing S–R analyses or in fact much in the way of detailed analysis of complex behaviors, (2) in an interest in theory and mathematics and the logic of theory construction by Hull, (3) in the type of experimental work emphasized, and (4) in a greater emphasis on classical conditioning by Hull.

At any rate, the traditional learning theories have provided a framework which in their major aspects are highly similar. It should not eliminate the the need for a third-generation learning theory to note that the traditional learning theories, especially those of Hull and Skinner, were very important advances in the progress of the science of learning (which is what the area should be considered). In this era of traditional learning theories the area became the model for scientific theory construction in psychology. A great deal of animal research was conducted which greatly expanded the findings concerning the basic principles. Many different behaviors were also subjected to experimentation. Moreover, great strides were made in experimental methodology, for both animal and human research. Perusal of experimental journals a few decades ago will reveal much less experimental sophistication in apparatus, procedures, and methods of design and analysis. The importance of this fund of knowledge should not be underestimated. These developments, and their systematization into general learning theories, it is suggested, will come to be ranked with the early achievements of the other natural sciences, even though these developments may only be considered to be the beginning.

Not all, or perhaps even a major part of this progress may be directly attributed to the basic learning theories themselves. However, it is the case that even when the experiments to test the different theories were not crucial themselves, they were in many cases the vehicles by which methodological advances were made. It is also true that the major theorists made direct experimental and methodological contributions which were influential. Moreover, the theories performed a guide to many investigators who might have gone into other areas of investigation without the impetus the theories provided. This is not to say that there were not other contributors whose efforts were unrelated to the major theories. The "functionalist" school of investigators, for example, conducted a great deal of research on verbal learning, as one example. Most of this work was not theory oriented, but rather was based upon acceptance of a common experimental methodology. It is possible to present subjects with paired-associate or serial learning tasks and get systematic changes in learning as one manipulates different variables. This field is perhaps one of the best examples of how an experimental field grows without a formal theoretical direction. That is, most of the field's experiments are derived from previously conducted experiments, and there has been no real theoretical systematization of the various findings. Nevertheless, again, this work yielded general progress in experimental methods both in terms of procedures as well as in terms of design and statistical analysis, although most of the experiments in this area will not in the opinion of this author fall into the mainstream of the development of the science.

To continue, however, in the history of science we may see many examples of advances in theory which at first were large contributions in the context of the times, but which later become anachronistic and retarded further development until finally replaced by a more advanced view. It may be suggested that the traditional learning theories constitute examples of this type of progression; great contributions in their context, but presently inadequate guides to further advances. Before offering an outline of a third-generation theory in learning, a moment may be spent briefly mentioning the areas of weakness of the traditional learning theories.

To begin, it is suggested that the major theoretical philosophy of the traditional learning theories is incorrect. That is, as has been indicated, it was accepted widely that the task of a learning theory was to put forth a set of higher-level statements, more abstract than the facts of learning, that would *explain* the principles of learning. This method has been succinctly summarized by Spence (1944).

> The physicist is able to isolate, experimentally, elementary situations, i.e., situations in which there are a limited number of variables, and thus finds it possible to infer or discover descriptive, lower-order laws. Theory comes into play for the physicist when he attempts to formulate more abstract principles which will bring these low-order laws into relationship with one another. Examples of such comprehensive theories are Newton's principle of gravitation and the kinetic theory of gases. The former provided a theoretical integration of such laws as Kepler's concerning planetary motions, Galileo's law of falling bodies, laws of the tides and so on. The kinetic theory has served to integrate the various laws relating certain properties of gases to other experimental variables [pp. 47–48].

The perusal of the principles of scientific theory construction methods by psychologists, as this statement shows, has yielded very important knowledge. It may be suggested, however, that unlike the examples cited above, and as will be discussed further, the higher-order principles for a general learning theory are not more abstract formulations than the laws of learning. *The higher-order principles of the learning theory are the laws of learning themselves.* This suggestion is a major revision of strategy. The major orientation to theory construction in the traditional learning theories, it is thus suggested, was incorrect. The basic philosophy of science is correct but its application to learning, and psychological theory in general, erred. When it is recognized that the laws of learning are the higher-order, more abstract principles themselves, even though obtained through experimentation, the nature of the theory construction task can be made clear. That is, *the task is to employ these higher-order learning laws to explain, deal with, and integrate the lower-order principles of behavior.* This will be exemplified further on.

Central to the role of a theory, it may be suggested, is its function in guiding the information gathering activities of scientific research. The theory rests upon findings already made, but it serves as a structure which directs further experimentation of various kinds. The manner in which the theory provides these guides may be very explicit—for example, in the way that Hull's theory spawned research to specify the relationship of habit and drive that he posited, or in the way that Skinner's formulation has spawned a great number of studies which vary reinforcement schedules. The guides which a theory sets forth may also be implicit in various ways, including an implicit injunction not to be interested in certain problems when the theory does not touch upon those problems. An example might be Skinner's implicit injunction not to make S–R analyses of complex behavior by not doing so himself.

At any rate, the direction provided by the traditional learning theories has been and is inadequate at various levels. Thus, as one example, without a philosophy of theory construction that included the importance of human level research, the traditional learning theories have not been extended intensively into the various areas of psychology to which learning is central. That is, one role of a learning theory of great significance is its status as a general conception for understanding and dealing with man and his problems. The learning theory has failed in this test of its generality and significance if it does not indicate the manner in which human level research, theory, and treatment activities relate to the basic theory. The theory must include explicit recognition that it is to be extended into *various* areas of human behavior, cutting artificial boundaries established by accidents of history and current theoretical Balkanization. In this task the commonality of principles underlying different behaviors, and behaviors considered under different terms, must be shown, and the learning theory must indicate a philosophy and methods for performing these integrations.

The learning theory must also show that it is a theoretical structure that unifies the principles of the basic animal laboratory, experimental studies of simple human behaviors, and that it extends equally to more and more complex human behaviors of all kinds: child and adult, normal and abnormal, individual, group, and cultural, behaviors of a sensory–motor variety, emotional behavior and motivation, intellectual behaviors, social behavior, ethical behavior, or what have you. Presently, there is great diversity and antagonism between different parts of psychology and between theoretical orientations. The lack of a traditional theory that serves as a comprehensive guide and integrating agent has prevented psychology's entrance into the full status of a science by preventing the emergency of common goals, methods, principles and a common philosophy.

It should be noted that not only have the traditional learning theories been inadequate as a guide on this level, they have not provided guides for the advancement of research even at the basic levels. The direction and impetus provided by Hull's theory was to experimentally develop and test the specific statements of his theory—for example, as already mentioned, his statement of a multiplicative relationship between drive and habit strength. Much experimentation was of this variety, but interest in this has begun to wane as interest in the specific aspects of Hull's theory has decreased. Perhaps the greatest specialization (in an evolutionary sense) of this development has been the growth of the mathematical models approach to learning theory. Hull had attempted to employ mathematics in specifying his theoretical terms, and the math models approach has evolved into a central emphasis on this characteristic.

Skinner's basic theory, on the other hand, has stressed the central nature of the continued experimental analysis of the principle of reinforcement, to the exclusion of the use of other experimental procedures or other aspects of learning principles. He has also stressed the unique importance of the probability (rate) of behavior which has had an inhibiting effect all of its own. It has been said by followers of this orientation that unless rate of behavior is being measured, the experiment is not of much worth. In basic work this has led in many cases to a stereotyped concern with the study of schedules of reinforcement, with little innovation or extension into other areas. It may be suggested that the popularity of this type of research will decline and will in later years not be considered in the mainstream of the science of learning. Thus, although each theory has stimulated important types of research, the traditional approaches presently do not guide even basic research in innovative paths, and in some cases even prevent such developments. One area of basic research that requires expanded support and interest that does not derive with sufficient force from the traditional learning theories concerns the interaction of the two major principles of conditioning, instrumental and classical conditioning.

Furthermore, still on the basic level, the traditional learning theories do not provide a guide for the systematic study of the complex ways that stimuli and responses can be combined into complex constellations in human behavior through the organism's learning history. That is, the aim of the basic field of learning has been to investigate the elementary principles of learning in their most simple setting. It is the establishment of the elementary principle that is of interest, and this is best ascertained when dealing with the most simple case. This means dealing with the case where one stimulus and one response are involved, with other complications excluded by experimental controls.

But it is also important to discover how more complex learnings of multiple stimulus and multiple response events occur, while still analyzing the complex combinations into their basic principles. A few of the possible combinations (S–R mechanisms) have been indicated and investigated, such as response hierarchies where one stimulus tends to elicit one of several responses. However, there is much human research whose importance lies in indicating the complex S–R mechanisms that can be learned. Usually, because there is no recognition of the explicit need of studying the various S–R mechanisms, such studies are considered only in their specific role as an example of problem solving, or concept formation, or some such specific behavior, rather than for investigating an abstract, general S–R mechanism. The learning theory must specifically indicate the place of the study of the learning of complex S–R mechanisms in the basic theoretical structure. The theory must also indicate the importance of the study of complex S–R mechanisms in the analysis of significant, functional, human behaviors of varying kind.

In short, the traditional learning theories are no longer frameworks for indicating what the science of learning is and where it should be headed. The traditional theories are also inadequate in indicating the relationship of learning theories to other science areas as well as to various areas in psychology itself. Furthermore, the traditional theories are inadequate even on the level of constituting formulations by which to organize basic learning research and by which to generate new research. While the means to remedy these deficits cannot be dealt with in a brief chapter, an outline of a suggested larger learning theory is herewith presented.

III. PROGRAMMATIC OUTLINE OF A LEARNING–BEHAVIOR THEORY

As indicated, it is only possible in a brief article to outline the major points of the learning theory that is being proposed; I will not be able to examine specific experimental citations for the most part, or to describe the research controversies involved with some of the principles. Each of the major aspects of the learning theory to be discussed calls for elaboration which a more complete future work will provide. Nevertheless, the approach can be characterized and some of its main features presented. As will be indicated, the learning theory has three levels which differ in the extent of abstractness and generality. The higher-order, most abstract level consists of the set of basic conditioning principles—those of instrumental and classical conditioning. At the second level, the general principles of stimulus–response combinations (S–R mechanisms), derived from the higher-order principles, are stipulated. The lower-order aspects of the theory concern the integration and explanation of the observations and empirical concepts of behavior, especially human behavior, through use of the principles and S–R mechanisms.

A. The Basic (Higher-Order) Principles

It should be noted that a novelty of the present theory-construction method is to accept the experimentally established principles of conditioning as the higher-order laws of the theory. This does not mean that they are assumed or immutable, rather they are established by experimentation and will be altered in the same way. It is not the intent, however, to present the research underlying the principles, or the present research issues involved.

Classical and Instrumental Conditioning. The principles which form the most basic higher-order principles of the learning theory are those of classical conditioning, as first experimentally isolated by Pavlov, and instrumental conditioning, as first experimentally isolated by Thorndike. (It should be noted that in each case there were previously employed philosophical principles of behavior based upon naturalistic observations that coincided with each basic conditioning principle.) The findings involving these basic learning principles were later employed in the systematizations which constitute the traditional learning theories. There have been theorists, such as Hull and Guthrie, who did not distinguish the types of conditioning. The higher-order principles they proposed were respectively that conditioning (of either type) took place through reinforcement (drive-reduction) or through contiguity (the simple pairing of stimulus and response). Later theorists such as Mowrer and Skinner have suggested that there are different principles involved in the types of conditioning. Classical conditioning has been said to take place through contiguity, while instrumental conditioning demands reinforcement. Skinner has taken great pains to separate the two types of conditioning, and has emphasized the primary role of instrumental conditioning. Through this type of separation the study of classical and instrumental conditioning has largely taken place in isolation as investigators usually work in one area or the other. Moreover, the symbols used to stand for the stimulus and response events in the two areas have been formulated in isolation from one another so that any relationship between the two areas has been obscured. One of the important items in a learning theory must be to employ a notation system that shows the relationship of the two types of conditioning, thus providing for a theoretical system in which both can be considered together in behavior analyses. As will be seen, although the procedures involved in producing the two basic types of conditioning are different, there is considerable overlap and interaction between the two. Whether distinctly different learning mechanisms are involved is a moot question.

To continue, however, the empirical principle of classical conditioning is that if one stimulus elicits a response in an organism, if that stimulus is presented, paired with another stimulus that does not elicit that response, the latter will come to do so. A stimulus that elicits a response in the organism, without prior preparation of the organism by the experimentalist, is called an unconditioned stimulus. This type of stimulus should be denoted as ^{UC}S. A stimulus that does not elicit a response but which comes to do so because it is paired with an unconditioned stimulus is itself called a conditioned stimulus. The symbol standing for a conditioned stimulus is ^{C}S.

It may be noted that the general principle to be followed is that all stimuli will be symbolized by S. The superior prefix will be employed to indicate what kind of stimulus is involved. Actually, there are many physical energy sources in the environment which may be called stimuli. There are air vibrations (sounds), light waves (sights), mechanical energies (touch), and so on. Not all of these physical energy sources will serve as stimuli of any kind for a particular organism. Whether or not a physical energy source will serve as a stimulus for an organism has to be established empirically, over species and individuals, since there are differences.

To continue, however, Fig. 1(a) diagrams the classical conditioning process. The ^{UC}S is shown by the *solid* line to elicit the response in the beginning. The ^{C}S is presented with the ^{UC}S, just preceding the ^{UC}S for greatest conditioning, so the diagram includes a time dimension moving from left to right. The line between the ^{C}S and the response is dotted, to indicate that this stimulus does not at first elicit the response, the conditioning trials only serve to strengthen the "association." In Fig. 1(b), the ^{C}S is shown by itself eliciting the response, and the line is now solid. This indicates that the conditioning is now strong and the ^{C}S through the pairing process has come to elicit the response on its own, although previously being neutral with respect to the response.

It may be noted here that the response elicited by the unconditioned stimulus is not exactly the same as the response which through conditioning comes to be elicited by the ^{C}S. The conditioned response may only include components of the original response, the unconditioned response, elicited by the ^{UC}S.

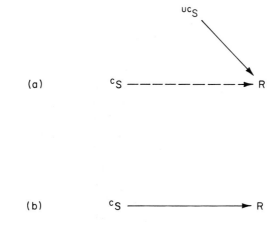

FIG. 1.   Classical conditioning.

As an example of classical conditioning, let us say that the ^{UC}S employed was an electric shock. The electric shock if aversive would elicit in the subject a variety of responses. His heart rate would change, the blood volume in his blood vessels in different parts of the body would change, the sweat gland activity in the subject's skin would change, and so on. Each of these is an "emotional" response elicited by such aversive unconditioned stimuli. If, for the subject, a ^{C}S was presented and followed by the ^{UC}S, and this was repeated, soon the ^{C}S when presented alone would elicit responses like these. The subject would now be responding to the ^{C}S much as he would to the ^{UC}S. This is thus an example of the higher-order (abstract) empirical law of classical conditioning.

The empirical principle of instrumental conditioning isolated by Thorndike has been stated by Skinner in the following way. A motor response that occurs and is followed by a reinforcing stimulus (such as a bit of food) will occur more frequently. It is suggested, however, that the stimulus situation which is present must be included in the principle although Skinner does not include this element in his statement. That is, a more adequate statement of Thorndike's principle is that when a response occurs in the presence of a stimulus (or stimulus situation), and the response is followed by reinforcement, the stimulus will come as a result more strongly to elicit the response on future occasions.

At any rate, there are two types of stimuli involved in this type of conditioning. There is the stimulus (actually a stimulus complex) present when the organism makes its response, and there is the stimulus which is presented following the response which acts as the reinforcement. The first stimulus, regardless of its complexity, may be called a discriminative stimulus. The symbol for such a stimulus is ^{D}S. It is important to include the action of such a stimulus in the very first instrumental conditioning process, unlike Skinner's custom. That is, reinforcing a response does not increase the organism's frequency of response in general—the process strengthens the response in the presence of particular situational stimuli.

The stimulus which serves to reinforce the conditioning may at this point be simply called a reinforcing stimulus and symbolized as ^{R}S. More will be said of the types of stimuli which can serve this function, as well as the relationship of such stimuli to others described. Fig. 2 depicts the process of instrumental conditioning. In Fig. 2(a), the response is shown to occur in the presence of a ^{D}S. The response is followed by the occurrence of a ^{R}S. At first, as shown by the dotted line, the tendency for the ^{D}S to elicit the response is weak. In Fig. 2(b), after a number of such conditioning trials, the tendency for the ^{D}S to elicit the response is strong, as shown by the solid line. The response will occur to the ^{D}S on any particular occasion, whether or not it is followed by the reinforcing stimulus.

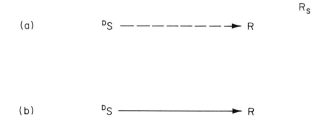

$$\text{(a)} \qquad {}^{D}S \;-\!-\!-\!-\!-\!-\!-\!-\!\longrightarrow\; R \qquad\qquad R_s$$

$$\text{(b)} \qquad {}^{D}S \;\longrightarrow\; R$$

FIG. 2.   Instrumental conditioning.

As an example of instrumental conditioning, let us say that a child was used as a subject. Let us also say that the conditioning situation consisted of a room in which there was a chair and a panel from which a knob extended. If the knob is pulled out, it activates a device that delivers a reinforcer (such as an M & M candy). Suppose that after a time the child makes the knob-pulling response and receives a reinforcing stimulus. It will then be seen that the response occurs with less delay next time. Each time the process is repeated the response will occur with a higher rate until some maximum rate in that situation is achieved. It should be quite apparent that the response is being strengthened to the stimuli that are present, especially those to which the child must attend in making the response (for example, the sight of the apparatus, the feel of it, and so on). That is, upon leaving the room, and the discriminative stimuli in the room, the knob-pulling response would not be elicited in any greater-than-usual strength. The conditioning would be specific (or relatively so) to the stimuli in the conditioning situation.

Parameters of the Basic Principles. The preceding discussion gives a general statement of the basic principles of classical and instrumental principles. There are a number of conditions (independent variables) that can vary and by so doing affect the strength of the conditioning. Some of these may be summarized to indicate what is involved. Some of these variables are exactly the same for both types of conditioning. In other cases the variables are the same but there are characteristics that are specific to each type of conditioning.

To begin with, the number of conditioning trials will affect the strength of conditioning, up to some maximum point. Within that limit the greater the number of conditioning trials, the greater the strength of the conditioning. There are also time elements which affect the strength of conditioning in similar ways. In classical conditioning the time between the occurrence of the ${}^{C}S$ and the ${}^{UC}S$ is important, with almost immediate contiguity (0.5 sec interval) being the most effective. A similar relationship between the ${}^{D}S$ stimulus and the occurrence of the response and the subsequent reinforcing stimulus would probably pertain. However, in instrumental conditioning the situational ^DS is always present when the response is made, so this time factor has not been so systematically studied. It would be possible to do so, however.

The time interval that has been studied in the context of instrumental conditioning is that between the response and the occurrence of the reinforcing stimulus. Immediate presentation of the reinforcing stimulus results in the greatest conditioning. As the interval is increased less strong conditioning results. In animals, experimental results suggest that the maximum interval is about 30 sec.

The magnitude of the stimulus affecting the conditioning is also a significant variable. In the case of classical conditioning the magnitude of the ^{UC}S, and thus the strength of the response elicited, appears to affect the strength of the conditioning. In instrumental conditioning the magnitude of the ^RS also appears to affect the strength of the conditioning. The greater the reward, the greater the conditioning. A variable which appears to be related to the magnitude of reward in instrumental conditioning is the effortfulness of the response itself. Effortfulness itself is aversive, and may be considered to subtract from the amount of reward which follows the response. The effects of aversiveness following a response will be summarized further on in discussing the subprinciples of instrumental conditioning.

A word may be said here concerning measures of response strength. In classical conditioning, for example, it would be seen that as the number of conditioning trials increased, presentation of the ^CS would with a higher probability elicit a response. In addition, as conditioning increased, the extent of the response would increase, and the latency between presentation of the ^CS and occurrence of the response would decrease. Limits of response strength growth are involved in each case, of course.

It may be suggested that similar measures of response strength are implicit in the characteristics of instrumental conditioning. The probability that the response will occur in the stimulus situation (^DS) increases with conditioning trials. The fact that the response is related to the occurrence of the stimulus situation is not seen because the stimulus situation is present during the whole period of observation. If presentation of the ^DS was not continuous, however, it is suggested that it would be seen that latency of the response to the ^DS would decrease, as is the case for classical conditioning, and extent of the response (or intensity) would increase. Again, limits of response strength growth are involved.

Subprinciples of Classical and Instrumental Conditioning. There are a number of subprinciples that involve classical and instrumental conditioning that elaborate the circumstances under which the learning takes place. As with the parameters of conditioning just described, there is considerable similarity in these subprinciples over both types of conditioning. Thus, in most cases the subprinciple will be described for both classical and instrumental conditioning.

1. *Positive and negative stimuli in conditioning.* In instrumental conditioning, it should be noted, not every stimulus will have a reinforcing effect for an organism. That is, there are stimuli that could be presented after a motor response had occurred that would have no effect upon the future strength of the response in that situation. The stimuli would be neutral, and would not be called reinforcing stimuli. Whether or not a stimulus will be reinforcing for an organism is a matter for empirical specification. There may be species differences, such as the types of food stimuli that are reinforcing for carnivores versus for herbivores. As will be indicated further on, moreover, differences in what stimuli have reinforcing value for the individual may be a function of past learning history.

It is important to indicate, however, that the concept of the reinforcing stimulus is not a circular one, as has been claimed, nor one that can be ascertained only after the fact. That is, in any particular case, at one time or another, it is necessary to establish through observation what stimuli are reinforcing (without training) for the members of a species. However, once this has been found, knowledge of reinforcing stimuli will generalize to other responses of the organism, as well as to other members of the species. That is, having found that raw meat constitutes a reinforcing stimulus for a newly observed animal, for one response in one situation, it will be found that this will hold for other responses in other situations. (This generality has not always been recognized, as will be discussed further on. See, for example, Premack, 1959.) Moreover, other members of the species subjected to the same conditions will behave in a like manner. Later on, it will be seen in another way how the concept of the reinforcing stimulus is not circular, for it is possible through utilization of the principles of conditioning to *produce* stimuli that are reinforcing for the organism.

To continue however, it has been indicated that of the universe of stimuli that can be sensed by the organism some will act as reinforcers and some will not have a reinforcing effect. This may be elaborated by saying that only the case of the *positive* reinforcer has been described, and there is a negative case as well. That is, there are additional stimuli which if presented following a particular response will not increase the frequency of the response, but will have just the opposite effect—the response will occur less frequently in that situation in the future. Thus, there are positive reinforcing stimuli (rewards) and negative stimuli (punishments).

The basic principle of instrumental conditioning may be further elaborated. That is, it has been said that presenting a stimulus following a motor response may have either a strengthening or a weakening effect upon future occurrences of the response if the stimulus has reinforcing properties. It is important to add that *taking away* a reinforcing stimulus that is already present, following a motor response, also has an effect. In this case the effect is just opposite that when the stimulus is presented. That is, presenting a positive reinforcer following a response will strengthen the response. However, if the organism "has" a positive reinforcing stimulus and following a response the reinforcing stimulus is taken away, that response will occur less frequently in that situation. Taking away a positive reinforcer thus acts like a punishment.

On the other hand taking away a negative reinforcing stimulus following a response will act as a reward. When a response occurs and is followed by removal of an already present negative reinforcing stimulus, the organism will be conditioned to make that response more frequently in that situation in the future. Behaviors that diminish punishment become learned.

Thus, in instrumental conditioning there are positive and negative stimuli. The same may be said for classical conditioning. There are stimuli that can serve as ^{UC}S in that they will elicit positive emotional responses in the organism. Food, sexual stimulation, warmth of a certain level, and so on, will elicit positive emotional responses in the organism. On the other hand, there are ^{UC}S that elicit emotional responses in the organism that are of a negative variety. Intense sounds, extremely bitter substances, and so on, and the wide variety of stimuli we call painful, will all elicit negative emotional responses in the organism. In either case, the emotional response will be conditioned to any contiguous ^{C}S. As a later section will indicate, the stimuli that serve a positive or negative emotional eliciting function in classical conditioning are the same as those which serve a positive or negative reinforcing fuction in instrumental conditioning.

2. *Stimulus generalization.* Conditioning is not highly specific to a perfect replica of the controlling stimulus, whether it is a ^{C}S or a ^{D}S. That is, for example, once an emotional response has, through classical conditioning, come to be made to a particular sound (as the ^{C}S), the response will be elicited by sounds that vary from the original. The closer the ^{C}S is to the original, however, the greater will be the strength of the response to the stimulus. The same principle holds for instrumental conditioning. A response reinforced in a particular situation will also occur more frequently in similar situations (^{D}S), to the extent that the latter situations are similar to the original.

3. *Stimulus discrimination.* As the author has suggested previously (Staats, 1963), it is important that organisms have evolved to function according to the principle of stimulus generalization (as well as to the other basic principles). That is, for example, the principle of stimulus generalization

is adjustive to the organism, since if learning were highly specific the organism would have to learn each response in each slightly different situation. However, learning does generalize. Having learned an appropriate response in one situation, the organism will behave in the same way in similar situations.

Nevertheless, there are cases where it is not adjustive to make a response previously learned in one situation in a slightly different situation. The child may be reinforced for speech ranging from the normally loud to the boisterous in the home. In a similar building structure called a church, however, he will not be so reinforced for normally loud speech.

Fortunately, fine discriminations between the responses made to similar stimuli can occur through additional conditioning, classical or instrumental. An organism classically conditioned to respond to a light of a particular intensity will respond similarly to a stimulus of a slightly different intensity. However, if the conditioning is conducted further where the particular ^{C}S light is followed by the ^{UC}S and the similar lights are never followed by the ^{UC}S, a discrimination will occur. The organism will come to respond to the former and not to the latter.

The same is true for instrumental conditioning. Let us say that the organism has been reinforced for a response in the particular situation, as the child pulling the knob in the previous example. Let us say that we change the situation by introducing a noticeable tone stimulus from time to time. The tone would only be a slight stimulus change, and the child would continue responding as before. Let us also say, however, that the response is only reinforced when the tone is present. A discrimination will then occur. The response will come to be made only in the situation when the tone is present, not when the tone is not present. This would constitute a stimulus discrimination between the situation with the tone and the situation without the tone.

The extent of the fineness of discrimination between two similar stimuli will depend upon the nature of the organism's conditioning experience with respect to the two stimuli, as well as upon the sensory acuity of the organism. Extremely fine discriminations in the various senses can occur for humans, depending upon the fineness of the discrimination training.

4. *Extinction.* It was suggested that organisms have evolved biologically so that learning generalizes under usual conditions, but can come under finer stimulus control in the learning process called discrimination. This type of evolution would be expected because it is generally adjustive. It may be suggested that organisms follow the laws of learning because they are *all* generally adjustive. This accounts for the universality of the basic principles of classical and instrumental conditioning. For example, when a stimulus that elicits a response is paired with one that does not, it is generally adjustive

for the organism if he comes to respond to the one that does not in the same manner as to the stimulus that does elicit the response. For example, the herbivorous animal that looks at a new plant and samples a piece, only to retch, is conditioned to respond to the plant with negative emotionality—an adjustive process. The same holds true for instrumental conditioning. The baby deer who smells a strange odor and shortly after is prodded into flight by its mother will later in life come to run away when experiencing such odors.

But if an organism was so constructed that once learning had occurred it would be immutable, the organism would not have attained a maximal level of adaptability. That is, although many aspects of the environment remain the same, there are also changes that occur. The animal may be reinforced for making certain locomotive responses in the presence of certain geographic stimuli by finding water. The geographic stimuli will come to be the ^{D}S that controls the locomotive responses. If the learning was immutable, however, the responses would occur even after the water hole had dried up. The animal continues to exist (and to procreate) because the learning is not immutable. In the present case, when a response is no longer reinforced the control of the ^{D}S is weakened on future occasions.

The general principle holds for both classical and instrumental conditioning. When the ^{C}S is no longer followed by the ^{UC}S, the ^{C}S after some trials loses its power to evoke the conditioned response. When the response is no longer reinforced in the presence of the ^{D}S, the stimulus no longer comes to elicit the instrumental response. The process of extinction actually underlies the principle of stimulus discrimination. That is, it is when a response is extinguished to one stimulus, while still being conditioned to a similar stimulus, that discrimination occurs.

5. *Intermittant conditioning trials.* The environment in real life is not nearly so consistent, either in always having conditioning trials, or in never having conditioning trials. Not every time, for example, is a strange odor followed by the rush of a predator. However, unless the conditioned fear response to the strange odor occurs each time the ^{C}S occurs, the deer may not survive. As another example, with instrumental conditioning, the primitive hunter's or fisherman's behavior was indeed reinforced by securing food. However, not every time. Nevertheless, unless the behavior is maintained in good strength without continuous conditioning, the primitive man will not survive.

Organisms have thus evolved in such a way that the strength and character of the organism's learning molds itself to the strength and character of the conditioning. Let us take the example of the animal reinforced by water when it locomotes in a certain manner under the control of geographic stimuli. Let us say that for this animal the water hole is always full, with no exceptions. Then one day there is no water in the hole. This animal may return again at a later time, but in relatively few trials his behavior will extinguish.

Let us take another animal under similar circumstances. However, in this case the animal has had experience where sometimes when he goes to the hole it contains water. Other times it is empty. After such experience, if the water hole goes dry and remains that way, this animal will return to the former drinking place many more times than will the other animal. The intermittant reinforcement will have made the animal more resistant to extinction than has the continuous reinforcement for the other animal. In short, reinforcement environments that reinforce the animal for performing the response continuously even though the response is only sometimes reinforced will produce more persistent behavior in the face of nonreward than will reinforcement environments in which the response is reinforced on every trial.

Moreover, the behavior of the organism adapts itself to the conditions of reinforcement in various ways. An individual who is reinforced for the number of responses made—thus more rapid responding is more quickly (effectively) reinforced—will be conditioned to respond more rapidly. If the reinforcement environment is set up to reinforce only responses that occur after a long pause, the organism will learn this mode of behavior. Skinner and his followers have concentrated their experimental efforts upon the detailed study of various possible patterns of intermittent reinforcement and the effects upon the behavior of the organism. Much of this work stems from no other rationale than that a variation in schedule will produce effects upon behavior, and the work will probably not lie in the mainstream of the development of the science. However, the major principles in this area are important to an understanding of behavior, and Skinner's work has contributed heavily to this knowledge.

The effect of intermittant conditioning upon the character and resistance to extinction of the conditioning has been described in brief for the instrumental case. There are analogous findings for classical conditioning That is, for example, if the ^CS is sometimes presented and followed by the ^{UC}S, and sometimes the ^{UC}S does not follow, it will be found that the amplitude of the classical conditioning is less. The conditioned response will not be as intense as if the ^{UC}S always followed the ^CS. Furthermore, if this intermittant conditioning has occurred it will be found that the conditioned response of the organism is more resistant to extinction. The ^CS will continue to elicit the conditioned response when it is never followed by the ^{UC}S for a larger number of trials in the intermittant conditioning than if the conditioning has been continuous. These principles are relevant to all of the types of emotional conditioning that can occur to an organism and to other types of classical conditioning as well.

It may be noted here that resistance to extinction has also been employed as a measure of the strength of conditioning. As shown here, however, resistance to extinction is affected by the schedule of reinforcement in addition to the other variables which underlie strength of response.

6. *Deprivation and satiation (drive) conditions.* It has been said, for example, that a reinforcing stimulus such as a piece of food if presented following a response will result in that response occurring more frequently in the future in that situation. This is the paradigm for instrumental conditioning. A necessary corollary to this basic law is that the organism must first have been deprived of food for a time. That is, with an animal that has just been satiated for food, a piece of food following a response will not have a reinforcing function. Moreover, the reinforcing value of a stimulus varies according to the deprivation–satiation conditions of the organism with respect to that stimulus. As the organism is deprived of units of the reinforcing object, such units increase in reinforcing value for the organism. As the organism receives greater quantities of units of the reinforcing stimulus, the reinforcing value of each additional unit decreases.

In general, the same principle is relevant to classical conditioning. The dog that is satiated for food will not classically condition in the situation in which food is to be used as the ^{UC}S. That is, the food will not elicit a response such as salivation in the same strength, and thus the response cannot be conditioned to a contiguously presented ^{C}S. In general terms, when the organism has been deprived of units of a stimulus that elicits a positive emotional response (such as food) each unit will elicit more strongly the emotional response. Satiation, on the other hand, reduces the value of the stimulus for that type of elicitation.

7. *Relative reinforcer strength.* As the author (Staats, 1963, 1964, 1968a, b) has indicated, the reinforcing stimuli that are functional for an individual or organism may be considered to be in a hierarchical system. That is, the reinforcers in the system will have different *relative* strengths, and individuals, for example, can differ in their behavior because of differences in the relative strengths of the reinforcers in their reinforcer systems. To illustrate: two organisms reinforced for one behavior by a stimulus which for both has exactly the same strength will nevertheless learn different behaviors if for one organism, but not the other, there is another reinforcing stimulus of even greater strength that is made contingent upon a different behavior.

At one time in experimental psychology investigators were interested in studying the relative strengths of "instincts" or "drives." Thus, the investigator might test the intensity of electric shock an animal would take while crossing a grid to obtain a particular object, in comparison to another object. We may see such studies as measures of the relative reinforcing value of different stimuli. These studies were more interested in the concept of drives or instincts, rather than with the principles of the reinforcer system, however. Relevant concepts of a hierarchical "need" system have also occurred in the social sciences (see Maslow, 1954; Samuelson, 1958), but again not tied in with the principles of conditioning.

More recently, Premack (1959) has discovered facts of reinforcement that may be used to suggest the relative strengths of reinforcers. However, he has done so in the context of certain additional principles which make for unnecessary difficulties. He constructed an experimental situation in which organisms make responses in different rates. Moreover, he found that if one made a high-rate response contingent upon a low-rate response, the high-rate response would act as a reinforcer for the low-rate response. But he found that the low-rate response would not function as a reinforcer for the high-rate response. He thus concluded that reinforcers do not have general properties, that a given reinforcer will not strengthen *any* response (Premack, 1959).

This is in error, however. A given reinforcer should strengthen *any* response provided that the reinforcing properties are greater than the effort (aversiveness) of the response. Premack made his conclusion, it is suggested, because he confounded in his experimental work the reinforcing stimulus with the response (few behaviors are inextricably linked with particular reinforcers) as well as relative and absolute reinforcing value. In any particular situation it may appear that a stimulus does not have reinforcing power, if there is a stronger reinforcer which is present. The stronger reinforcer will control the behavior that occurs in that situation, but the weaker reinforcer may nevertheless have reinforcing properties when it is presented alone. As a matter of fact, it could be demonstrated easily that a lower-value reinforcer can help strengthen a behavior that is usually maintained by a higher-valued reinforcer. For example, although social reinforcement is not as strong a reinforcer as food for chickens, it has been found that a chicken will eat more when in company than when alone. That is, the social reinforcement plus the food reinforcement has a greater reinforcing effect than the food alone, although the social reinforcement itself would not be sufficient to maintain eating behavior. Premack's procedures only allowed assessment of the relative strengths of reinforcers, and they are specific to that situation.

The variables that help determine the relative value of reinforcers in human reinforcer systems have been discussed more extensively (Staats, 1968b). For example, the manner in which deprivation, extinction, counterconditioning, and so on, affect the relative strengths of reinforcers have been described. Consideration of the differences in the relative strengths of reinforcers in individual's motivational systems is extremely important.

Further basic work is indicated, as well as further elaboration of the principles of the motivational system in the context of human behavior.

Derived and Theoretical Subprinciples: Interactions of Classical and Instrumental Conditioning. In the above summary of the basic learning principles, in each case the principle was described as it pertained to both classical and instrumental conditioning. This was done to emphasize one of the present approach's main points, that is, that the two types of conditioning are not two distinct and separate phenomena, as has been implied in some of the accounts that have separated classical and instrumental conditioning. One of the most important tasks of a new learning theory, it is suggested, is to indicate the interrelationships and commonalities of classical and instrumental conditioning as well as the manner in which the two types of conditioning interact in their operation. The next section includes several other derived or theoretical extensions of the basic principles. However, its main emphasis will be upon indicating some of the areas of *interrelationship* between the two major principles which must be considered.

Interactions of Classical and Instrumental Conditioning.

1. *Overlap of reinforcing* (^{R}S) *and classical conditioning* (^{UC}S) *functions of stimuli.* Ordinarily, in traditional learning theories, food may be discussed at one point as a ^{UC}S which elicits emotional responses in the individual such as salivation. Later, when the topic is instrumental conditioning, the same stimulus of food will be symbolized as an ^{R}S (using Skinnerian notation). The principles are discussed separately and the fact that the same stimulus serves both a classical conditioning and an instrumental function is not made explicit. The obvious fact is, however, that some stimuli that are ^{UC}S will also function as reinforcing stimuli (^{R}S). The notation system should be constructed to allow one to see this relationship. The author has suggested a system in which the multiple functions which some stimuli have can be depicted. Thus, an unconditioned stimulus that elicits a response, but which also has reinforcing properties and could serve to condition an instrumental behavior, would be denoted as a $^{UC \cdot R}$S, an unconditioned reinforcing stimulus. The two functions of the stimulus are shown. In the positive case, where the stimulus elicits a positive emotional response and will serve as a positive reinforcer, a plus sign is added ($^{UC \cdot R^+}$S). In the negative case, where the stimulus both elicits a negative emotional response and will serve as a negative reinforcer, a minus sign is added ($^{UC \cdot R^-}$S).

2. *Classical conditioning within instrumental conditioning.* One value of indicating the double function of some stimuli in this notation system can be seen in the consideration of instrumental conditioning. That is, the typical

terminology indicates that when a motor response is followed by a reinforcing stimulus (traditionally denoted as an S^R) the response increases in frequency. When the reinforcing stimulus is symbolized as a $^{UC\cdot R}S$, however, it is immediately seen that there will be other concomitants than the simple strengthening of the motor response. That is, the notation indicates that the reinforcing stimulus also has the properties of an unconditioned stimulus in a classical conditioning sense. One then has to ask what the other stimuli are that are present when the $^{UC\cdot R}S$ is presented, because the emotional responses elicited by the $^{UC\cdot R}S$ will be conditioned to any other stimuli that are present. The stimuli of the situation are present, of course, among others, and any emotional response elicited by the $^{UC\cdot R}S$ will be conditioned to these stimuli. Thus, at the same time that the stimuli of the situation become a $^D S$ which will tend to elicit the motor response, the stimuli of the situation will through classical conditioning also come to elicit the same emotional responses that the $^{UC\cdot R}S$ elicits. Thus, classical conditioning takes place within instrumental conditioning. This is one of the interactions of the two basic principles. Actually, this occurs in a more complex manner than has just been described, and we will return to this topic again.

3. *Conditioned reinforcement.* One process that occurs in the situation just described, but which also has even more general relevance, concerns the principle of conditioned reinforcement. That is, it has been suggested that there are stimuli that, besides serving as a ^{UC}S which will elicit emotional responses in the organism, will by virtue of this quality also serve a reinforcing function in instrumental conditioning. Thus, such a stimulus has two potential functions and is symbolized as a $^{UC\cdot R}S$. In the preceding case of interaction, it was shown how classical conditioning occurs in the instrumental conditioning procedure. A similar overlap occurs in the opposite direction. Within the process of the classical conditioning of an emotional response, stimuli (reinforcers) are produced which will function in an instrumental sense.

That is, when a neutral stimulus is paired with a ^{UC}S that elicits an emotional response, the neutral stimulus will come to elicit the emotional response. It should be remembered that the ^{UC}S by virtue of eliciting the emotional response will also be a reinforcing stimulus, the stimulus is thus a $^{UC\cdot R}S$. Well, in the classical conditioning process, as the neutral stimulus comes to be a $^C S$ and elicit the emotional response, it also comes to be a reinforcing stimulus. The neutral stimulus in the pairing process acquires the several functions of the stimulus with which it is paired. The neutral stimulus thus becomes a $^{C\cdot R}S$, a conditioned reinforcing stimulus. This may occur in the negative case, where the stimulus will elicit a negative emotional response and also serve as a punishment, or in the positive case, where the stimulus will elicit a positive emotional response and serve as a reward.

4. *Secondary (higher-order) conditioning.* The principle of primary classical conditioning can be considerably expanded in scope and importance when it is added that a stimulus which reliably elicits a response can serve as the ^{UC}S in a further conditioning process with a ^CS. This type of conditioning has been called "higher-order" classical conditioning (the term "higher-order" in this use is not related to the term "higher-order" as used in indicating the higher-level, more abstract, principles in a theoretical structure). The expansion involved is that the reliable response to the stimulus need not be one which was built into the organism by biological development. A stimulus which has reliably come to elicit a response on the basis of past conditioning can now serve as the ^{UC}S in further conditioning. That is, it was suggested in describing primary classical conditioning that if a neutral stimulus, let us say a sound, was paired with an electric shock, the emotional responses elicited by the shock would be conditioned to the sound. The sound would then be a ^CS for the emotional responses.

After this conditioning was quite reliable, however, it would be possible to employ the ^CS to affect conditioning of the emotional response to yet another neutral stimulus. The ^CS would then serve as the ^{UC}S and the neutral stimulus would never have to be paired with the stimulus that originally elicited the response as a reflex, on the basis of the organism's biological structure. Real-life circumstances provide the conditions necessary to produce very reliable conditioning because many, many conditioning trials extending over periods of years are quite ordinary, and, moreover, there is intermittant conditioning which produces great resistance to extinction. Thus, examples occur where the ^CS may be far removed from the original ^{UC}S, and yet come to elicit a conditioned response.

The principle of higher-order conditioning is one which has been considered solely for classical conditioning. However, this is another case where there is overlap between the classical and instrumental conditioning. That is, when the principle is stated in its general form the relevance of the principle for instrumental conditioning may be readily seen. The general principle is that when any stimulus reliably elicits a response, a new stimulus presented in contiguity with the first stimulus, and thus with the response also, will come to elicit the response. A ^DS may be a stimulus which reliably elicits a response—a motor response. According to this theoretical principle, then, pairing a ^DS with a new stimulus should result in the new stimulus also coming to elicit the response, even though in this process the response is never followed by reinforcement. As with classical conditioning, it is suggested that the higher-order conditioning of instrumental responses may take place purely on the basis of contiguity. The author has suggested empirical results which suppoft this principle on the human level (Staats, 1966, 1968a) and such procedures as paired associate learning may be considered as one type of example. However, additional research on this principle (as with some of the others) is needed on the basic level in the animal laboratory.

5. *The ^{C}S, ^{R}S, and ^{D}S interaction.* It is not possible herein to deal with the various principles of interaction of classical and instrumental conditioning. An additional example will be added, however, to indicate how the three functions of a stimulus—the conditioned stimulus, the reinforcing stimulus, and the discriminative stimulus function—are inextricably interwoven for the organism (see Staats, 1959, 1964, 1966, 1968a,b). This interrelationship is not necessarily built into the organism—and in this sense the principles are not basic or higher-order principles—but the interrelationship is inexorable in the conditioning history of the organism so that the principles for all practical purposes are basic.

That is, it has been stated that in the instrumental conditioning situation the reinforcing stimulus (either a $^{UC \cdot R}$S or a $^{C \cdot R}$S) elicits an emotional response which is conditioned to the ^{D}S. Thus, as the conditioning process progresses, in addition to the overt motor response being conditioned to the ^{D}S (the situation), the emotional response is also conditioned to the ^{D}S. The results of the conditioning process produce the following associations:

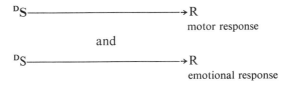

$$^DS\text{———————————}\rightarrow R$$
motor response

and

$$^DS\text{———————————}\rightarrow R$$
emotional response

Another important principle must be introduced here, although it will only be described more fully later, in order to realize the further results of the instrumental conditioning situation. That is, responses may in general be considered to have or to produce stimulus characteristics. In common-sense terms it may be said that we "feel" the way we respond. This is true for emotional responses—we have different sensations for positive emotional responses than we do for negative emotional responses, as one example. It is also true for motor responses where we also sense our responses.

In the present case this is important for the following reasons. As the instrumental conditioning process continues the ^{D}S comes to elicit a positive emotional response, which itself has stimulus characteristics. This means that the instrumental response is being reinforced in the presence of the emotional response and its sensations. Since any stimulus present will come to serve as a ^{D}S for the instrumental response being conditioned, the emotional sensations will also come to be a ^{D}S. This result may be schematized as follows. That is, in instrumental conditioning the ^{D}S comes to elicit an emotional response. The stimuli of the emotional response come to elicit the motor response which is reinforced in that situation:

^{D}S————————→R————————→^{D}s————————→R
(the external   (emotional   (the emotional   (instrumental
   situation)   response)   sensations)   response)

This result may be considered to be the inevitable outcome of *any* instrumental conditioning process involving reward. The organism inevitably will have a vast number of such conditioning experiences in his history. This means that positive emotional responses generally will come to elicit a number of different instrumental responses, namely all those instrumental responses which are learned under the action of reward. This class of responses will be identified by the characteristic of striving *toward* or *for* the stimulus involved, in contrast to escape and avoidance types of behaviors. It should be noted that various motor responses will be involved here depending upon the type of organism and the organism's learning history for motor behaviors. These "striving for" behaviors constitute a class of responses in that they tend to be elicited by positive emotional sensations. (Which particular response will be elicited in any case will depend upon the other stimulus features of the situation.)

This principle means that anything which increases the tendency of a stimulus situation (^{D}S) to elicit a positive emotional response in the organism will increase the tendency of that situation to elicit one of the "striving for" responses that the organism has in its repertoire. Thus, classical conditioning procedures that condition an emotional response to a stimulus will also increase the power of that stimulus to elicit overt instrumental behaviors. In this way classical and instrumental conditioning are inextricably inter-related. The results of recent experiments may be interpreted within this theoretical principle. That is, for example, Trapold and Winokur (1967) have shown that prior classical conditioning which establishes a stimulus as a ^{C}S will later enhance the ^{D}S value of the stimulus. Tying this in with what has already been described herein, it may be said that when one classically conditions a positive emotional response to a stimulus, that stimulus will also come to have positive reinforcing value. In addition, that stimulus will also gain discriminative stimulus value and tend to control the class of "striving for" responses that the organism has already learned.

Analogous circumstances would also be expected in the negative case. In this case, however, "striving away from" responses are involved rather than "striving for" responses. That is, when a negative emotional response is conditioned to a stimulus it also becomes a negative reinforcing stimulus. The organism is then reinforced for escape from the stimulus and the negative emotional response (and its stimuli). Through this experience the stimuli of negative emotional responses come (as ^{D}S) to elicit escape and avoidance responses. It would be expected, thus, that negative emotional classical conditioning to a ^{D}S would make that stimulus a ^{D}S that would elicit any of a large class of escape and avoidance behaviors. This should be tested.

It may also be briefly noted that in the instrumental conditioning situation the emotional responses elicited by the reinforcing stimulus are also conditioned to the stimuli of the motor response. Mowrer (1960) has suggested that this is the basis for motor conditioning, which may be seen to be an oversimplified view. Nevertheless, in instrumental conditioning employing a positive reinforcer, the motor response may be expected to come to elicit a positive emotional response and thus acquire positive reinforcement value. In the use of punishment, the response would come to elicit a negative emotional response and thus have negative reinforcing value.

6. *Additional classical-instrumental conditioning overlap.* Finally, there is also accumulating evidence that there is not a distinct separation between classical and instrumental conditioning in other ways. Thus, the author suggested in 1959 that reinforcement could strengthen the learning of a classically conditioned response in higher-order conditioning (Staats, 1959a). The possibility of affecting through reinforcement the change in responses that are ordinarily classically conditioned has been shown using various responses (Miller 1966). For example, Engel (1966) has shown that the heart-rate response can be conditioned to a slower rate when reinforcement is made contingent upon a slower rate response. Thus, it appears that instrumental conditioning changes can result from classical conditioning procedures, and also that classical conditioning changes can be affected by instrumental conditioning procedures. It should be noted that instances of classical-instrumental overlap can be theoretically derived. The phenomenon of *behavioral* contrast refers to the fact that in instrumental conditioning it has been observed that rate of response to one ^{D}S is a function not only of the reinforcement schedule involved but is also due to the reinforcement received in responding to another ^{D}S. When the conditioning sessions for the two ^{D}S are alternated, rate of response to one ^{D}S will be enhanced as the response to the other is contrastingly weakly reinforced. The " strength " of responding to one ^{D}S is affected by the conditioning to the other. The principle of contrast should be studied in classical conditioning, employing two ^{C}S and different intensities of ^{UC}S for eliciting positive (and positive-negative) emotional responses. Experimentation to systematically test the various theoretical statements of classical-instrumental overlap and interaction should be conducted.

Stimulus–Response Elaborations of the Basic Principles. There are other extensions and corollaries of the higher-order laws of classical and instrumental conditioning that require statement. One of the important aspects of this elaboration is the systematic indication of the types of stimuli and responses that can operate and are important in understanding the behaving organism. In this context, it should be noted that in any particular experiment, including the discovery of the original principles, the stimuli or responses involved should be considered to be only samples of a much larger class. For example, one might employ a sound stimulus as the ^{C}S in classical conditioning and food as the ^{UC}S, with salivation constituting the response. It should be noted, however, that in each case the findings pertain to a universe of stimuli in each class and a universe of responses. One of the goals of the science of learning must be to stipulate these respective universes, on a basic level as well as in the realm of important human behaviors. This is as true of instrumental conditioning as it is of classical conditioning.

A few of the general considerations involved may be mentioned here. There are various types of responses that may be classically conditioned. Thus, there are motor responses, such as the patellar reflex, as well as internal responses of various kinds. As has already been noted, the author (Staats, 1959a) first suggested in a modern learning context that an additional type of response that is of great importance in human behavior is that of the sensory response. The suggestion here is that stimuli to which the organism is sensorily sensitive actually elicit a response process in the organism. One may ask what the value is of suggesting that "sensations" are responses. The answer, in part, is that the concept that the sensation is a response suggests that sensations have response and thus stimulus characteristics. Thus, sensory responses should follow the laws of classical conditioning, for example. This has already been shown to some extent (see Staats *et al.* 1960). At this point the concept of the sensory response may be considered to be largely theoretical, still needing further evidence to become an empirical concept, as is the case with some of the other principles.

There are also various responses that can be instrumentally conditioned. The traditional concern has been with simple motor responses. It should be indicated, however, that there are classes of these responses. Thus, for example, an important class of motor responses which have common characteristics are speech responses. Another such class might be called "attentional" or "sense-placing" (receptor orienting) responses (Staats, 1968a). It should be noted that indication that any particular important type of human activity is an instrumental behavior is important. That is, this indication again suggests that the laws of instrumental conditioning will apply to the response. An important part of the science of learning is to explore the limits of response definition. As has been noted, this will include specification of the responses, formerly thought to function only according to classical conditioning principles, but which may also function according to instrumental conditioning principles.

One additional item may be mentioned here; there are response terms in the learning theory which must be derived from indirect observation. Not all of the responses the organism makes are open to direct observation. For example, in the human much language behavior takes place in a manner that is covert, the external observer ordinarily has no access to the internal language events. The question arises concerning how one can make statements about such events—such as suggesting that such covert language events are actually responses that have been learned according to instrumental conditioning principles and which function according to conditioning principles.

In answer, one could investigate the principles of speech learning employing overt speech responses, and then infer that the internal speech followed the same principles as overt speech. However, it would be desirable, in some manner, to gain a method of "observing" internal speech. One way could conceivably be by some electronic detection equipment (see Hefferline, 1963). Thus, there was at one time an attempt to observe the presence of internal speech by the muscle potentials from the throat, or the muscle potentials from the fingers of deaf individuals who employed sign language. As has been mentioned and as will be elaborated in the next section, responses have stimulus properties. One of the ways of stipulating an internal, unobservable, response may also be by "tagging" an overt, observable, response to the stimulus produced by the internal, unobservable response. One can then observe the occurrence of the internal response indirectly through the observation of the external response (see Miller, 1935).

The same types of specification are also necessary in dealing with stimuli. The stimulus or stimuli employed in any experiment are only members of a universe of stimuli which could function in the same manner. An item for systematic research is to indicate the various stimuli that can function as such, especially for humans. As one example, can the absence of something which has just been present serve as a ^DS? The fact that young children learn to say "allgone" appropriately indicates this to be the case. In order for learning people to be able to analyze natural environmental circumstances into stimulus components, there has to be systematic indication in the learning theory of an interest in such stimulus specification.

It may also be noted that there are certain theoretical issues concerned with the question of what represents a stimulus. One important item here is that of internal stimuli which are not available to direct observation. It has already been suggested that it is necessary to include in the domain of study covert responses which take place within the organism and are thus not naturalistically susceptible to direct observation in the intact organism. The same rationale applies to certain stimuli which do not arise from external circumstances. Thus, for example, there are internal sources of stimulation in many internal organs. The stomach may produce stimuli when empty, a dry throat is a stimulus, a pounding heart produces sensations. In addition, there are sensory mechanisms attached to the muscles and tendons involved in bodily movement. The movements or position of the parts of the body thus provide sensations. Russian experimentalists have been concerned with showing the stimulus properties of the responses of internal organs also (Razran, 1961).

In principle these stimuli should be able to serve the very same functions in a learning sense that other stimuli can serve. These stimuli can become conditioned stimuli for some classically conditioned response. The stimuli can come to be reinforcing stimuli, or discriminative stimuli. Thus, a response can occur which itself produces a stimulus which serves as a ^{C}S, ^{R}S, or ^{D}S, or all three. There are many types of behavior which cannot be understood without reference to these sources of internal stimuli.

Again, it may be asked, if these stimuli cannot be directly observed, what justification is there for a concept of internal, response-produced stimuli. The answer is that there are ways of indirectly observing the action of such stimuli. That is, one can anatomically see the nerve fibers in the muscles and tendons. One can also electrically monitor their action. Moreover, it is possible to show that responses can be conditioned to the stimuli that are produced by internal, unobservable, responses (Miller, 1935; Razran, 1961).

In conclusion, it may be suggested that the world is made up of various physical energies. Some of these can serve as stimuli for different organisms. One of the tasks of a science of learning is to indicate what these are. Any stimulus to which the organism can respond can become a ^{C}S, ^{R}S, or ^{D}S, provided there is no interfering circumstance, such as the stimulus already being a ^{UC}S for an incompatible response. In the task of showing how stimuli can come to determine the behavior of the organism through learning principles, it is necessary to indicate the stimuli that are functional for the particular organism.

B. *Second-Order Principles of Learning: The S–R Mechanisms*

The goals of the discovery, isolation, and detailing of the higher-order, (abstract) principles of conditioning, including also the various subprinciples, constitute the focus of the basic science of learning. In this task the aim is to establish the principles in the simplest, most controlled circumstances possible. That is the goal in any experimental science in establishing its elementary principles. In the present area of study it means selecting a simple sample of a response, a simple sample of a stimulus, preferably using simple organisms with whom the effects of prior experience can be controlled. Experimental control demands that a single stimulus be manipulated and the effect upon a single response be observed. Thus, the elementary principles of learning are usually based upon the study of simple stimulus–response (S–R) mechanisms.

Behavior in life situations is rarely so simple. Human behavior in naturalistic circumstances, for example, is usually quite complicated. Ordinarily, the individual learns complex combinations of stimulus and response events. Most human acts involve several principles, as well as many stimuli, controlling many responses. For this reason, an important part of a learning theory in general, as well as one that is to be significant in the human realm, must include specification of the ways that the principles of learning can operate to produce more complex learned S–R mechanisms in the organisms. Critics are quite correct when they say that human behavior cannot be adequately described in terms of single S–R events. To serve as a model of various human behaviors (or even complex behavior of lower organisms) the learning theory must outline some of the general ways that complex S–R mechanisms can be formed.

Isolation, derivation, and experimental description of the general complex S–R mechanisms has not been seen as an explicit task of a learning theory. This is not to say that various experimental papers have not dealt with such complex S–R mechanisms. There are a number of such experiments, ordinarily conducted with a different purpose in mind. However, the place of the principles of S–R mechanisms in the basic learning theory has not been seen—nor indeed the necessity of knowledge of the S–R mechanisms for understanding more complex behaviors. The S–R mechanisms are not basic principles themselves, they are derived from the basic conditioning principles. *The S–R mechanisms, on the other hand, must be seen as abstract principles independent of the particular behaviors involved in their study, for the S–R mechanisms when abstracted can be seen to apply to many different types of behavior.* It is important to note that systematic research and theory on the abstract S–R mechanisms must be considered an essential part of the basic theory.

The Component Stimulus S–R Mechanism. Let us take an example which should be seen as a study of complex S–R mechanisms, that is, a typical concept-formation task. In such a study, let us say that the subject of the experiment is presented individually with stimuli each of which constitutes a complex stimulus event. While all the stimuli differ in their various complex stimulus characteristics, with some of the complex stimuli there is a common stimulus attribute. Let us suppose that the subject is reinforced for making a response in the presence of these particular stimuli, which means that the subject is reinforced for making the response in the presence of only the common stimulus element, across stimuli that differ in other respects. This study elaborates the basic principle of instrumental conditioning by indicating that one element in a stimulus complex can come to control a response. Part (a) of Fig. 3 shows a response being reinforced in the presence of three different stimuli each of which has a common stimulus component. As part (b) of Fig. 3 shows, the conditioning process results in the common stimulus component (S_a) coming to elicit the response. This process has been termed concept formation (Hull, 1920) which misinterprets the importance of such a study. This should not be considered a general model of concept formation as there is much human behavior which would be considered conceptual that does not involve such a paradigm (S–R mechanism). It is important, on the other hand, to see the learning of such a mechanism (where a common part of several different, complex stimuli elicits the same response) as an abstract principle. The mechanism should be studied as a general principle that can apply to *various* types of behavior, including some examples of concept formation, but also many other be-haviors. The author, for example, has shown this S–R mechanism to operate in children learning reading units from whole-word reading training (Staats, 1968a). Confusing the abstract S–R mechanisms with specific types of behavior like concepts, problem solving, communication, creativity, and so on, has obscured the general import of the mechanisms, and given over-simplified views of the complex behaviors involved in these areas.

The Response Sequence S–R Mechanism. Another S–R mechanism that is important to an understanding of many complex behaviors is that of the response sequence. That is, as has been indicated, responses can be thought

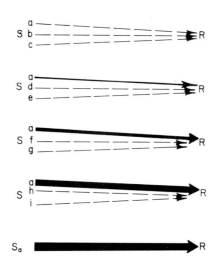

FIG. 3. The common stimulus component S–R mechanism. The common stimulus element in all the stimulus compounds comes strongly to elicit the response, the other stimulus elements gain only weak elicitation strength.

to have stimulus characteristics. Thus, any time a response occurs just following a preceding response, the second response will be conditioned to the stimulus of the first response.[3] Much of the importance of the study of serial learning with animals and with human verbal responses, it may be suggested, is simply in demonstrating this S–R mechanism. It is important to study the characteristics of the formation of sequences of responses and the manner in which such sequences are important to adjustive human behavioral repertoires. For example, the establishment of sequences of responses appears to be essential in understanding aspects of language (such as grammatical speech), problem solving and reasoning, and mathematics. Unfortunately, the field of verbal learning has not realized that its role is studying the S–R mechanisms that man can learn, as well as the functions of such mechanisms in his cognitive functioning. Rather, for example, the field attempts to employ serial learning research to investigate memory—an implicit assumption being that there is a unitary process or faculty of memory. As a result of this inadequacy, the field of verbal learning has gotten bogged down in inconsequential tangents to its major role in developing an adequate learning theory. This example may be extended to other areas of psychology. If such research tried to study the acquisition and functioning of S–R mechanisms, rather than trying to pin down the "will-o'-the-wisps" of the mind (such as the faculty of memory), the research could produce data that would be in the mainstream of the development of learning proposed.

A line of experimentation that can be straightforwardly derived from an understanding of response sequences is that which has been referred to as verbal mediation studies. That is, Russell and Storms (1955) showed that subjects could learn a response sequence of R_a–R_c more easily if, as a result of previous learning, the subject had learned the response sequence R_a–R_b as well as the sequence R_b–R_c. The reason the subsequent a–c response sequence is easier to learn is because of the two sequences already acquired (the a–b and b–c sequences). That is, the a element already tends to elicit the c element because a elicits b and b elicits c. The only additional point that must be added is that when a response occurs, it tends to elicit the responses that have been conditioned to its stimuli. The second response may be covert and still function to elicit the third response. The subject may even be unaware that he makes such a response to the first word. It should also be noted that response sequences much longer than two or three elements would seem to function in complex human behavior. The characteristics of response sequences in language, and the manner of the functioning of such response sequences in reasoning, communication, problem solving, learning through language, and so on, should consciously be seen as an area of study in the elaboration of the learning theory. Unfortunately, again, the *general* nature of S–R mechanism principles has not been seen, and present study

---

[3] This is not to suggest that in a serial learning task, or in paired-associate list training, that each response will come to elicit only the following response. "Associations" will occur to other members in a response sequence than the one directly following any response. These elaborations do not have to be considered here, however.

of verbal response chains is again in large part tangential to the task.

As another example that really involves response sequences, there are studies variously called sensory preconditioning, semantic generalization, and mediated generalization that involve this S–R mechanism. For example, Shipley (1933) first trained his subjects so that a light stimulus and a tap-to-the-cheek stimulus both elicited a common response, an eye-blink. Then in a further procedure he trained his subjects to respond to the tap-to-the-cheek stimulus with an emotional response. He found, then, that when the light stimulus had been presented it now elicited the emotional response, although it had never been involved in any emotional conditioning. The reason this occurred was because in the second phase of the training the emotional response was conditioned to the eye-blink response—a response sequence was formed. Later, the light when presented elicited the eye-blink response and this response in turn elicited the emotional response. When this same paradigm is expanded to include sensory responses as well as emotional and motor responses, various areas of experimental study can be considered within the same S–R mechanism. Moreover, various types of human behavior can be understood in terms of the S–R mechanism of response sequences.

Multiple-Stimulus-Controlling-Behavior S–R Mechanisms. Another mechanism that is important to consider involves multiple stimuli controlling behavior. Let us say that S_1 through conditioning has come to tend to elicit a response. Let us also say that S_2 has come to tend to elicit that same response. Each stimulus alone has a tendency of a certain strength. The two stimuli combined will have a greater tendency to elicit that response. This is a case where more than one stimulus tends to elicit a response. This is an important type of S–R mechanism.

Moreover, there are variations of this mechanism that have additional import. Take for example the case where S_1 elicits one response and S_2 another response. When the two stimuli occur together, both responses will tend to be elicited. If they are not incompatible they both may occur together. Much novelty or originality resides in the fact that a *new* combination of responses occurs because the individual experiences a new combination of stimulus elements, each element of which elicits a previously learned response. The mechanism of multiple stimulus elicitation of behavior is thus important in understanding originality. In the case where the responses elicited by a combination of stimuli are incompatible, either one or the other will occur, this also has importance for understanding behavior in complex situations. That is, people frequently criticize a learning approach for its uncertainty in nature, sometimes the organism makes the response and sometimes not. This is taken as evidence for free will. Such variation can occur, however, because of multiple stimulus effects. While one stimulus in a situation may tend to elicit a response—and will do so under conditions where this tendency is not neutralized in some way—there may be other stimuli in the situation which tend to elicit an incompatible response. There may also be stimuli in the situation which tend to elicit "not making" that particular response. For example, a good friend as a stimulus has some tendency to elicit dirty-joke-telling behavior, let us say. However, when a maiden aunt is also present such behavior is unlikely to occur because the maiden aunt tends to elicit "no-dirty-joke-telling" behavior. The multiple elicitation of responses may be schematized as the following S–R mechanism:

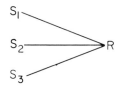

It is interesting to employ an example of such multiple stimulus effects upon a response in the area of language, since it helps introduce the next S–R mechanism. That is, there are many examples in language where more than one stimulus tends to elicit a particular word response. Thus, for example, the Russell and Jenkins norms (1954) indicate that the words *bed*, *dream*, *comfort*, and *deep* as stimuli all tend to elicit the word *sleep* as a response on a word association test. It would be expected that a person with such a learned word association mechanism would be more likely to give the response "sleep" if each of the word stimuli were present than if only one were present.

The Single-Stimulus-Multiple-Response S–R Mechanism. Another important and general type of S–R mechanism is that the organism may have learned more than one response to a particular stimulus. Thus, presentation of that stimulus will have tendencies to elicit more than one response. If the responses are mutually incompatible, the strongest will occur. If the responses can occur at the same time they will. Many behaviors may only be understood in terms of the fact that a particular stimulus tends to elicit more than one response. The multiple elicitation of responses may be schematized as the following S–R mechanism:

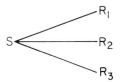

One can see such mechanisms easily in language. That is, there are stimulus words that tend to elicit more than one word response. For example, if the word *tender* was presented as a stimulus to a person in a vocabulary test he might respond by saying *money* at one time and by saying *fragile* or *loving* another. The one-word stimulus would tend to elicit not one response but a hierarchy of responses.

Multiple-Stimuli, Multiple Response Combinations. These last two S–R mechanisms may be combined into even more complex mechanisms in the realm of language. Thus, a sequence of word responses may actually be a sequence in which the stimulus produced by one response controls more than one following response, with more than one such stimulus controlling any particular following response. Thus, in our language culture, the stimuli of the word *give* will be followed in the child's experience by the personal pronouns *him*, *her*, and *me* and thus acquire tendencies to elicit each of those responses, among others. This will also be true of the word responses *throw* and *push*. A relatively simple sequence of these multiple S–R mechanisms which everyone in our language culture would have acquired through his language experience is here depicted:

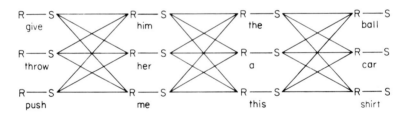

It should be noted that in saying any one of the sentences in the above example the particular word sequence uttered would also be determined by the various other stimuli present in the naturalistic situation. It is suggested that an articulate person may be considered to be a compendium of such S–R verbal mechanisms, many of them of great complexity.

The fact is that in general people can and do learn fantastically complex sequences, hierarchies, combinations, and arrays of responses under complex stimulus-eliciting conditions. It is time to realize self-consciously that one of the requirements in developing the basic learning theory is the elaboration on a theoretical level of the abstract types of S–R mechanisms that can be formed. Moreover, the basic task must also be one of showing in experimentation how such S–R mechanisms can be learned—and, once learned, how the mechanisms function in behavioral acts of various kinds. This area must also include demonstrations of the different kinds of responses that can enter into S–R mechanisms. There are certainly combinations of emotional, motor, verbal, and sensory responses involved in different S–R mechanisms. This area of study must also include the exploration of the basic principles of learning in the context of the study of the S–R mechanisms. This must be done to relate the higher-order basic principles to the second-order level theory concerning the S–R mechanisms. And, finally, the learning theory at the S–R mechanism level must be related to the next lower level of the theory construction task, that is, the analysis of different aspects of human behavior in terms of the S–R elements of which it is composed. Some of the examples given in the present section actually constitute instances of the extension of a S–R mechanism to a realm of human behavior. This was done in illustration, but in actuality many aspects of human behavior cannot be understood unless one can analyze the particular behavior into the S–R mechanisms of which it is formed.

C. *Lower-Order Principles: The Logic of Behavior Theory Construction*

The purpose of the higher-order principles in a theory is to explain and integrate a variety of seemingly diverse empirical events. Thus, Spence (1944) stated that "Theory comes into play for the physicist when he attempts to formulate more abstract principles which will bring these low-order laws into relationship with one another [p. 47]." As has been suggested herein, there is additionally a task at the higher level of the theory in deriving some of the basic laws not yet clearly shown in the laboratory, in positing the relationships between the learning principles, and in deriving the principles of the S–R mechanisms. More generally, however, a major role of theory in the science of learning must be seen as just the type of explanation that occurs in the physical sciences. That is, the basic learning theory can be employed to integrate and relate a variety of seemingly diverse empirical events. To some extent this may occur with the behavior in the animal laboratory. However, the central point here is that the seemingly diverse empirical events of interest to psychology—the ones of the greatest complexity and significance—are those of human behavior. Every observation we have of a human behavior, every systematic principle or empirical concept that has been stated in the various areas of psychology as well as other social and behavioral sciences, education, and so on, provides a potential empirical event of human behavior to be explained and related by means of the basic learning theory. It is suggested that the task of doing this, after establishment of the basic principles of conditioning and the S–R mechanisms, should be seen as the primary theory-building objective. It should be emphasized that the task in principle is the same as that of Newton's theory of gravitation which accounted for and integrated Kepler's and Galileo's empirical laws and the laws of the tides, and so on.

It is not possible in this one chapter to show in any complete way the manner in which the learning theory can serve to explain and integrate diverse empirical observations and concepts of human behavior, even within the field of psychology. However, some examples can be given that will indicate the general strategy of theory development. Actually, as will be seen, there are examples that go back into the early history of the learning approach; however, the significance of the individual studies for the general task of theory construction has not been seen.

Let us take as one example, the early study of Watson and Rayner (1920). They showed that if a white rabbit was presented to a child (as a ^{C}S), along with a loud, aversive, sound (^{UC}S), the negative emotional response to the sound would be conditioned to the sight of the rabbit. (The present more sophisticated learning theory would also predict that the rabbit would also become a negative reinforcer—since the sound was actually a $^{UC \cdot R}S$—as well as a discriminative stimulus for avoidance behavior.) The study thus showed that fears were learned by the nature of the child's experience, according to conditioning principles—albeit, conditioning principles only primitively stated at this early time. In this example, an important area of observed differences in people's behavior to the same stimulus—individual differences in fears—could then be accounted for by the learning theory.

Let us thus take the example a little further, to indicate more fully how seemingly diverse empirical events and concepts can be interrelated by the learning theory. In the field of social psychology the study of attitudes is one in which many studies have been conducted and many concepts suggested, many of them disparate from each other and quite unrelated, and most of them unrelated to the basic principles of learning. This has been true even though most of the theorists in the field of attitudes include in their conception that attitudes are relevant to emotional or affective responses. The manner in which the learning analysis may be employed to integrate the diverse concepts of attitudes as well as the observations that underly these concepts would require a great deal of space. The following excerpt, however, will illustrate the integrational possibilities. The excerpt is of a passage that employs the present author's learning theory of attitudes with which to interrelate empirical concepts and observations of human behavior ordinarily treated as disparate, antagonistic, or unrelated. Greenwald begins by quoting some of the variegated definitions of human attitudes:

An attitude is a mental and neural state of readiness, organized through experience, exerting a directive or dynamic influence upon the individual's response to all objects and situations with which it is related (Allport, 1935).

... an attitude is a predisposition to experience, to be motivated by, and to act toward, a class of objects in a predictable manner (Smith, Bruner, & White, 1956).

Attitudes are predispositions to respond, but are distinguished from other such states of readiness in that they predispose toward an evaluative response (Osgood, Suci, & Tannenbaum, 1957).

An attitude is a disposition to react favorably or unfavorably to a class of objects (Sarnoff, 1960).

. . . attitudes are enduring systems of positive or negative evaluations, emotional feelings, and pro or con action tendencies with respect to social objects (Krech, Crutchfield, & Ballachey, 1962).

Attitude is the affect for or against a psychological object (Thurstone, 1931).

Attitude is . . . an implicit, drive-producing response considered socially significant in the individual's society (Doob, 1947).

Staats' formulation of the three functions of attitudinal stimuli will provide the basic language to be used here for comparing attitude definitions, [see Staats, 1968b]. The three stimulus functions of attitude objects identified by Staats are: (a) conditioned stimulus function—attitude objects elicit emotional reactions; (b) reinforcing stimulus function—exposure to an attitude object may function as a reward or punishment; and (c) discriminative stimulus function—the attitude object serves as a signal for the performance of a variety of instrumental responses.

The first two definitions listed above (Allport, 1935; Smith et al., 1956) identify attitude broadly as a readiness to respond. These and other similar definitions may be said to stress the discriminative stimulus function of the attitude object, with minor emphasis on the conditioned stimulus function (since it may be assumed that a portion of the response tendencies in relation to an object may be emotional).

Definitions that refer to readiness to respond but specify an evaluative dimension (Krech et al., 1962; Osgood et al., 1957; Sarnoff, 1960) appear to lay approximately equal stress on conditioned and discriminative stimulus functions. That is, the tendency to respond favorably, say, may include the tendency to respond with positive emotional reactions (e.g., affection) and instrumental responses (e.g., "striving for" to use Staats' term).

Attitude definitions that refer to affective reactions to an object (Thurstone, 1931) or to "implicit drive-producing" reactions (Doob, 1947), have apparently focused the conception of attitude on the conditioned stimulus function.

None of the attitude definitions sampled here makes explicit reference to a reinforcing stimulus function. Although those definitions that refer to a conditioned stimulus function may be seen as implying a reinforcing property (due to the acquired reinforcing properties of classically conditional stimuli), nonetheless such a function is typically not stressed in conceptual definitions of attitude. Staats' own treatment is, of course, an exception to this observation (Greenwald, 1968, pp. 362–363).

The important point is the demonstration of how the learning principles can be employed to integrate the various empirical concepts. It should be noted that in each case the attitude concept was based upon systematic observations of human behavior, some obtained in controlled laboratory study, but the empirical concepts referred sometimes to different aspects of the observations and were not unified by a common set of theoretical principles. Thus, the conceptions have remained disparate and competitive.

The article of the present author (Staats, 1968b) to which Greenwald refers uses the same higher-order learning principles to also integrate and explain aspects of the lower-order empirical events in other areas of study such as behavior therapy and behavior modification as well as social interaction which comes under the heading of imitation, leadership, persuasion, identification, conformity, communication, and the like. In addition, the acquisition and function of word meaning, the principles of social reinforcement, human motivation, personality theory and personality assessment by means of questionnaires, as well as the motivational systems of different social groups and social institutions, are integrated and explained in part by the same set of higher-order theoretical principles. It is suggested that such theoretical endeavors are in principle of the same type as those seen in the classic theories of the physical sciences.

It should be noted that this represents the use of only a small portion of the learning theory in dealing with only a small portion of the empirical events and concepts in the realm of human behavior. As another example, the simple straightforward basic law of instrumental conditioning can be employed to explain various behaviors and to indicate their relationship. Thus, there are studies which indicate that the acquisition of reading, number-concept learning, writing, various aspects of language, and so on, all involve the same higher-level conditioning principles. Other studies which have applied the principle to an aspect of human behavior may be seen to have the same significance for the general theory. To give a few examples: it has been suggested that the abnormal behavior of psychotics is learned and may be changed according to instrumental conditioning (Staats, 1957) and experimental evidence has been gathered to support this (Ayllon & Michael, 1959); regressed crawling in children may be altered by the same principle (Harris, Johnston, Kelley & Wolf, 1964); social isolation in children may be treated in the same way (Allen, Hart, Buell, Harris, & Wolf, 1964); temper tantrums also (Williams, 1959); improved attention in the classroom (Bushell, Wrobel, & Michaelis, 1968), as well as autistic children (Wolf, Risely, & Mees, 1964), and so on.

On a theoretical and experimental level it has been possible to consider within the basic learning theory human behaviors from all of the areas of psychology ranging from intelligence, attention, imitation, grammar, language universals, originality, problem solving, general cognitive development, sensory–motor skill development, motivational problems in the schools, toilet training, crying behavior, social reasoning, dependent behavior, and many others. Again, the important point here is that each extension of a learning principle to a human behavior represents development of the theory at the lower-order level. Much of the experimentation on human learning may be considered to serve this purpose. However, it should be noted also that much research which is considered to be in human learning does not fall within this endeavor. That is, the research or theory which does not draw on the basic learning principles does not contribute to this theory-construction objective (although the empirical results may on theoretical reanalysis be turned to this purpose). Much traditional research in human behavior and human learning, it is suggested, will not turn out to be basic in any sense, since it will not relate to any basic set of principles. On the other hand, much research which is considered to be applied will in time come to be seen as basic because it derived from and articulates with the basic learning theory.

It may be suggested that it is at this lower-order of theory development that the learning theory becomes a behavior theory. The two must be distinguished. A learning theory constitutes the statement of the basic, abstract, principles of the manner in which behavior is acquired and by which the behavior of the organism functions. The principles of such a theory are derived from laboratory studies in which the stimuli and the responses employed are inconsequential. The elementary principles are the focus of attention, the stimuli and responses are samples which are chosen for the practical purposes of research (for example, observability, duration, naturally occurring, and so on). Salivation as a response is chosen not for its intrinsic importance but because it is a response that has certain experimental advantages. The same is true of an animal traversing a runway or pressing a lever. This also applies to the stimuli investigated in the basic learning research on S–R mechanisms. Stimuli are also chosen in terms of the practical needs of the laboratory.

The generality, the basic nature, of the theory adheres in the fact that the principles are meant to apply to a great number of different specific events— many different responses and many different stimuli. Thus, for example, the previous basic statement concerning reinforcing stimuli, ^{R}S, is an abstract principle and should be generally applicable. As such food, for example, may be considered but a sample of the universe of $^{UC \cdot R}S$. Moreover, any $^{C \cdot R}S$ dealt with represents a universe in which the same principles should apply. Thus, as an example, a word which has been paired with a $^{UC \cdot R}S$ or a $^{C \cdot R}S$ should become a conditioned reinforcing stimulus also, and function as such, as has been shown (Staats, 1964, pp. 205–213, pp. 291–295; Finley & Staats, 1967; Pihl & Greenspoon, 1969). It is an easy jump to consider the whole class of words which have emotional and hence reinforcing value. Thus, statements of value and attitude and interest should also function as conditioned reinforcing stimuli and there is evidence accruing that this is the case (see Byrne, Young, & Griffit, 1966; Reitz & McDougall, 1969; Staats, Carlson, & Reid, 1970). Titles should also serve the same function and individuals with titles that are conditioned reinforcing stimuli should themselves have such reinforcing properties in various types of social interactions. The abstract principles have an unlimited number of extensions as lower-order experimental hypotheses.

If one is interested in human behavior, for example, one can analyze a behavior in which one is interested into its S–R constituents. The stimuli acting upon the individual (because of his past learning) will be either ^{R}S, ^{D}S, ^{C}S, or ^{UC}S, or some combination of these. The behavior itself will be some combination of instrumental and/or classically conditioned responses. When the analysis into S–R elements has been made it constitutes a theory of that behavior. That is, the principles involved are empirical principles which stipulate that if such and such antecedent conditions occur, a particular type of behavior will follow. One can thus derive a lower-order hypothesis concerning the behavior and subject it to test in the laboratory, or in the naturalistic or clinical situation.

At this point the learning theory—the set of abstract, higher-order, conditioning principles and S–R mechanisms—has become a behavior theory. It should be emphasized that verification of a lower-order hypothesis, derived from the theoretical analysis of a type of human behavior, has several levels of significance for the theory. That is, the logic of theory construction suggests that at the lowest level the specific experimental hypothesis may receive experimental support. Moreover, the same experimental verification gives support also to the more general subtheory of the type of human behavior. On a more general level, however, any of the abstract S–R mechanisms involved in the subtheory or in the experimental hypothesis gains substantiation in the process, as do the higher-order conditioning laws on which the S–R mechanisms are based. Finally, verification of any of the S–R mechanisms or higher-order conditioning laws tends to verify the entire set of mechanisms and laws in the general theory. The general point here is that in a hierarchical theoretical structure, which at the top consists of higher-order principles and which progresses downward through the derivation of lower-order principles, verification of the immediate experimental (lower-order) hypothesis derived from the theoretical body produces verification all the way up the line. (See Braithwaite, 1955, for a discussion of similar principles of scientific explanation in the physical sciences.) In this process the learning theory has all the characteristics of the classic theories in the physical sciences. This has not been recognized in psychology or the other sciences. The importance of this understanding cannot be underestimated since acceptance of psychological theory as having the characteristics of theory of the physical sciences catapults it to a much higher level of scientific status. Psychology should be oriented towards producing such advancements in theory, and experimentation should be conducted with both the general as well as the specific theoretical import in mind.

Thus, it is suggested that the basic learning theory involves abstract principles that potentially apply comprehensively to many, many behaviors (especially human). When these abstract principles are employed in analyses, experiments, and treatments of behavior, the learning theory becomes a behavior theory with experimental, theoretical, and practical significance of the most general quality. The learning theory must be constructed to serve these various purposes, which was not the case with the traditional learning theories, and which accounts for some of their inadequacies. This is stressed because the behavior analyzed in terms of the learning principles is an essential part of the theory. The depth, comprehensiveness, and explicitness with which the theory is developed in the context of human behavior is an essential feature of its development. As the author has suggested a number of times, it must be expected that many of the lower-order empirical observations relevant to the theory will be outside of the laboratory. There will be lower-order observations and concepts in the naturalistic conditions of the social and behavioral sciences (such as sociology, economics, anthropology, and so on), the medical and psychological clinic, education, history, ethics, and so on. See Staats (1968b; 1970) for a description of this *social behaviorism*.

D. The Need for Unity of Science in the Study of Man

There has not been an adequate philosophy of science and philosophy of psychology within the field of academic experimental psychology by which to include the study both of basic principles as well as the significant behaviors of man and the problems of such behaviors. In the history of psychology applied and basic work have been divorced. The principles that have been studied by the basic scientist have not been used in the applied fields of psychology, or in other social and behavioral science fields. While the basic worker was discovering his elementary, analytic, principles of learning, the applied worker was discovering techniques and principles with which to work with real problems of behavior. The applied worker, however, did this through the systematic study of naturalistic rather than laboratory events, and his methodology and concepts differed from those of the basic experimentalist or theorist.

Thus, basic and applied work were actually quite separate. The work of the applied psychologist did not have the sophisticated methods or logic of the experimentalist, nor were experimentally derived principles used in applied work. The experimentalist, it may be added, also developed negative attitudes toward applied work, for it was not conducted with the same scientific finesse that the experimental psychologist held in high value.

Moreover, because of the scientific goals of the field of learning—that is, the need to attain the characteristics of a classical, experimental, science in competition for status as a natural science—there has been a value against dealing with samples of functional human behavior. Thus, in experimental psychology, when one sees a label that would *seem* to apply to some functional human behavior, perusal of the experimental task will ordinarily not show a relationship to the human behavior customarily given that label. In most traditional experiments the use of the terms problem solving, concept formation, verbal learning, or what have you, will be no guarantee that any general information about that type of behavior in functional human activity will be the object of investigation. It is not unfair to say that one of the measures of the status of an experiment in academic psychology has been the extent to which the behavior has been an artificial task—not a socially important behavior, or one that could easily be seen to be representative of such a behavior.

Thus, a basic experimentalist will tend to do a concept-formation study employing nonsense figures, geometric forms, Chinese characters—preferably with monkeys—rather than with the learning of reading units by young children. To exemplify the reason for this, it may be said that the physicist, chemist, or biologist would be likely to say about an experiment on concept formation with reading units in children, "Reading, oh yes, that's in education isn't it?" and thereby read the experiment out of the realm of science. There is a real pecking order in science (which is followed in psychology). The order is determined by the extent to which the accoutrements of science are employed in one's work, that is, the sophistication of one's laboratory, apparatus, mathematics, and so on. While such characteristics of some scientific endeavors have had and do have great importance, each such development is a tool or product, not a guiding purpose or assumption of science, or an end in itself.

The fact of the matter is that much so-called basic research in human learning manipulates conditions of learning unspecified in basic learning principles or S–R mechanisms. The research then does not derive from or relate to either in any way, and thus to basic theory, and yet it does not relate to any defined universe of human behavior and cannot suggest useful procedures for dealing with that behavior. It is suggested that such work will have no relevance in many cases to the later development of the basic science. It also has no practical significance. Thus, it cannot boast of being either basic or applied.

It has been stressed that one of the dimensions of progress in elaborating the learning theory is in extending its abstract principles to a variety of behaviors in every way possible, phylogenetically of course, but most importantly to the much greater variety of behaviors we see at the human level. At the behavior theory level, the more representative the sample of behavior is the better. There should be a positive striving to increase the representativeness of the samples of human behavior dealt with to the point of ultimately dealing with the real thing in the naturalistic circumstances in which it occurs. Studies must be designated basic or applied (in a pejorative sense) according to whether or not they employ basic principles and methods; by their contribution to the theory construction task, not by the functional significance of the sample of behavior dealt with. In actuality, the label basic or applied will in the future come to be determined by whether the emphasis of the study is upon the basic, abstract principle, or whether the emphasis is upon extension of a known principle to a new behavior for the focal purpose of understanding the behavior, not the principle. Since both endeavors will relate to the same theoretical task, however, any pejorative content to the terms will be inappropriate.

The further fact is that when the type of theoretical structure described herein is in action there is movement up and down the theoretical structure. So far the present account has indicated only how the downward movement occurs. That movement involves the derivation of the S–R mechanisms from the basic principles, and the further derivation of the lower-order hypotheses from the S–R mechanisms and basic principles. It should be noted, however, that productive contributions are produced also from the work at the lower-order level. These contributions can also change the nature of the higher-order levels of theory. This is seen dramatically when the observations of the lower-order end are discrepant in terms of the reigning theory and thus constitute a pressure toward major alteration in the theoretical structure, thus causing creation of a new theory. We see many examples of this in the history of science, for example, the change from Newtonian physics to the theory of relativity. In any event, lower-order observations are central.

The influence from the lower-order principles to the higher-order is suggested as an essential part of the development of a learning theory. That is, when the basic principles are applied to the human level it will be seen that certain additions, changes, or restructuring may be necessary. As one example, the interactions of the basic principles suggested by the author in the present analysis and elsewhere came in part from experiments on complex human learning as well as naturalistic observations of human behavior. Thus, as illustration, it was seen that words that elicit emotional responses also will serve as reinforcing stimuli, and as a consequence will also have a discriminative stimulus function. The basic research to verify these various expectations, as a matter of fact, is largely yet to be conducted.

As another example, the hierarchies of reinforcers that have been described (Staats, 1968b) is another basic principle that emerged also, albeit in unsystematic form, from social and clinical observations. For example, it has been proposed that humans have a hierarchical need system (Maslow, 1954). The observations which underly this naturalistic conception, when the biological interpretation is removed, may be seen to refer to the individual's learned system of reinforcers. That is, reinforcers have differing intensities and thus have a relative relationship as well as an absolute value. In a situation in which one response is followed by a reinforcer of one value and another response by a reinforcer of another value, the response which is followed by the higher value reinforcer will occur more frequently. If the behaviors are mutually incompatible, the other behavior may not occur at all. Moreover, deprivation and satiation may affect the relative as well as the absolute values of reinforcers. Again, the analysis which is derived from the human level suggests some of the basic research which should be conducted. As another example, it is theoretical demand at the lower-level (the human level) of the theory that dictates a systematic formulation of the aspects of the theory concerned with S–R mechanisms. The behavior of lower animals is not as complex, nor indeed so interesting as human behavior as to demand S–R analyses so that the behavior can be produced expeditiously, and at will.

The major point, however, which may be reiterated, is that the learning-behavior theory suggested is an integrated system in which the various aspects are relevant and important to each other. In this analysis there is no place for the antagonism and separatism between workers at the different levels. The work of each adds to the other. It is only in the joint effort that the full characteristics of a classic theory can be achieved. Moreover, it is in this way the social or functional potentialities of learning theory will be harvested. Although many traditional experimental psychologists are prejudiced against extension of the basic science to important human behaviors because they feel this demeans the science, the reverse is actually the case. The tremendous status of the sciences that have "arrived" is in great part gained from the fact that the theories apply not only to the artificial circumstances of the laboratory, but also to the events and problems of the real world. The science of learning has this potential in as great or greater measure than our presently most cherished science areas.

In conclusion it may be stated that the present-day field of learning (and psychology in general) consists of unorganized striving in large part, and great separatism. It is in a prescientific state in which there is much idiosyncracy, and individuals still see the "innovation" of minor concepts that deviate from past formulations as a step toward distinction. But the science of learning has great basic constituents. It has the experimental methodology, basic learning principles, sophistication in the logic of science, and a comprehensive subject matter that goes from the simple to the very complex. It is a fund of knowledge and technique that with the concentration of a guiding framework—and the participation of a large number of the science's members—could enter into the first rank of sciences. It is a science on the verge of making it big. These possibilities are obscured by the elements of